YOUNG ISLAM

PRINCETON STUDIES IN MUSLIM POLITICS

Dale F. Eickelman and Augustus Richard Norton, series editors

A list of titles in this series can be found at the back of the book

YOUNG ISLAM

The New Politics of Religion in
Morocco and the Arab World

AVI MAX SPIEGEL

PRINCETON UNIVERSITY PRESS
Princeton & Oxford

COPYRIGHT © 2015 BY PRINCETON UNIVERSITY PRESS
Published by Princeton University Press
41 William Street, Princeton, New Jersey 08540
In the United Kingdom: Princeton University Press
6 Oxford Street, Woodstock, Oxfordshire OX20 1TW

press.princeton.edu

Library of Congress Cataloging-in-Publication Data

Spiegel, Avi, 1975-
Young Islam : the new politics of religion in Morocco and the Arab World / Avi Max Spiegel.
pages cm. — (Princeton studies in muslim politics)
Includes bibliographical references and index.
ISBN 978-0-691-15984-3 (hardcover : alk. paper) 1. Islam and politics—Morocco.
2. Islam and politics—Arab countries.   3. Muslim youth—Morocco.
4. Muslim youth—Arab countries.   I. Title.
BP173.7.S72 2015
320.55′70964—dc23

2014032950

British Library Cataloging-in-Publication Data is available

This book has been composed in Linux Libertine O and League Gothic

Printed on acid-free paper. ∞

Printed in the United States of America

1 3 5 7 9 10 8 6 4 2

CONTENTS

A NOTE ON LANGUAGE

One of the many challenges of representing Arabic speech in English texts is that no formal transliteration system exists to depict the diverse and distinct colloquial varieties of spoken Arabic—the languages of everyday life in every Arabic-speaking country in the world. Modern Standard Arabic—the formal, shared, and regularly written language of governments, books, party platforms, and news reporting—is relatively more accommodating: it is transliterated here following a simplified version of the well-known *International Journal of Middle Eastern Studies* guidelines.[1]

For colloquial Moroccan Arabic, a primary language of research for this book, I have opted to formulate an approach that seeks to reflect the ways in which words and phrases are pronounced and expressed in day-to-day life. Admittedly, local variations and nuances abound, including long clusters of consonants, and fragments of words and sounds inspired by different varieties of Amazigh (Berber), French, and Spanish. To make Moroccan Arabic discernible, even intuitive, to the non-linguist, the idiosyncratic system adopted here avoids macrons and dashes. It indicates long vowels (also known as full or stable vowels) as "aa," "ee," and "uu"; double consonants are used to indicate their elongation, which even occurs at the beginning of words. The consonant *ayn* is marked by ʿ. I also employ an "e" to indicate a *schwa* sound: the ubiquitous quick "uh" often represented elsewhere by the visually unwieldy upside down, backward "e."[2]

No method of transliteration is without its faults, and, at times, certain spellings and abbreviations might be off-putting to specialists. But my hope is that this approach will help general readers navigate this terrain more seamlessly, and appreciate both the distinctiveness of colloquial Arabic *and* the diversity of linguistic expression in the modern Arab world.[3] Thus, when Arabic or French terms are common in English (and can be found in English language dictionaries), I use the English version for ease. Names of well-known movements or individuals mirror general usage (the style of the Associated Press is the guide)—e.g., "Ennahda" in Tunisia or "Al Adl wal Ihsan" in Morocco. In citations, I aim to preserve the transliteration used by the original author.

A NOTE ON ANONYMITY

Social scientists, and ethnographers in particular, often take steps to safeguard informant anonymity, but the need to do so in this instance is not simply academic. This book relies substantially on the thoughts and reflections of young Islamist activists. Allegations and critiques similar to those found in these diverse narratives have recently landed young Moroccans in jail.[1]

During the course of my research, certain Islamist activists (especially those from an illegal organization) claimed we were being followed or watched by plainclothes intelligence officers; such assertions could never be verified. The only overt encounter with police I experienced took place during a protest march in Rabat in July 2013, when I was personally accosted by an officer after he suspected I was using my mobile phone to take pictures of the demonstration. (He tried to confiscate my phone, but I managed to get away after a crowd of Moroccans gathered around us—and after I asserted repeatedly that I am American.)

It is important to note that at no other point did anyone ever attempt to stop me from doing my research. Unlike in other countries in the region, my official research clearance did not put any limit on the scope of research I could perform.[2] To the contrary: most individuals in positions of power were helpful and supportive, including the leadership and staff at the Moroccan British Society, led by the king's cousin, Princess Lalla Joumala Alaoui, as well as a number of officials with the Moroccan Ministry of Islamic Affairs (*Habous*), Ministry of Education, and the Ministry of Youth and Sports.

Yet, developments in Morocco increasingly suggest that young citizens do not always operate with this same impunity, independence, or privilege.[3] According to Freedom House, Moroccan journalists who criticize the king are routinely subject to physical beating. The organization ranks "Freedom of the Press" in the country as "Not Free," the lowest possible designation and the same one assigned to Egypt, Libya, Iraq, and Afghanistan.[4] One journalist I interviewed, for example, was arrested by police in his home a few months after our meeting; his website was also blocked.[5] Based on allegations of "insulting the king" or "attacking the nation's sacred values" or "offending a state institution," authorities have also pursued charges against young people for specific Facebook posts, YouTube videos, and even online rap songs.[6]

In these pages, I recount private details about people's lives, but I also relay, among many other things, a range of their criticisms against the Moroccan state. Direct quotations by individual activists appear throughout the book, and are sourced from my own interactions with them (most often from recordings or field notes), unless, of course, a different source is specifically cited.

Because some of the words quoted echo those that have resulted in jail time for others (and even, in some prior cases, for those being quoted), and because being quoted here could be construed as a "public" act, I have taken concrete and affirmative steps to safeguard informant anonymity. Because I cannot possibly judge which specific comments (or portions thereof) could be considered by authorities to be "incendiary" or "insulting" (nor should that be the role of an academic), I use only first-name pseudonyms for most of the people quoted in this book. Out of an abundance of caution and when warranted, I have also taken steps to remove, change, or transpose any overtly identifying characteristics. I do quote public officials and well-known scholars in Morocco and the Arab world by name, unless they specifically requested that I not do so, in which case I employ a general term such as "party official" or "professor."

YOUNG ISLAM

Introduction

ISLAMIST PLURALISM

"I don't like *other* Islamists," said the young Islamist. Mustapha, twenty-eight, was in the midst of his standard recruiting pitch.

"Some wear silly clothes—long black socks and even longer robes," he whispered in Arabic to the high school students beside him. I had to lean in to hear. "Who do you think was responsible for 11th September?" he asked. "Well, not them exactly, but people who look like them." Other Islamists are "sell-outs," he said, "just like their Muslim Brotherhood partners. The state says bark like a dog; they say, how loud?" Only *his* group, Mustapha insisted, one of the major Islamist movements in Morocco, was truly committed to political reform.

This was Casablanca in the decade before the Arab Spring, before outsiders were paying attention, before young Arabs were considered significant political actors or North Africa was deemed consequential. But here, before anywhere else, new Islamist rivalries were starting to take shape.

This book is about these emerging rivalries—rivalries that are transforming political systems across the Middle East and North Africa. It is about how overlooked developments in Morocco through the last decade can offer important clues to understanding this new competitive era of Arab politics. And it is most of all about people like Mustapha, the young activists who play a substantial role in Islamist movements, yet seem to disappear into the background in books written about them.[1]

When I first met Mustapha, I was standing outside a roadside café on the outskirts of Casablanca—an overpopulated commercial capital with little of the intrigue or romance of its cinematic rendering. I was on a preliminary research trip exploring Islamist strongholds, and Morocco was my first stop. I came here because even then, before the Arab Spring, both the largest opposition party in parliament *and* the largest opposition force in the country were Islamists.

It was early summer. The heavy desert sun overpowered a quiet coastal breeze. The air smelled of mint tea and car exhaust, of aftershave and charred corn, of seashells and backed-up latrines. Teenage boys hawked their wares: Marlboro packs by the cigarette, shoe shines by the shoe, and water by the glass. The picture on a small television inside the café alternated between a European football match from the night before and a documentary about Qur'anic recitation. There was something here for everyone.

Mustapha—single, with two part-time jobs, a university degree, and two mobile phones—wore a grey hooded djellaba and yellow *babouche* slippers. A counterfeit Boston Red Sox hat shaded his bearded face. Tall, intense, and inquisitive, he is both a close and a fast talker: he pushes his face almost next to yours, and once he begins to speak, he rarely pauses to look up. He might occasionally punctuate a sentence by asking *fehamtee?* ("you understand?"), but he will seldom break for confirmation. In his spare time, he transcribes Celine Dion songs to practice his broken English.

His one real moment of rest comes on Fridays when, after mosque, after the midday *jumuʿah* prayer, he goes home—to his parents' house—to share a large plate of couscous with his immediate family. He eats slowly and carefully with his right hand, carving each bite into a small, sticky ball, always conscious of not taking too much for himself. He also slows down a bit late at night, when he likes to fall asleep to episodes of *Walker, Texas Ranger*, the 1990s series starring Chuck Norris that long aired on Saudi satellite television. "I like how he's tough but tender," he later told me. It is his dream to move out on his own and marry some day soon, very soon. He talks about women the way an uncle talks about his niece: with pride, affection, and detachment.

There is a part of Mustapha that misses the old days, the days before he and his friends were inundated with multiple choices: television programs, clothing, living spaces, even potential spouses. But he is conflicted in his nostalgia. He adores the multiple technologies at his fingertips, loves chatting with new friends, exploring different cultures and ideas, leaving his world without leaving his country. "I don't want to go back fourteen centuries, to the caliphate," he likes to joke, "what would happen to my mobile phones and my computer?"

Yet, Mustapha was certain about one thing: the task of recruiting potential Islamists used to be a lot more straightforward. He used to promise discipline, order, and a straight path to God, but there are many who offer that now. Clear lines once seemed easier to draw. His old sales talk, once crisp and convincing, used to revolve around the singular theme of sickness. He was "sick," he used to say, "of the status quo." Of Muslims being humiliated militarily. Of politicians promising change, but never delivering. Sick of being given "false promises over and over and over again." The problem he saw with bureaucrats—"the slaves of dictators" who won sham elections and dominated Arab politics for the last half century—was not simply their lack of faith. It was their lack of efficacy. Their impiety was a proxy, a gateway: it led to corruption, to indolence and, ultimately, to disappointment. These were the lessons of his childhood, the conclusions any young person in his circumstances could be forgiven for drawing: that correlation was tantamount to causation; that secular politicians simply made bad politicians.

Mustapha did not have to look far for corroboration. One of his role models, Sheikh Abdessalam Yassine, a onetime Sufi spiritualist with a long, grandfatherly grey beard, once called non-Islamists "bestial" and likened them to "Satan." Their policies, he said, were based on the "imported ideologies" of either capitalism or communism, were "poisoned by superficiality" and by a "chronic disease of weakness."[2]

For Mustapha, the world seemed different now, and his adversaries seemed different, too. He and his diverse Islamist counterparts were increasingly encountering opposition from an unexpected source: each other. He was not the only one who was taken aback by these developments. Even after graduate training in the religions and politics of the Middle East at Harvard and Oxford, and following service in the U.S. Peace Corps in Morocco, I was still puzzled by the wrangling and backbiting I was witnessing, by the level of enmity being saved for supposed brothers. Recruiters like Mustapha once talked of an Islamic pact, of uniting all religiously inspired activists under one solitary Islamic state. Now they barely spoke to one another.

But why? Wouldn't it make more sense for them to cooperate? Their shared goals would be easier to achieve; alliances would allow them to reach wider audiences. They were all Sunni Moroccans, who recognized, even if they sometimes rebutted, the central authority of the nation-state. While there may have been minimal theological distinctions between them, these distinctions were blurring. And they all appeared to desire a more expansive role for religion in politics, a state ruled in some form by Islam. Indeed, early Islamist writings often counseled a commitment to unity, to sticking together in the face of oppression.[3]

For much of the last quarter of the twentieth century, cooperation here was, indeed, the norm. The two main Islamist movements in the country—Mustapha's group, the Justice and Spirituality Organization, or Al Adl wal Ihsan (Al Adl), and their main rival, the political party modeled after the Muslim Brotherhood, the Party of Justice and Development (PJD)—used to send representatives to each other's meetings.[4] They also used to march together, even issuing joint communiqués on issues ranging from Palestine to prisoner abuse.[5] Yet, in both of their cases, they were now more likely to forge alliances—to march arm in arm—with non-Islamists (those old Satanists) than with each other. "We have *new* brothers and sisters now," Mustapha would tell me, with no hint of regret. A member of his rival group once described to me how he spent a portion of his university years trying to find common ground between Islamist groups. But he eventually gave up. "That was an impossible dream," he said.

What was happening to Islamism? The collective effort to apply Islamic teachings to the practice of politics could no longer be blithely conflated with terrorism; it could also no longer be assumed to be monolithic. Its varied proponents had moved from personal calls for piety to a sophisticated force in Arab politics, from purveyors of social services to political machines, from unwieldy umbrella movements to localized, plural forms of protest. Nonviolent mainstream Islamist groups had been gaining in popularity, but new power struggles also seemed to be making this shifting landscape even more complex to navigate.

It was apparent that I had many questions, and Mustapha suggested we share a glass of overly sweetened mint tea, his fifth of the day. "Moroccan whiskey," he called it, mischievously invoking the name of the country he hopes to lead one day and the alcohol he would never dare touch. By the time I left Mustapha, it was nearly dusk. I was drunk on sugar and my mind was racing. But I wasn't going anywhere. I set out the next day with a goal: to immerse myself in this puzzling new world—the world of competing Islamists.

I did not come to the topic lightly. I was wary of overstating discord, of writing Middle East politics through clumsily constructed binary oppositions such as secular/religious, moderate/radical, Sunni/Shi'a, or fundamentalist/nonfundamentalist. It seemed as if such divisions could sometimes be manufactured merely by their continuous declaration. After all, the citizens and identities I had come to encounter were more intricate and intersecting than such blunt categorizations suggested.

And yet, to capture the politics of the Middle East and North Africa today and for the foreseeable future, one particular relationship seems almost inescapable: this is the dawn of the era of Islamist versus Islamist. It is only through finally focusing on the factions and fissures between and within Islamist movements—viewing them as complex, competing organizations and not as crude, coherent entities—that we can begin to uncover the shifting nature of the Islamist project itself. That was the aim of my research, and it is now the aim of this book.

This book is based on extensive ethnographic fieldwork among the young and divided Islamist rank and file in Morocco (including intensive participant observation, in-depth interviewing, and textual analysis)—the challenges of which I will uncover in the following chapter. It does not rely on the familiar framework of state-opposition relations. Instead, it begins to unlock the incipient industry of Islamism.[6] This is, at its core, a work of political sociology, informed, most of all, by scholarship in social movement theory, comparative politics, and the sociology of religion. But to make the material accessible to a wide variety of readers, I have also aimed to write in a lucid, narrative style. In my nearly four years in Morocco, I witnessed firsthand the development of political Islam in one place.[7] But these experiences also shed light on what is happening in other parts of the Arab world.

★

This is the story of the future of political Islam as told by those already living it: young Moroccan Muslims. When I first met them, activists like Mustapha had no way of predicting that they would soon be given an opportunity not just to vie for power, but to hold it. Nobody did.[8] A textbook published in April 2010 as part of a series on the "Contemporary Middle East" included this sentence in its final paragraph: "It does seem clear that political change in Tunisia will not come about through some dramatic event that suddenly replaces the existing order with a new one."[9] Yet, astonishingly, that is exactly what happened.

By now, the tale of the Arab Spring is a familiar one. In December 2010, young people in Tunisia and then Egypt and then across the region, in different forms and phases, began to shake themselves free of the shackles of authoritarianism, chipping away at decades of repressive rule that was once deemed indestructible. After the protest signs were put away, after the revelry faded, after the horns of merriment stopped blaring in the streets of the Middle East and North Africa, a new Arab world was born. Except it didn't quite look the way everyone wanted it to.[10]

It became popular to proclaim, especially among Western political analysts, that the Arab Spring descended into a long "Islamist winter"—that moves toward freedom only managed to pave the way for ostensibly dark days of Islamist rule. *Washington Post* columnist Charles Krauthammer, for example, forecasted Islamism writ large as the "new totalitarianism."[11] And, at first glance, the evidence appeared straightforward enough: in nearly every Arab country where elections took place in 2011 and 2012— in Egypt, Tunisia, Kuwait, and Morocco—Islamist parties posted historic victories.[12]

Then, in the summer of 2013, the Egyptian military signaled that it had had enough: it deposed the government led by the party affiliated with the

Egyptian Brotherhood and arrested the new president, Mohammed Morsi. And, soon, analysts began asking a new question: was the Islamist project dead in the water?

A fixation on this apparent "rise and fall" misses a more consequential story, however, one that scholars have yet to tell. Even as Islamists continue to expand across this contested region, intense struggles between and within their movements are mounting. Islamism is splintering. Nowhere in the Middle East or North Africa does a single Islamist group hold a monopoly on popular mobilization. Everywhere the dilemma confronting young Arab Muslims has become not *whether* Islamism, but rather, *which* Islamism.

This is still evident in Egypt, where at least fifteen Islamist parties materialized after the fall of Hosni Mubarak.[13] Even so-called Salafi activists—who once joined Al Qaeda in condemning political participation as unjustly appropriating God's work—have entered the electoral fray. In the Egyptian parliamentary elections of 2011, for example, they went head to head with the triumphant Muslim Brotherhood, ripping down their posters, poaching their members, and eventually placing a startling second. When the military initiated its coup in 2013, many Salafis even preferred to side with them over the Brotherhood. And the Egyptian case is now even more comparable to Morocco: with the country's largest Islamist movement again relegated underground as the vestiges of an authoritarian regime once seemingly on the wane now shows continued signs of endurance.

Thus, over the course of mere months, what was once a Moroccan anomaly—rampant Islamist infighting—suddenly became a regional reality. The age of competing Islamists is officially upon us. What will happen in this next phase of the Islamist movement? What will happen when Islamists have to compete not just with non-Islamists, but also with *each other*? How, in the face of new rivalries, will Islamists work to win the hearts and minds of Arab citizens? These are the questions driving this book, and the questions that are set to define the future of the Middle East and North Africa.

★

The central argument of this book is that Islamist groups that emerge from this dynamic marketplace—from this wild, disordered arena of inter-Islamist contestation—will bear little resemblance to the Islamists of yesteryear.

To find out how, we first need to move beyond a tendency to conceptualize Islamist movements almost exclusively in relation to the state and not in relation to one another—to what the scholar of Islam, Bjørn Olav Utvik, calls "the wider Islamic environment that is their immediate habitat."[14] Realities on the ground now demand a more fluid analytical framework: a move beyond a focus on Islamism *as* opposition and toward an approach that appreciates oppositions *within* the opposition.

We need to look not simply at the multiplicity of movements, but also at the force of their collisions—not simply at how they compare, but how they compete.[15] Examining movements in this way will allow us to see that they are shaped not just by structural constraints and conditions, by political openings and opportunities afforded to them from the state, but also by their relationships with each other.

Second, we need to recognize the Islamist movement for what it is: not a single, united, overarching mission, but rather a dynamic and complex amalgamation of competing organizations and orientations. Thus, despite calls to regard them as aberrant or somehow distinctive, Islamist groups are, at their core, complex social movement organizations and, like such organizations the world over, survival—self-preservation—is their primary aim.[16]

Competition has grown fierce because in order to expand, to increase, or even to maintain membership, each needs adequate commitments of time, skills, and money—and most of all human power. This intensifying race for limited resources—for relevance in the midst of rivalry—invariably propels them to change the way they do business, including how they attract new members, what messages they relay to them, and which members they target in the first place. Put another way: in order to continue to remain a viable competitor, to stay in the game, each Islamist rival has no choice but to respond to one another.

This race for resources is, above all else, a race to recruit. Despite the many differences among Islamist groups, there is one feature that characterizes them all: demography. Two-thirds of all Arab Muslims are under the age of thirty. Or as one activist once told me: in the Middle East and North Africa, "kulshi shabaab." Everyone is a youth. Put bluntly, young people are the new currency of political Islam—the coveted constituency that each movement requires for self-preservation.

What happens next contradicts much of what has been predicted. In the face of stiff competition and a scramble for similar pools of potential young recruits, Islamists do not necessarily try to "outbid" each other, to rush toward the extreme, to be one acute thing to one specific set of people. They also do not seek out a broad uniformity, to dilute the scope of religious authority so much so that they can be everything to everyone—trying to generalize their message to appeal to what political scientists call the "median voter."[17]

7

Rather, something else is taking shape, something I call "Islamist plural-ism." The movements I studied are working internally, even contorting themselves, to be as many things to as many different kinds of young peo-ple as possible, making room for a multitude of activists and multiple ave-nues to activism—all at the behest of those they seek to attract: young peo-ple. They are reshaping and reinventing, in short, to offer a place where new members can be *who* they want to be.

Some analysts still maintain that the fundamentals of Islamist recruit-ment have remained unchanged since the 1950s.[18] My research, by contrast, uncovered multiple forms of activism within these robust and layered or-ganizations, especially with their varied political, social, and religious wings. A leading scholar of political Islam once sought to show how young Islamists were primarily "recruited by insistent mosque preachers, crude revolutionary pamphlets."[19] But very rarely are such preachers or even their texts the first ones to engage potential recruits. More often than not, the first people youth encounter are each other. And, contrary to public perception, young Islamists in this competitive milieu increasingly attract one another not by selling organizational rigidity—firm lines of hierarchy and control—but rather by promising and preaching personal choice, au-tonomy and freedom, by offering the ability to carve out what young peo-ple want: their own individual identities.

The lives of young people are simply too complex and too multilayered for all to follow reflexively the same path or even the same individual leader. Just as there is no such thing as the monolithic Islamist movement, there is also no such thing as the singular Islamist activist. We need to rec-ognize their diverse and fluid identities, ideologies, backgrounds, person-alities, and desires. Youth now have a multitude of choices, new opportuni-ties to sample Islamic wares: trying one on for size before moving on, coming and going between groups as they please. A decision to join one movement is always embedded in a decision *not* to join another. Each young person sets her or his own course, constructing what "religion" means—and, in the process, challenging already fading monopolies of po-litical authority and Islamic interpretation. Young Moroccan Islamists like Mustapha—actors for whom religion and politics were once considered al-most congenitally intertwined—are now at the forefront of reimagining categories that were long deemed fixed.

In the end, Islamist pluralism is born out of strategic realities. When I confronted young activists with this heterogeneity, I was not met with de-nial or consternation or embarrassment. Instead, most embraced it. This is a sampling of some representative responses that I will expand upon in later chapters: "Everything must be reinterpreted." Or "Yes, it's ok, it is something different for everyone." Or "This is just my own understanding." When considering a point of interpretation, one longtime Al Adl activist told me, "not everyone feels this way—you will find others in the group who think something different." "And that," he said, "is good." Mustapha himself once noted the efficacy of this tractability: "It is because of our multiple parts and approaches that we are successful."

By design, different identities not only co-exist within these organizations—they are *encouraged* to coexist. Their complex organizations make room for such internal pluralism; Islam itself allows for it; the competitive milieu demands it; and the diverse orientations of young people call for it.

★

Thus, to understand how Islamists are responding to competition, we have to focus once and for all on those that their groups are fighting so intensely to attract: the youth that eventually become known as the rank and file, the foot soldiers, or the base. The chapters that follow will take us to Morocco to offer a close-up look at who they are, what they want, and who they do (or do not) listen to. The four sections of the book are meant to unfold like the peeling of an onion, carefully uncovering and unraveling various parts of their activism, and engaging and unwrapping assumptions that too often shroud our understandings of them and their movements.

Part I, "Relationships," is devoted to developing the proposition that Islamist movements cannot be understood in isolation—that, in short, all Islamism is relational. But before I go into the roots of the relationships between the two main movements in Morocco, I explore my relationship to each of them.

Chapter 1 looks at the methods and challenges involved in studying both legal and illegal Islamist movements up close. How does one go about engaging diverse rank-and-file activists and would they even talk to me? How also could I trust what I would be seeing or would be told?

Then, in chapter 2, I seek to understand how these movements have evolved over time, and, in the process, provide important background on the political and religious contexts of the movements in question. Why, for example, would an Islamist group that had previously exhibited little interest in forming a political body—and had formally rebuffed them and even decried their existence—suddenly move toward forming its own quasi-political party? These are similar questions to those being asked of Salafis in Egypt and across the region, for example, who long shirked the political arena, but suddenly embraced it in 2011. They are different actors in different contexts with different histories, but common threads mark their behavior. Egypt in 2011 and Morocco in 1997 shared one connection: it was the year that the largest Islamist group in each country formed a political party—the Muslim Brotherhood's Party of Freedom and Justice (FJP) in Egypt and the PJD in Morocco.

The answers to understanding these evolutions lie not in a change of heart, but rather in a change in the competitive environment. I show that Islamist movements coevolve. To use a biological analogy, movements are less like organisms and more like species: alive, moving, and functioning not in individual isolation, but in strategic interaction within a wide ecosystem in which they develop alongside other beings.[20] Thinking about them in this way is helpful because it forces us to focus not just on big, broad strokes—their success or their failure—but instead on diverse movement activity, on the back and forth, on complex relationships that, in reality, tend more to ebb and flow, not rise or fall.

Next, the two chapters of part II—"Identities"—grapple with a central yet elusive puzzle of contemporary political Islam: what drives young people to join one Islamist movement *over* another? It is a deceptively complicated problem. For half a century, social scientists have studied why individuals would join social movements at all. For at least two decades, they have hypothesized about why they might join the Islamist movement in particular.[21] But these efforts have focused largely on only part of the equation: on what leads people to rise up in the first place, to give up their time and energy and sometimes freedom, especially when they could gain similar benefits simply by watching, by free-riding. To join or not to join—that has been the question.

But the multiplicity of actors, players, and contenders across the Middle East and North Africa now demand different kinds of questions. How, we must ask, do young Arab Muslim citizens navigate this changing landscape, where they choose among a selection of Islamist groups and often alternate among them? We will see that, contrary to popular assumptions, deciphering these puzzles is not as straightforward as retracing the paths of their parents or siblings or neighbors or even friends—or finding out who offered them the most generous good or service or even whose prayers or doctrines they most heeded.

In fact, these are new questions that can only be answered in new ways: by peering into and behind the places and faces that tend to be overlooked, at the parts of young people's lives that, in the words of political anthropologist Yael Navaro-Yashin and the sentiment of philosopher Walter Benjamin, often "escape formalized articulation, normalization, citation, sit-ing."[22] I show in these two chapters that we cannot begin to understand what motivates young Islamists—what drives their decisions, what informs their politics—without understanding the textures of their daily lives. Their multiple experiences in the world around them shape how they seek to change that very world. The clothes they wear, the roads they live off of, the designs of their homes, the websites they look at, their shifting prospects of marriage, the sources of their news, the food they consume: it all matters.

This is terrain that is, admittedly, not normally traversed by policy makers or even most political scientists. It is a decidedly messier vantage point than that offered, say, by district-level voting data, raw polling numbers, or macroeconomic trends—or even by the cold texts of party platforms. But there is meaning to be found in what is too often dismissed as the mundane.

The chapters of parts III and IV investigate and reassess young Islamists' relationships with competing authorities—first with the state (part III) and then within their organizations (part IV).

The anthropologist Saba Mahmood has argued that Islamism has long been cast as a "historical anomaly" largely because it "frames its object as an eruption of religion outside the supposedly 'normal' domain of private worship."[23] Mahmood writes under the shadow of classic democratic and civil-republican theory, with its normative assumptions of secular-liberal politics.[24] Yet, in Morocco and, for that matter, many Arab states, the eruption of religion outside the private sphere is far from abnormal. To the contrary, an eruptive *absence* of religion in *public* space would itself constitute a "historical anomaly." As the theorist of religion Talal Asad has noted, even within supposedly secular states, the state is constantly faced with the function of defining and crafting and regulating the religious domain. The state, according to Asad, is never "that separate."[25]

Many Arab regimes have explicitly sought—for their own benefit—to define, craft, and institutionalize Islam "outside" the realm of the private. It can be said with some confidence, for example, that, since its inception, the modern Moroccan monarchy has sought to do just that. In part III— "Shadows"—I explore the reach of the king's religious authority in a globalized age, an age of unprecedented competition, antagonism, and rivalry. How do young Islamists relate to the authority of this modern Arab state? And, how, in turn, does such a state exercise its supposedly vast authority in a variegated world—a world where a ruler's voice is only one among many, a world where authority itself is necessarily multiple?

The answers, I argue, lie not simply in deciphering state policies but also in looking at how they are understood—in uncovering the multiple social worlds in which young people and the state interact. To this end, this section is devoted to analyzing numerous such encounters—including Islamist group gatherings, meetings, and conventions held in homes, cafés, city halls, official state buildings, instances of police action, and diverse applications of administrative law.

In the final part of the book—"Individuals"—I turn my attention to the internal dynamics of Islamist groups. Here, I look closely at who young Islamists listen to or do *not* listen to within their organizations, at who they might look to for direction, and at how they make sense of those who are purportedly guiding them. To answer these questions during my field-work, I wanted to move past a reliance on the isolated pronouncements of movement elders or the talking points of movement elites. It is difficult to assess how religious authority is constructed, for example, when the only data being analyzed are the words of clerics themselves.[26]

Such a methodological approach and its reliance on religious texts only manage to reify the perception of young people as disempowered by-standers. It is tantamount to studying a sermon, even listening to it up close, but not talking to audience members afterward to find out what they were thinking or how they interpreted the words being uttered. It is also equivalent to imagining a sermon being delivered to an empty room or, if the room is full, assuming everyone in the audience digests the sermon wholesale.

Instead, I chose to listen to activists making sense of the world around them, not merely others envisioning the world for them. To borrow the terms of anthropologists Gloria Raheja and Ann Gold from a different context, I aimed to "listen" to, not just "watch" the voices of young activists.[27] And, by doing so, my goal is to make the subtle yet significant point that the pronouncements of old men in grey beards are no more important than the voices of young activists in blue jeans, djellabas, and multiple mobile phones.

The diverse stories of mobilization we hear—and the organizational charts drawn by members that we will examine—belie predominant accounts of Islamist movements: of uniform submission, of undue deference paid to certain figures, of Weberian charismatic authorities hovering above all, of the "wise leading the blind."[28] A reference book on Islamism, for example, declares this as fact: "The rank and file member does not enjoy freedom of opinion."[29] Another describes a "cult of personality devoted to their general guide."[30]

The chapters that follow reclaim the role of young activists as thinkers—and important ones at that. They are neither blind followers to those supposedly directing them nor passive spectators to events unfolding around them. Far from being absent from the process of organizational change, they are on its front lines, continually crafting ideas and socializing others to them. Confronting competition for similar supporters, every young recruiter becomes a reinterpreter; every individual Islamist becomes an independent interlocutor. And through these dynamic interplays of ideas, new models of Islamist activism are born—from the bottom up and the inside out.

★

I want to pause for a moment to clarify my terms. What, the reader might ask, does "Islamist" even mean? I remember one of the first times I considered this question. It was late one afternoon in Rabat, and I remember it because it was cloudy and wet. The streets were empty. The stores were late in opening up from the lunchtime siesta. Rabat, like most places with near perfect climates, does not quite know how to manage in the rain. The only person around was a newspaper vendor. Merchants like him arrange dozens of publications on the ground, often on a makeshift sheet; this spot had a large umbrella above it to keep it dry. People just hover. They stare, sometimes for hours, at the magazines and newspapers, peering at the pictures, the bold letters, the black and white print. Headlines and cover stories are particularly important in these publications—for these are often all the passerby will ever see. As I stood among the crowd, waiting for the city to wake from its slumber, one magazine cover in particular managed to catch my attention.

The banner headline was provocative and, in retrospect, prophetic. In bold Arabic type it read: "What Will Islamists Do If They Gain Power?" Its language was deliberate—and revealing. It employed the Arabic plural of "Islamist": *Islamiyyūn*.[31] Large, overlapping photos of *two* men jumped out from below the bold typeface. Even on a single newspaper cover, no one group occupied the page. Pictured were the leaders at the time of the two main Islamist groups in the country: Abdessalam Yassine, the founder and "spiritual guide" of the banned and illegal Al Adl (Mustapha's movement) who died in December 2012; and Saad Eddine El Othmani, then the head of the legal and electorally included Party of Justice and Development or PJD. Both men had beards, though Yassine's was longer, scragglier, and greyer. (Othmani became the country's foreign minister in 2012.)

As we will see, there are other groups, even within Morocco, but like the newspaper that day I focus here on the two largest ones.[32] PJD, as noted earlier, was formed as an outgrowth of a movement inspired by the Muslim Brotherhood model.[33] Like its Egyptian ideological prototype, the Moroccan Brothers also overcame early violent roots. A top Al Qaeda thinker (Abu Musa al-Suri) once even referred to the 1970s group that gave rise to PJD as a "paradigmatic Jihadi group."[34] But its members, many who have risen to the rank of government minister, cling to the conviction that change is most effectively pursued from within the political system. This has been the party's hallmark, beginning with (or, indeed, as a basis for) its licensed admission by Moroccan authorities into the electoral process in 1997.

Al Adl, on the other hand, complicates casuistic categorizations of religio-political activism. It is illegal but nonviolent, repressed but thriving. Its members boycott elections, but are also politically engaged. Officially formed more than three decades ago, its founder, Yassine, was once a prominent Sufi spiritualist leader. And, while the group is organized in part like a traditional Sufi brotherhood, it also functions like a modern political party, replete with a political wing (or "circle"), official spokespeople, compound organizational charts, internal elections, and multiple websites. It has not shied away from calling for the—nonviolent—overthrow of the Moroccan regime and for an entirely new system of government. It remains today the largest single opposition force in the country.[35]

When I use the term "Islamist Movement," I do so to refer to groups such as these. I use it, in sum, just as the vast majority of the citizens of the Middle East and North Africa do: to signify the individuals whose largely nonviolent efforts to engage or participate in the political process, usually in the form of political parties and movements, are guided or animated by Islam or Islamic principles.[36] Despite their diversity—and despite their vast grievances with the postcolonial Arab state—these actors nonetheless accept and function within the authority of such states. And even though not all take part in elections—some boycott them and others remain illegal—all recognize the political process itself as legitimate or, at the very least, lawful. Such activists increasingly come in the form of conventional politicians, bureaucrats, legislators, and current or wanna-be parliamentarians.[37]

The members of groups such as the ones in Morocco or *Ennahda* (Renaissance) in Tunisia, *Islah* (Reform) in Yemen, or the Muslim Brotherhood–linked parties in Egypt or Jordan need no modifier; they are simply Islamists. To proceed otherwise would be deceptive: it would imply that the majority of Islamists are today violent. Instead, it is those who eschew politics or still employ arms that require the caveat of a modifier.[38]

To complicate matters even more, the umbrella terms "Al Adl" or "PJD" or "Muslim Brotherhood" do not by themselves come close to capturing the varieties of activism associated with their numerous allied associations and movements, the complexity and dynamism of which I will disentangle in part IV of the book.

Some, no doubt, will take issue with the label "Islamist" itself. Some consider it a Western invention. But I adopt it here largely because the activists I lived among employed it—and often proudly. "A Muslim," in a formulation more than one articulated, "is simply a person who performs rituals." But an "Islamist," on the other hand, is "someone who strives to establish a state based on Islam."[39] "We're not just regular Muslims," I would also often hear with pride, "we have a project and are doing our best to implement it."

Thus, I am not focusing here on violent extremists—the global Jihadi movements of the Al Qaeda or ISIS type—who exist squarely outside the realm of the modern nation-state and who condemn as apostates anyone who engages politically with such a state. I am also not focusing on militants, such as Hamas or Hezbollah, who experiment in electoral politics, but simultaneously engage in violence. Such groups have straddled the line between national liberation movements and full-blown domestic insurgencies.[40] And even though they now often play outsized roles in local governance, it remains largely impossible to disassociate them from their military wings, which still plan and plot terrorist operations.[41] Simply put, regardless of how some might continue to mislabel them, such movements do not represent the mainstream of political Islam.[42]

★

My arguments took shape, inductively, in the cities, houses, secret gatherings, and public protests of Morocco, but they can also help us think about the development of political Islam elsewhere.[43] I want to spend the remaining pages of this chapter dispelling frequent misconceptions about the North African country and addressing a question that many readers will no doubt be pondering: What can Morocco tell us about the rest of the Arab world?

When the novelist Paul Bowles first caught a glimpse of Morocco in the 1930s, he became convinced it was a "magic place."[44] The Moroccan government long ago embraced this fantasy, selling itself as a bastion of calm in a troubled region, the Arab world's model of reform.[45] Yet, for all that the Moroccan regime has done to hold itself out as inimitable, political developments over the last three decades there have shared much in common with its neighbors.

This was the job description that could have been applied to most of the region's leaders, including Morocco's: an authoritarian leader with almost total control of the institutions in the country, one who has built a repressive police apparatus, which engages in torture, and curbs press freedoms, peaceful demonstrations, and active political oppositions; has paid mere lip service to the pervasive problems of corruption, cronyism, unemployment, and socioeconomic inequality; and, despite the rhetoric of reform, has constructed weak legislative bodies with limited governing authority.

Every index of Arab governance (including those by Transparency International, Freedom House, World Bank, and the Arab Human Development Report), rank Morocco not as outstanding, but as decidedly average or even below average.[46] Contrary to the fantasies of Moroccan exceptionalism, reform in the country has stalled for much of the last decade. While Morocco has often been spared the political unrest of some of its neighbors, national elections in 2007 and 2011 were noteworthy not for who voted, but for who abstained. Intentionally spoiled ballots reached their highest level in Moroccan history. If one counted those blank or spoiled ballots, that total would easily represent the largest vote getter, surpassing any party.[47]

It is no coincidence, therefore, that the word most commonly used by Moroccans to describe the governing elite is *makhzen* or warehouse—for the bulk of the power of the country's major institutions has remained tightly stored within its confines. Secret U.S. State Department cables released by WikiLeaks in 2010 accused the Moroccan government of profound corruption and "appalling greed." The documents expressed in writing what most citizens already suspected: "major institutions and processes of the Moroccan state are used by the Palace to coerce and solicit bribes."[48]

Some might rightfully note (as I pointed out earlier) that the king of Morocco maintains a powerful religious role, and claims direct descent from the Prophet Mohammed, but so too does the king of Jordan. And, for that matter, Hosni Mubarak, the Assad family, and the presidents of Algeria, Iraq, Yemen, Tunisia and most every leader in the region (not the least of which the Saudi royal family) went to great lengths to control and dominate the religious sphere, sometimes even engaging in what one scholar cleverly called "prophet sharing."[49] Thus, the myth of the "secular" Arab autocrat was never quite so. Throughout the last half century, the constitutions of Egypt and even Tunisia long declared Islam as the official religion of the state; Egypt's even prescribed Islam as "the main source of legislation."[50] In fact, in a comprehensive survey tracking government regulation and favoritism of religion in the Middle East, Morocco ranked statistically in the middle of all Arab states.[51] Moreover, as I show in part III, Islamism is policed in Morocco less by the force of the king's religious aura than by varied social mechanisms available to most leaders.

To be sure, much has been written about the differences between Arab kings and presidents, between monarchies and republics. The systems of rule certainly influenced which authoritarian leaders were deposed from office in 2011 and beyond (it is undoubtedly easier to banish a president than a monarch, especially one such as Morocco's whose family has ruled in some form since the seventeenth century). And it is also true that monarchies, bolstered by the confidence of the throne, made slightly more room for opposition actors to emerge. But, in the end, regime type had little impact on the ways citizens living in these countries experienced reform—or lack thereof.[52]

Morocco also does not represent an economic utopia in its region—just as it does not represent a political one. Throughout the 1990s and 2000s, many economists and policy makers touted North Africa's economic progress. "Today," wrote one glowing economics professor in August 2010, "less than nine per cent of Moroccans are considered 'poor,' compared to 16.2 percent a decade ago." This particular adulatory piece was entitled: "Morocco's Economic Model Succeeds Where Others Fail."[53]

But the African Development Bank has shown how poverty in Morocco and throughout North Africa is more complex than such figures suggest. Many statistical studies rely on outdated definitions of poverty; and seemingly low absolute numbers obscure vastly unequal distributions of wealth within and between regions. Daily life in Morocco, as we will see, regularly illuminates these incongruities: one sees slums next to mansions, panhandlers outside five-star hotels, and, in Rabat, unemployed medical students on daily hunger strikes in front of the ornate, cordoned-off parliament building.[54]

Morocco, like its North African neighbors Tunisia and Egypt, remains stuck as an emerging economy where resources are scarce, but labor is abundant. And, despite mostly top-down liberalization efforts of the 1990s and 2000s, certain structural factors continue to depress a still struggling labor market. Economic turmoil in the nearby Euro-Zone has affected an increasingly interconnected Morocco: tourism revenues, the need for migrant laborers in Europe, and the amount of remittances being sent are all down. Due largely to improving healthcare standards, fertility has slowly decreased, but not before the years between 1990 and 2010 produced what has been called "the greatest labor force pressures from young male and female workers" in the country's history.[55] Indeed, the increase in education among women ironically has added even more stress to an already distended labor force. This is true even while female labor force participation in the Arab world remains among the lowest in the world.[56]

One additional point: Morocco is also not immune to terrorism. On April 27, 2011, to use but one example, a student walked into my office and asked if it was safe to study in Morocco. "Definitely," I said. The next day seventeen people were killed in a suicide bombing in Marrakesh's main square, at a popular café that I had frequented dozens of times. (Fortunately, the student still planned to go.) The deadliest attack in recent memory occurred on May 16, 2003, when suicide bombings across Casablanca killed forty-five people over four locations: a tourist hotel, a Jewish-owned restaurant, a European consulate, and a Spanish social club. It has come to be known as Morocco's 9/11. As they are in Iraq and the Arabian Peninsula, Al Qaeda affiliates in North Africa are still active. In September 2013, for instance, Al Qaeda of the Islamic Maghreb called upon all Moroccans to wage jihad.

Of course, in the end, there is no such thing as an archetypical Arab state. All possess distinctive political, historical, economic, social, and cultural characteristics. But if the Arab Spring demonstrated anything, it was that the Arabic-speaking countries to the west of Egypt demand more of our attention. The main countries of the Maghreb—Morocco, Algeria, Tunisia, Libya—have consistently been understudied, overlooked in favor of the more recognizable or seemingly significant countries of the region, such as Egypt, Syria, Jordan, or Lebanon. Yet, the events in North Africa in 2010 and 2011 that spearheaded both widespread regional reform and tumult prove that the Maghreb can no longer be ignored.

Part I

RELATIONSHIPS

in search of the offices or headquarters of the banned Islamist group, Al Adl, he would not find them. If he looked to recent measurements of Islamist mobilization favored among social scientists—election results or incidents of violence—the largest Islamist group in the country would also not be on display. If he went to the souq or market in the old medina or even to one of the ornate bookstores that line the wide boulevards of the new city and asked shopkeepers for material by the movement's founder, Sheikh Yassine, he would be met, as I often was, with only suspicious or purposefully unknowing stares. Even if he peered inside a mosque looking for all forms of Islamist activism, only certain legal groups would be visible. And if he ventured beyond the major cities, where Al Adl, for one, often operates under different organizational umbrellas to evade repression—with names, I discovered, such as al-Waha or al-Manar—he would have an even harder time tracking them down.[3]

It would be as if certain Islamists did not exist. And yet, all this time, the legal political party, PJD, with its official offices, daily newspaper, public parliamentarians, and published policy papers, would be in full view.[4] But, contrary to popular assumptions, what is excluded electorally or even repressed does not simply disappear. Rather, in terms familiar to a deconstructionist or even a psychoanalyst, such movements "return to unsettle every construction, no matter how secure it seems."[5]

★

How does one locate something that is purposely hidden? When Sigmund Freud, for one, first asked an American audience to consider the "repressed," he invited them to conjure up the image of *two* rooms: a large hallway that led to a smaller space. Perched between these areas stood a single gatekeeper with the power to decide who could proceed from the big room to the smaller one—from the oversized yet crowded and uncomfortable realm of the unconscious to the vaunted gateway of the conscious.[6] This is often a confused, competitive process, Freud described, as both rooms are filled with those who constantly "jostle one another." The inhabitants, one analyst wrote later, are "like a crowd of suitors hoping for an audience."[7] In the end, that single gatekeeper, like an authoritarian ruler or military dictator, ultimately decides what is "inadmissible to consciousness."[8]

Freud's spatial rendering, he admitted at the time, was "crude"—just as it is in this instance to evoke the overlapping relationships within and among Islamist movements. In the case of Morocco, the metaphor helps us imagine an Al Adl held back, trying to propel its way to the forefront of national politics, constantly challenging both the guard—and its fellow Islamists—only to be relegated to that large, unruly room. It is here where they continue to exist, where they occupy an often hidden (and too often ignored) methodological underworld of cybercafés, téléboutiques, text messages, mirror websites, contraband DVDs, photocopied pamphlets, cell phone screensavers, sleepovers, private house meetings, illegal or unsanctioned protest marches, semi-public avenues of democratic contestation, and student, not necessarily national, elections.

PJD, on the other hand, by virtue of its legality and its electoral inclusion, has been granted entry into the visible, accessible, familiar domain of the conscious: a world of existing datasets, parliamentary elites, government representation, state-run mosques, electoral results, polling, ministry offices, party headquarters, and even newspapers. These are Islamists who have come in from the cold.

In this light it makes sense that the vast majority of studies by social scientists, policy makers, and journalists suffer from what one of their own once called an election "preoccupation."[9] It is so much simpler and more straightforward, for example, to research groups such as PJD, whose members sometimes converse in French, whose activists are listed in the phonebook, and whose leaders invite you for sweetened tea at their plush parliamentary offices. Who would want to risk getting arrested when doing his or her research?

The U.S. government, for one, has not had much luck or interest in deciphering the multiple varieties of Islamist activism. A classified 2008 cable to Washington, DC from the embassy in Rabat—released via WikiLeaks—revealed that diplomats could not even figure out what to call Al Adl (was it Justice and Charity Organization or the Justice and Spirituality Organization?).[10] The authors also seemed shocked that the group "may be moving toward political participation"—even though the formation of its "political circle" had taken place a full decade earlier. This confusion was understandable. The embassy admitted that it had not had any communication with the group for at least seven years—because the last time they tried to make contact with Al Adl, the Moroccan government "protested." In a practice that has become all too common, the United States relied on a foreign government to determine which of its nationals Americans would engage.

★

It is true that working with a banned, illicit movement involves obvious methodological challenges. But, as with most assumptions related to the region, the story on the ground reflected a more intricate reality. It was certainly more straightforward to locate PJD initially, but not always easier to get them to agree to talk to me or, more specifically, for them to allow their members to converse openly with me or to move beyond the formal strictures of party positions and documents. Al Adl was more difficult to find, but once accessed, they proved far more eager and willing to speak freely.

This paradox is best understood by extending the psychoanalytic metaphor discussed earlier. Let's return, for a moment, to Freud's two rooms, to the realms of the conscious and unconscious. Imagine, again, Al Adl as the unconscious: hidden, even forbidden, and challenging to access. The task involved is so onerous, so steeped in pitfalls, that Freud once suggested that making the unconscious conscious was the overriding task of psychoanalysis itself.[11] But once an analyst accesses a patient's unconscious, often through painstaking daily sessions of analysis, she is rewarded with less inhibition and constraint. PJD was at first easier to contact—to see—but it was nonetheless more difficult to penetrate their "conscious defenses" or "barriers."[12] Their very consciousness presented as "perpetual awareness."[13] They often exuded cooperation, yet seemed nervous or reluctant to want me to take a closer look around.

Take, for example, my first encounters with each movement. Looking back, the patterns were evident even then: the formalities, the necessary connections, the protectiveness of PJD. And then there was Al Adl: infinitely more difficult to uncover, but ultimately much more disposed to allow me to stay (and visit) after I had managed to find the door—and proved my willingness and ability to understand what I was seeing.

I first met Al Adl's second in command, Fattalah Arslane, early on in my fieldwork. When I finally reached him by mobile phone after many tries (I had succeeded in tracking down the number from a contact in England), he gave me only the name of an avenue where I could go to meet him. He asked if I had a mobile phone and then told me to call him for further instructions when I arrived. The street, it turned out, was one of the largest in Rabat. Twenty minutes into the trip there the taxi driver glanced over at me as if to ask for directions. I asked him if we were on the correct street, Shari ʿal-Majid. He laughed and said we had been on Shari ʿal-Majid for nearly ten minutes.

I decided to call the house. A young woman answered and immediately (and convincingly) declared that Arslane was not there, sounding as if I had dialed the wrong number, as if no one by that name actually lived there. I told her about my arranged meeting. She then asked me to hold.

She returned to the phone and asked that I get dropped off at a bank on the avenue. Luckily, we had not yet passed it. The taxi driver soon deposited me in front of the closed, deserted bank. The street was empty, almost silent. No one was around except for a man selling freshly squeezed juice for a dirham a glass from a small cart out front piled high with oranges. I waited for about ten minutes. A man suddenly emerged out of a block of nearby apartments and walked toward me from across the street. This was not Arslane but rather Hassan Bennajah, a younger man, one of his deputies, and, it turns out, the head of the youth branch. (Bennajah would later become a major leader of the country's Arab Spring protest movement, coordinating marches to challenge and topple the monarchy.) It was surprising that Hassan was there that day considering that I had only told Arslane in passing, over a noisy phone connection, that I was interested in talking to young activists. Hassan then escorted me inside one of the nearby buildings.

When we entered the apartment, Arslane was sitting on a couch in his salon. A short, stout, slightly overweight man with a full dark beard and the build of a wrestler, Arslane has been with the movement since its inception and was often seen at Yassine's side. "I am ready to answer all your questions," he began. "It is better that you will hear from me than read the wrong information about us in the newspapers." Thank you, I said politely. He then allowed me to turn on my digital recorder and we sat in his living room for almost three hours. Hassan walked me out and scheduled a follow-up meeting with me so that we could talk more.

When we next spoke, Hassan again expressed his appreciation: "It is us who thank you. Just as Mr. Arslane said last time. We encourage communication. You, at least, have come to us and are ready to listen, unlike others who just judge us with little information." In the coming months, his fellow activists would often share with me a Moroccan proverb to make a similar point: "Elli ma'arfek kheserek" (He who doesn't know you, loses you). The colloquial meaning was discernible, but was nonetheless invariably followed by an explanation: if someone never takes the time to get to know you, they cannot possibly claim to understand you.

★

The experience of tracking down the head of PJD at the time, Saad Eddine El Othmani, the man who became the country's foreign minister in 2012, was different. His email address was found through a routine Google search; his fax number was listed on the party's website. But it took months for him to finally agree to see me. When I first arrived at the party's main headquarters, a repurposed grand villa on a leafy residential street in Rabat, I sat in the waiting room for close to an hour. The secretary, a veiled woman probably in her late thirties (but looking more like her late fifties), asked if I was a Muslim—and continued to grill me, while feigning friendly banter, about my intentions. She eventually agreed to escort me up the stairs, past the outdoor courtyard, to the secretary general's office.

Othmani, a lanky man of medium stature with a soft grey beard and a slightly high-pitched voice, greeted me at the door, smiling. A psychiatrist of Amazigh or Berber origin from the working-class southern transport town of Inezgane, Othmani is a serial smiler. He peppers his statements with grins so often that it is difficult to find a photograph of him *not* smiling. One cannot help but wonder whether he was, all this time, consciously trying to lend a happy, benign face to the often-feared Islamist party.

"Tefeddal" (Please), Othmani said, as he pointed to the formal sofa, next to his desk. A large, burly man with a thick mustache was sitting on a sofa opposite me, quietly mumbling my name to himself as if to sound out a puzzle, or perhaps unnerve me. Maybe that was his role. "Spee-gul." "Shpee-gal." "Sipee-gil." It was as if he was attempting to decrypt my name in his head: "American?" "German?" "Brit?" "Israeli?" "Jew?"

Othmani spoke over him and asked first about an old professor of mine at Oxford, who he knew had written articles about the party. He was concerned that he had not read all of them and made me promise that I would send him additional copies. "Did you see that I was in the United States?" he then asked. "I received an award in Washington!" He was referring to being named "Muslim Democrat of the Year" by the Center for the Study of Islam and Democracy. His voice then got higher and he smiled even wider, if that was possible. "Waash shuftee sondage?" (Did you see the poll?) He was referring to a controversial poll sponsored by an American NGO that showed that his party would post large gains in the upcoming national elections.

I nodded, and he then asked me why I wanted to see him. I cautiously said something about wishing to understand why young people were supportive of PJD. I meant it, I suppose, as a gentle introduction, a polite ice breaker. But Othmani quickly became defensive, as if wary of admitting too much success. "How do *you* know they do?" he quizzed me. "What evidence do you bring me to maintain that youth do support us?" He wanted proof. He then asked me what I thought before he offered his answer. I tried to pivot: "Well, these are the sorts of questions I came here to have answered." Frustrated, he grabbed his mobile phone on the large, rectangular coffee table in front of us and called the person who was serving as the head of the party's youth wing, Aziz Rabbah. "Aziz will tell you what you want to know," Othmani said, pointing to the door. He was kicking me out. But this was actually a welcome gesture—as I had been trying (unsuccessfully) to reach Rabbah for months. After Othmani's intervention, I had a message from Rabbah that evening.

Rabbah, who would go on to become the country's minister of transportation in 2012, agreed to meet me at the party headquarters later that week and then again at the courtyard cafeteria of his office in the prime minister's building, where he worked as a technology consultant, and where we shared a tagine, a slow cooked stew. The next time I saw him, a few months later, was at his party's convention, to which he had invited me. On the second day of that convention, I got out the questionnaires I had prepared in Arabic and began passing them around to young party activists.

Within minutes, a party official materialized in the seat next to me, several crumpled copies of my survey clutched in his fist. I had been discovered mingling, as I usually did, among the young party faithful. (I had snuck into the conference: with no credentials, I often waited for a large group to gather at the door, rattled off some greetings in Arabic, and then made my way past security.)

The interrogation was soon under way. Who was I? What was I doing there? Who invited me? I explained that I had met months earlier with the secretary general of the party, who in turn put me in touch with Rabbah, the head of the youth wing, who then invited me to the conference and even asked me (I think facetiously) to bring along some American "democracy trainers."

My interrogator scampered off for backup. When he returned, he grabbed my hand and escorted me outside. Standing there waiting for me was none other than Aziz Rabbah. We exchanged handshakes, kisses on both cheeks, and the requisite, repetitive greetings about his health and my family.

And then, suddenly, his tone changed: "Why did you not come to see me when you arrived?"

"I tried to find you," I fumbled. "You are very busy."

He edged his face closer to mine. "Well," he said, "you cannot pass out your questions. You need permission."

I could have apologized. I could have reminded him that I possessed an official government research clearance—not a small feat for a foreign researcher in this part of the world. I could have pleaded that trying to track down a well-known party leader such as himself was a bit like trying to have a word with Mick Jagger at a Rolling Stones concert.

But I was reluctant to allow this to become a lesson in proper obeisance, even in a country where citizens commonly kiss their monarch's feet. "Your party campaigns on a platform of transparency," I blurted. "What have you got to hide?"

In a flash of frustration—tempered by a hint of intrigue—he snapped back: "We believe in transparency—but organized transparency."

I was allowed to stay, but was relegated to a roped-off section in front. They said it was an honor, but now they could control the show. No more surveys for me, but plenty of opportunity for positive PR for them. But, it turned out, there was a reason that the party was so wary of outsiders.

★

As a relatively new political party, PJD had everything to lose by opening up to the foreign researcher. It had worked assiduously to construct its image, especially abroad, with its carefully assembled platforms and cautiously worded public statements. There is an understandable defensiveness that comes with increased visibility, like the presidential press secretary who hews closely to briefing books, afraid of veering too far off script lest she actually say something newsworthy. It is one of many paradoxes of modern democracy: the more a party participates in campaigns, the more guarded it seems to become.

There is also a certain protectiveness that comes with increased success. An avowedly secular academic friend of mine in Rabat, for example, has been embroiled in a legal dispute with his downstairs neighbor for almost three years. He was suing his neighbor for running a halal butcher shop out of his apartment without first obtaining a permit. The noise from chopping whole carcasses, the overflowing crowds, and, of course, the stench of rotting meat—not to mention the flies—had all become too much to bear. (They've since given up and moved.) But at the end of one of his long tirades against his butcher neighbor, my friend unintentionally demonstrated the challenges of a new political party. "And, you see, he's PJD," he moaned. "They say they are honest, but, look, they aren't." With this single, isolated example, my friend managed to dismiss an entire movement. With notoriety, it seems, also comes scrutiny.

To be sure, PJD activists, particularly leaders, tend to keep more demanding schedules than their Al Adl counterparts. Engaging in the bureaucracy of governance brings with it certain responsibilities: meetings, legislative hearings, conferences, conventions, and overseas trips. Many have jobs in parliament or even work for the movement's allied newspaper. When I met with the chief party strategist, Mustapha Khalfi, he was so busy, he said, that he insisted we meet at the train station on his way home after a long day at work. He has, at various times, edited the party newspaper, overseen its student wing, devised strategy for the party, and pursued a doctorate. (In 2012, it was almost as if it wasn't enough for him to be appointed minister of communications; he also assumed the position of chief government spokesman.) When I first saw him at the station, he was waiting to board his train, and he refused to sit down. While everyone else around us sat comfortably in chairs, we stood for ninety minutes at the counter at the café inside Rabat Central.

But even if his colleagues at times weren't as busy as they liked to suggest, they certainly relished appearing so—as if working legally gave them reason for their superiority. As one activist later noted to me, in sentiments repeated frequently, "We could do anything, but we work for Morocco. We believe that our home, our organization and our party need help from us. It is our responsibility to give what we can to our country. It is not merely to fill empty space in our schedules. No, it is about convictions. We try to give the best of ourselves to our country."

In contrast, Al Adl had very little to lose by talking to me. With its ability to produce its own propaganda severely limited by the authorities, almost anything I reported would likely be better than the current perception of them in the popular press: an illegal, surreptitious, revolutionary, cult-like, Islamist group. In many cases, simply by virtue of the fact that I was actually talking *with* them, seeking them out (and, therefore, not relying on third-person, largely negative accounts, or official narratives of state-run media), certain individuals categorized me as being receptive to their agenda. In this instance, even though it might not always be the case outside of the research setting, my mere presence was encouraging. As a group of young Al Adl activists once told me: "You are the first outsider we have ever met with. This is something new to us. A few years ago, we were afraid. But now we need to show people our aims, our objectives, our suffering. People need to know."

Take also the example of a research tool I would frequently employ: the digital recorder. PJD members often asked why I needed to use it, seemingly nervous of what I might I catch them saying. Al Adl activists welcomed it, eager for a mouthpiece, for any chance to get their message out. Those in PJD are also used to speaking with academics and journalists; they were skilled, tired, and likely wary of the exercise.[4] The by-product of being ignored (and being perceived as unapproachable) by outsiders is that Al Adl members are often very eager for any date to the dance. Also, its limited legal status and lack of formal headquarters meant that we most often met in more familiar settings—cafés, homes, etc.—where more prolonged discussions were easier. There is a certain intimacy involved when you visit someone in their own dwelling—when you see where they live, glance at pictures of their families, receive hugs without warning from their children, and if, even in passing, if even for a brief moment as they bring you tea or slip trays of cookies in front of you, you exchange greetings with their wives.[15]

When I would phone Al Adl members, I was consistently met on the end with a stalling technique: "Alo? Alo?" Pause. "Alo? Alo?" Longer pause. "Alo? Alo?" The skeptical silence was judicious: who was this person, with an unrecognized number, and a funny voice? Should they talk to me or just hang up? But my face-to-face encounters were usually different. When I would finally meet them in person, as I did that day at Arslane's house, they would almost always express gratitude *to me* for seeking them out. I recall being astonished by the very first thing Arslane said to me at our first meeting: "Shuukran" or "Thank you."

★

There was still an issue that concerned me: how could I trust what I would be hearing or seeing or being told? To study contemporary Islamism is to study quotidian competition. It invariably means being drawn into—and navigating—a netherworld of alternating beliefs, conscripts, games, and ploys, with each actor working to convince you, the researcher, that they are in the right. A typical day would involve seeing an advisor to the king in the morning, and then meeting those who wanted to overthrow the monarchy later that afternoon.[16] I would often finish that same day by attending a PJD event, talking with young people who tried to explain why working with the king was the best way forward—and why fellow Islamist groups actually presented the greatest obstacle toward progress.

My research, like the train line between Casa and Rabat, proceeded in constant motion—ambulatory, fluid, moving among cities and movements and multiple cohorts of members. I followed an approach that I like to call "shuttle ethnography."[17] I combined extended ethnographic fieldwork, more than two hundred unstructured interviews, and the analysis of texts and relevant survey data when available (and appropriate). Like a shuttle diplomat, I bounced between actors, challenging each group's pontifications with insights and objections culled from their competitors. I found that there was no better way to tease out their beliefs and positions than to invoke this contrarian view; and this allowed me to better understand the nuances and distinctions between and within groups. I observed and listened, but also interviewed and cross-examined.[18]

My aim was to try to move beyond the often-canned rhetoric (and talking points) of publicly prepared documents and statements, and instead to listen directly to the young people who make up the majority of these movements. It is a central contention of this work that the oft-ignored lives of these young people have meaning—that they represent significant unexamined texts of political Islam. Following the practice of political ethnography, I place their words front and center, as part of the text itself—for their lives, their thoughts, their experiences, and even my interactions with them, are portals into "the lived experience of the political." Because, to borrow the formulation of the great social scientist Charles Tilly, we cannot understand why things happen if we don't understand how they happen.[19]

I spoke to activists in their homes, and at cafés, party gatherings, protest marches, and group meetings. Anywhere, in short, where they would normally hang out. As political scientist Lisa Wedeen, who has carried out fieldwork in Syria and Yemen, has noted: "texts do not actually 'talk back'"—but "people in unstructured interviews do." This, she argues, enables "us to understand the effects of particular . . . actions, the multiple but nonetheless specifiable ways in which people *make sense* of their worlds."[20] More often than not, young people did indeed manage to make their leader's texts "talk back," critiquing and reinterpreting the tenets underlying—and guiding—their movements writ large.

Another approach I employed was to observe individuals and events over time, to make note of diachronic shifts in attitudes, feelings, or impressions. My research was not consecutive, but rather spread out over the course of many years (1997–2014). Even early on in Morocco, I began to notice that, contrary to the crisp chronological boundaries sought after by scholars, the ideas I encountered were not circumscribed simply by the periods of my presence. Fieldwork begins and then usually ends (perhaps a year or two later), but the people we study continue living.[21] Thus, the extended period of my own research has allowed me to take a wide view of these movements and their members—to follow their evolutions and life courses more comprehensively than is usually possible. It allowed for time to leave and then return, for time to consider conclusions, to re-question, to follow up.

It was also significant that we all spoke the Moroccan dialect of Arabic. Young people were not being forced to craft or fumble over sentences in a foreign language for my benefit, not responding to me in French or Modern Standard Arabic, languages they know but don't normally speak. Over time, I was able to become an active eavesdropper—participating by *not* participating. I wanted to be able to watch them interact with potential recruits, for example, and then compare the substance of their discussions with what they were telling me. If they were putting on a show for me, I ultimately concluded, then they were also putting on a show for everyone else.

Of course, there is, as it has been pointed out numerous times, no research without the *researcher*.[22] Despite our best efforts, despite an earnest hope that some "objective truth" could somehow be uncovered if only the right methods or techniques were utilized, we, researchers, are always there: seeing the world through our own eyes, being seen, even in multiple ways, through the eyes of others. I snuck into conferences, and lingered in the backs of crowds or the middle of protests; I was sometimes even asked if I was just a *Faasi* or a local pale guy from Fez. I still instinctively touch my heart with my right hand after shaking someone's hand—a practice I picked up from my years in Morocco. And, yet, however much I spoke the language, grew a beard, adapted local customs, or even managed to blend in, I was never "invisible"—for no researcher ever is.[23] But I nonetheless worked hard to hear and learn and listen to what activists were saying to each other, rather than just what they might have wanted to articulate purely for my own benefit.

After one of my initial interviews, when I left Arslane's house that very first time, and after his deputy, Hassan, said his good-byes, I remember, of all things, what the bus driver told me about the summer sun. I was sweating by then and as I got onto the bus, I referred casually, perhaps defensively, to the heat. "Skhuun elhaal," I said. He replied, laughing: "Haadi lbidaaya akhuya maazaal maazaal" (This is the beginning, my brother, just wait, just wait). He was, of course, talking about the weather, and about the looming start of summer. But I remember thinking, as I looked out at the rows of jacaranda trees lining the side of the road, and at the multiple overflowing intra-city buses changing lanes in front of us, that, for me, this was the beginning of a different sort: that my patience and perseverance in tracking down names and numbers and contacts and subjects would begin to bear fruit. And that I would soon gain entry to the remarkably expansive, once off-limits world of Islamist youth. This was the world that I had come to see.

Chapter 2

COEVOLUTION

When Itimad Zahidi was a student in the late nineties, she was precisely the kind of person any Islamist group would want to attract. Smart, well-spoken, and telegenic, she was studying to become a computer engineer. Even then, she held herself to high moral standards: she chose to wear the veil at an early age for reasons of modesty, and she came to adapt the conservative leanings of her family members—not because they told her to, but because she chose to. She also had a keen interest in politics. Her favorite book growing up was *La Mémoire d'un Roi*, an account of King Hassan II's reign by French journalist Eric Laurent.[1]

She studied elections closely. She watched—with what she says was "hope"—when elections took place in Morocco in the winter of 1997, in the thirty-sixth year of King Hassan's thirty-eight-year reign. Across the country, young people just like her observed how small signs of Hassan's often ceremonial attempts at political liberalization were beginning to appear from under the shadow of monarchal rule. Political scientists often cite these last parliamentary elections under Hassan II for the changes they brought to formal political institutions in the country.[2] When Moroccan voters went to the polls in 1997, they selected candidates who would become members of a newly formed bicameral legislature.

For the first time in Moroccan history, the person who would become their new prime minister, Abderrahmane Youssoufi, was a direct product of the election results—leading to, even if only in the most literal sense, the country's first ever "opposition" or *alternance* government. Youssoufi was not only the leader of the largest party in the legislature (Union Socialiste des Forces Populaires or USFP), but it was the kingdom's largest and most long-standing opposition party.

Itimad remembers thinking there was a chance that the new government could do something that no prior Moroccan politicians had been able to do: transform the static political system. But, just like for most citizens, these expectations and hopes never quite seemed to mesh with the realities of its rule. After assuming office in 1998, the Socialists stumbled and ultimately offered little by way of change. The perception over time was that instead of changing the system, it changed them. For her part, Itimad came to believe that real solutions could only come from the "moralization of politics." Her hope, from her own assessment of history and current events, was that a broken political system, a system of corruption and little result, could be improved by applying the lessons of her faith to the practice of politics.[3]

Itimad soon looked past Youssoufi and the USFP, and, instead, she began to pin her hopes on the small faction that finished ninth during the 1997 elections. That year, Moroccans sent—for the first time—nine Islamist candidates to parliament, paving the way for the creation the following October of the country's first official Islamist political party, PJD. A noted Moroccan scholar later reflected on the implications of that 1997 vote, remarking simply that "attitudes toward Moroccan Islamism will condition the democratic future of the country."[4]

This was certainly true for Itimad. Around her eighteenth birthday, she decided to join a political party, and she knew exactly where to go. In the town she lived in—Temara, just outside Rabat—she headed directly to the local office of PJD, the only legal Islamist party in the country. Her father advised her against it. He was worried that political activism would adversely affect her grades. But she was fortunate. Most of the party's events— conferences, meetings, get-togethers, rallies—were intentionally planned for weekends so that she could remain focused on her studies. When she first arrived at the party office, she remembers exactly what the man sitting there said. "You must be a rebel," he told her, she recalls even now with a smile and a sense of satisfaction, marveling at her own personal courage and conviction.

When I first met her in 2006, the party had identified her to me as a rising star. "I want to help others," she told me, "I want to work for the sake of the community, not for someone else—just like PJD." She would go on to become a member of both the party's central electoral committee and its governing youth board. By 2011, the year PJD swept national elections, she was elected to Morocco's parliament from Temara at age twenty-eight— the youngest woman ever to be elected to the body. When the party first placed her on the parliamentary list, she was working as a computer engineer and studying for a master's degree in finance. She quickly assumed positions as a member of three influential parliamentary committees: on Islamic affairs, on foreign affairs, and on Moroccans living abroad. In 2013, when I showed young PJD activists the pictures that I had taken of my first meeting with her, everyone immediately recognized her unchanged face. "That's Zahidi," they said. She was famous.

The stories of Itimad and of young Islamist activists just like her cannot be understood in a vacuum. Their paths provide important insights into their myriad motivations (which we will examine in the following chapter) as well as into the trajectories of the movements around them—the movements competing for their support. Making sense of Islamist mobilization means making sense of options, and at the time Itimad was considering political Islam, she didn't have many. If she was interested in a religious organization that offered avenues for formal political activism, there was only one major avenue available to her: PJD.

For its part, the other main Islamist movement in the country, Al Adl, had up until that point rebuffed efforts to form its own official political wing and denounced formal political activism in general. But that would soon change.

★

What would lead Al Adl, seemingly suddenly, to move toward organized political activism, to spawn what members would come to call "a quasi political party"? How did PJD even come to form a political party in the first place? What, in sum, explains these Islamist movements' paths to political activism?

In this chapter, I want to begin to answer these questions by telling a new story of Islamist evolution. It is one marked not simply by repression, but by competition—a competition to win the support of young people just like Itimad Zahidi. In this light, movements' behavior is best understood as a strategic calculation to survive in dynamic interaction not just with those setting the rules of the game (the authoritarian state), but with their movement opponents as well. They don't just evolve in relation to the state; they coevolve in relation with each other.

The premise of "coevolution" is far-reaching and straightforward: Social movements are shaped by regimes and also by other actors around them.[5] They develop not just based on their own ideas or even the specific openings or limitations afforded to them from above, but rather in competition with one another for success. This success is increasingly measured by attention, by resources, and most acutely by effective youth mobilization. In the midst of this competition, what ensues can partly be understood by a process theorists call "diffusion": political openings afforded to one movement, for example, spur the other to compete even more actively in the political sphere. One group's gain is another group's opportunity.[6]

But the textures of coevolution go beyond isolated incidences of contagion or diffusion, beyond one group piggybacking on another's opportunities. Instead, movements, like species, tend to evolve gradually—not always in dramatic shifts, but rather in small ways, over the course of "events" distributed over time across a variety of actors.[7] Understanding these processes, then, involves honing in on dynamic relationships that develop between them.

The goal here is not to provide exhaustive histories of these movements. Rather, I want to hone in on "events" over the course of three main stages of their evolutions: the *genesis* of their movements; the *building* of new formal organizations; and, finally, the *expansion* of separate and systematic political wings. The evidence is culled largely from the recollections and retellings of current and former Islamist activists from both movements.

The histories of PJD and Al Adl are usually told separately, with each assigned separate categories or chapters or even books of their own. Yet, their evolutions can only be fully appreciated if they are relayed in unison. "Theories of protest and social movements," write the sociologists Pamela Oliver and Daniel Myers, "must be theories of interaction and relationship."[8]

Along the way, these movements' responses to each other can almost always be understood as relational, but not necessarily linear or formulaic. They mirror one another depending on the competitive context, sometimes reflecting, sometimes refracting, sometimes borrowing, sometimes adapting or even reorganizing in order to keep up with the other.

In the last three decades of the twentieth century, an era of Islamist experimentation and expansion, the individuals and incipient groups that would go on to form what is today PJD and Al Adl saw models and potential in one another's successes and setbacks and consistently adjusted to these ebbs and flows, including regarding the use of violence. To gain legality and recruits, one movement (the future PJD) came to embrace the religious and political authority of the state while the other (the future Al Adl) refused, mirroring the monarchy in some ways, but ultimately seeking to replace it.

Their paths have been characterized not by inelasticity, but by fluidity and appropriation. Yassine, we will see, once worked for the state that he and his movement would later seek to topple. The future PJD head, Abdelilah Benkirane, was once a member of a movement who threatened the very state he would later serve as prime minister. Moreover, Yassine was once a leading member of a Sufi Brotherhood he would come to renounce— the same brotherhood that the state and, as a result, Benkirane's PJD would later come to embrace.

From the beginning of both Al Adl and PJD, neither one operated on separate planes. They have always had each other, and their competitive environment, in their sights. As early as 1987, Yassine once wrote that the Islamist strains in the country were so related that they would one day merge (with Al Adl presumably swallowing all else).[9] Yet, in the midst of increasing competition between the groups, few members of either movement would soon likely concur. It is a relationship, we will see, that would only intensify, as both movements grew and widened their spheres of support—and especially when, beginning in the late nineties, they *both* moved toward expanded political participation.

The three sections that follow trace these very paths, setting the stage for the continuing battle for hearts and minds that would ensue in the twenty-first century—the battle at the heart of this book.

THE GENESIS

When the seeds of the respective organizations that would go on to become PJD and Al Adl began to develop in Morocco, the Muslim Brotherhood, the world's oldest Islamist movement, had been operating for close to four decades in Egypt, having first begun in Alexandria, Egypt in 1928. Its writings and persona had been well known and well read the world over. Spurred by the model of the Egyptian Brotherhood, and even aided by some of its early members, the Islamist movement Harakat al-Shabiba al-Islamiyya (Movement of Islamic Youth) or Shabiba was formed—or at least legalized—in 1972 by schoolteacher Abdelkarim Mouti.[10] It had been operating secretly and behind the scenes starting in 1969. Though not an official part of the Brotherhood's network, it adapted its model of a comprehensive social, political, and religious movement and promulgated the work of its forefathers, Sayyid Qutb and Hassan al-Banna.

Morocco's first modern Islamist movement appeared during a time of domestic political uncertainty and unrest. Only a year after inheriting the throne from his father, Mohammed V, Hassan II proposed a new constitution in 1962 to introduce a legislature to the political system. He then spent close to a decade grappling with threats from opposition forces, most notably in the form of student riots, an increasingly vocal Left, and even from multiple coup attempts. He responded with brute force (against protesters), political assassinations (against Leftist leaders, most notably Mehdi Ben Barka), and with wit and wile (to survive multiple coups).

As opposition forces called for more open political rule, Hassan II consistently outmaneuvered them, crafting new constitutions in 1970 and 1972 and holding referenda (which won 98 percent of the vote) with claims that he wanted to see a more democratic system, but wanted to personally oversee that transition.[11] He also always fell back on the monarchy's religious roots. While the country's first constitution (1962) was largely borrowed from the French, there remained one overriding difference: the formal anointment of the king as the "Commander of the Faithful" or *Amīr al-Mu'minīn*.[12]

If the formation of an organized Islamist movement was new to the Morocco of the 1970s, political mobilization on religious grounds was anything but. Examples from Moroccan history abound.[13] At the turn of the twentieth century, for example, noted religious figure Mohammed al-Kattani mounted opposition to the sultan at the time. Later, the founder of the Independence party (Istiqlal) envisioned Islamic governance in newly postcolonial Morocco. Of course, this blending of religion and politics is embedded in the modern monarchy itself (an issue we will investigate in part III of this book).

During one of many episodes of constitutional revision during his long reign, Hassan II declared (in 1969) that he was limited in his ability to transfer power to legislators. He wanted a stronger parliament, he claimed, but a larger force constrained him. "Islam forbids me," he declared, "from implementing a constitutional monarchy in which I, the king, delegate all my powers and reign without governing." "I can delegate power," he went on, "but I do not have the right, on my own initiative, to abstain from my prerogatives, because they are also spiritual."[14] He ultimately settled on a special brand of "Hassanian" democracy, where parties could compete, but where the king would hover above all.

As part of his authoritarian rule, Hassan was careful not to let any opposition become too powerful, even bolstering some groups to offset others. Islamist movements did not escape these calculations. The regime initially had been open to the country's first Islamist group, Shabiba, as a possible counterweight to the rising Left—in what one Moroccan scholar called an "objective alliance."[15] And Shabiba's leaders did not hide their disdain for their non-Islamist competitors: one referred to the main Socialist party as one "of heathens that secretes atheism."[16] These Islamists' aims were the "social construction of Moroccan society" by "encouraging the Moroccan citizens to enjoin righteousness, virtue and reform through the implementation of Islam."[17]

Rampant unemployment, political stasis, and social malaise helped lay the groundwork for their rise. But, ironically, so did Hassan II's own machinations. To stamp out socialism and Marxism on campuses, for example, he forced universities in the early seventies to require Arabic courses and to form Islamic studies departments, which often displaced faculties in philosophy and the humanities.[18] Such action, not surprisingly, paved the way for the Islamicization of the country's main student union, a trend that continues today.

But even in the midst of its ascent, Shabiba did not go unchallenged. The same year it was formed another stream of Islamist activism also began to emerge. Some have suggested that what makes this second outlet unique, what distinguishes it from other Islamists in the country and particularly what would become PJD, is that it arose almost from nowhere, divorced wholly from historical antecedent or political analogy.[19] This *sui generis* trajectory contrasts, under such a reading, with PJD, which can be linked to Morocco's first Islamist movement, Shabiba, and from them, the Muslim Brotherhood outside Morocco. But such assumptions are misleading. Both Islamist movements developed in relation to one another, to other religious movements, and to the Moroccan state itself.

If Shabiba was modeled on the Muslim Brotherhood, this second stream was carefully modeled on the Muslim Brotherhood *and* a different kind of brotherhood: the Boutchichiya Sufi Tariqa. Such tariqas or orders are usually organized around "masters" or "guides," who help adherents cultivate spiritual and mystical connections with God, most often through specialized ritual practice. The Boutchichiya, the largest such order in Morocco, whose adherents number in the hundreds of thousands, formally eschews politics, but has nonetheless tacitly supported the ruling Alawite dynasty.[20]

As Shabiba's Mouti was building his organization and getting ready to legalize it, a forty-four-year-old former bureaucrat by the name of Abdessalam Yassine was becoming closer to assuming the head of another major one, the Boutchichiya.[21] Mouti and Yassine shared much in common. Both were former inspectors for the education ministry. Mouti even ascended to the position of secretary general of the Union of Education Inspectors.[22]

Yassine's interaction with the state was a consistent theme in his early years: first as an alumnus of the state-run al-Yusifiyya University in Marrakesh; then as a public school Arabic teacher; and finally, and most starkly, as a bureaucrat within the Ministry of Education.[23] It was from this staid perch as a lowly *fonctionnaire*—an inspector working for the government—that Yassine suffered what he called a "spiritual crisis," and transitioned to membership with the Boutchichiya.[24]

If a spiritual crisis led Yassine to join the Boutchichiya, how then did he come to leave it, just six years later? To find the answer, one would have to examine the events that transpired in 1971 in the northeastern town of Madagh, outside the major city of Oujda near the Algerian border, where the Boutchichiya Sufi order gathered for their annual pilgrimage celebration.[25] The year 1971, however, was a momentous one. Followers would learn of the appointment of their new master, the successor to the renowned Sufi master Sheikh Abbas. For the members of the Boutchichiya order, it was the Sufi equivalent to waiting for the white smoke billowing from the Vatican. The process, ostensibly apolitical Sufis will tell you, is far from a political decision. Unlike with the Pope, there are no favorites, there is no pre-game handicapping or preliminary polling. This was purportedly an executive decision made by a single individual.

By all accounts, the dying Sheikh Abbas had two choices before him to be his successor: his gifted son, Sidi Hamza, or a talented new disciple, Abdessalam Yassine. Yassine had been an active member since joining the brotherhood six years earlier at the age of thirty-eight. The succession was not, as genealogy might suggest, a foregone conclusion. The decision, according to Boutchichiya members, revolved around who was most equipped to handle and disseminate the divine inspiration, the *sirr* or se- cret of the Boutchichiya. There were, as one member of the Boutchichiya recalled, "many struggles between physical son and spiritual father." Ulti- mately, the spiritual father selected his biological son.[26] And less than a year later, Abdessalam Yassine left the order altogether.

The remaining part of the story is told in two distinct ways, depending on the person with whom you speak. According to interviews with current Boutchichiya members, Yassine lost his way. He departed from the world of the "spirit" and began experiencing the earthly qualities of jealously, envy, and hubris. He was passed over for the "promotion" and he did what most would probably do in that situation: he decided to quit to save what was left of his earthly pride.

The accounts one hears from members of Al Adl are different. Yassine did not fail the Boutchichiya; they failed him—and the rest of the country. It was not, they say, a personal falling out; it was a pragmatic split, perhaps even a deep division of conscience. Yassine had for some time been push- ing the Sufis to take more notice of the surrounding society and social con- ditions, the towns and villages that they lived in, and to do more for the world around them. But his plans did not mesh with his old Sufi brothers, and, according to Al Adl activists, there comes a time when a person has to be loyal to his heart and not merely to the organization to which he be- longs. And this, according to Yassine, required him to begin to think about forming his own organization.[27]

These were the roots of his Islamist activism—applying religious teach- ings to the world around him. Upset by the poverty and unemployment he saw, he became convinced that he could not be a "good Muslim"—or even a good Sufi—without working to help others. "You can't have spirituality, without transforming reality," one Al Adl activist named Younes said in recollecting those events.

And besides, Yassine felt that Sufism itself was changing; the asceticism that had marked its earlier days had been eclipsed by rampant materialism. Sufi spirituality, as Al Adl members now recall, suddenly became fashionable, with shiny new cars, "a lot of money," and "a lot of couscous."[28]

But there is evidence to suggest that Yassine did not simply come up with these ideas out of nowhere. When Yassine set out on his own, when he was even contemplating setting out on his own, even when he was pushing the Boutchichiya to take a more active approach to political affairs, there was a prototype, even an incipient competitor, closer to home. Yassine's departure from the Boutchichiya cannot be understood as simply a personal journey. Instead, the beginnings of Shabiba proved that the regime was open to Islamist activism, signaling that it was amenable to the formation of an Islamist organization. We also know that Shabiba was in Yassine's sights even back then. According to Yassine's family, the leader of Shabiba, Mouti, approached Yassine to form a partnership, but Yassine refused—preferring, instead, to set out on his own.[29] An elder member of the Boutchichiya told me that at the time Yassine left the Sufis, he had "become too concerned with power, with politics, with the Muslim Brotherhood."

Yassine was careful to sell a new product: to differentiate his work from the existing Muslim Brotherhood-type groups by creating a hybrid of the Muslim Brotherhood and a Sufi tariqa.[30] He hoped to bring attention to society and politics around him by combining a Sufi sensibility and a strict reading of the Prophet's Sunna. The eventual name of his future movement (not made clear until 1981) captured this hybridization: to combine *Adl* and *Ihsan*—justice and spirituality.[31] He aimed for a wholesale remaking of the individual and the wider body politic, beginning from the bottom up with individual Moroccans. His organization, driven by da'wa (or proselytizing), would soon seek to extend itself across all segments of society: from secondary schools and universities to trade unions and professional associations to women's organizations and athletic clubs. But his intentions went beyond propagation. Yassine laid out plans to create what he called "equivalent organizations in each of these areas," with the hope that these new organizations could ultimately eclipse, and even replace, the corresponding "official" ones run by the state.[32]

Boutchichiya members would later tell me that this effort was misguided from the start: that the idea of using Sufism for politics was "corrupt." And that once he left the Sufis, Yassine was no longer "authorized to guide souls." To make the point, the late Moroccan professor and Boutchichiya member, Zakia Zouanat, relayed to me the story of a young woman who came to them after following Yassine. She was, Zouanat described, "like a woman who had what seemed like a very deep illness, like a piece of chopped up liver, *kebda*, like dried flesh." Such an outcome, Zouanat said, was inevitable: Yassine's recipe of infusing Sufism with political concerns was so misguided to the Boutchichiya that it was literally sickening.[33]

The movement that Yassine himself would eventually go on to form, Al Adl, would constitute a wholly distinct body from the Boutchichiya. Yet Yassine's training during those formative years with the Boutchichiya was not in vain.[34] In fact, these institutional antecedents can be seen in Yassine's first public act in 1974, just two years after leaving the Boutchichiya.[35] It was then that he released his infamous one hundred fourteen-page "Islam or the Flood: Open Letter to the King of Morocco" (*Al-Islam aw al-Tufan: Risala Maftuha ila Malik al-Maghrib*), which set out a clear protest agenda.

While Shabiba at the time was taking a more conciliatory approach toward the state, Yassine set his future—and his group's—in opposition to it.[36] According to Yassine, the Moroccan state, including and most notably its king, stood in the way of progress. Yassine sought to replace the king by using the monarch's symbols, yet drawing on his own lineage and training—mirroring the king in opposition, in what political scientist Malika Zeghal once termed a *mimesis contraire*.[37] He dismissed the monarch as nothing more than his "brother," constructing an image of himself as an Islamic advisor or *'ālim*.[38] He alleged that the king had become an unworthy authority, a corrupt sellout to the West and Israel, and declared that the custom of *bay'a*, or allegiance to the monarch, should be reversed—that the king should prostrate himself to the people.[39] He made sure to point out that he too was descended from the Prophet; his family's origins of Ait-Bihi were Shérifs Idrissides from the region of Oullouz in the Souss (southern Morocco).[40]

The letter was such a bold and dangerous stroke—criticizing the monarchy publicly, even putting himself on par with it—that Yassine has said that he prepared his burial shroud upon completing it. This was not an entirely surprising choice in an era when the regime's political opponents were routinely murdered and/or "disappeared."

Instead, Yassine was sentenced to an insane asylum. In assigning Yassine's punishment, King Hassan's message was not accidental: only a crazy person would consider attacking him in this way. A senior Al Adl leader, Abdelwahed Moutawakil, told me that the real reason Hassan could not bring himself to assassinate Yassine was for religious reasons: he could not kill a holy man such as Yassine. Others maintain that there was a political rationale: killing him would have made Yassine a martyr, thereby making him even more influential. One Moroccan journalist took a more cynical approach: Hassan was a king with a playful side, he told me, displaying that he had a sense of humor.[41]

As Yassine stepped up its challenges to the monarchy, so too did Shabiba, but with one exception: Mouti's group allegedly turned to violence. Thus, Shabiba's legality was short-lived. In 1975, the first Islamist movement in Morocco was implicated in the assassination of the Socialist leader, Omar Benjelloun. Mouti was prosecuted for the assassination, but in absentia, as he had allegedly fled abroad (to Saudi Arabia, or perhaps Libya). Although the assassination was the stated reason for the prosecution, there were numerous underlying factors. Mouti's movement—which denied any involvement in Benjelloun's death—had perhaps grown too strong and had begun to form a threat of its own to the regime. When Shabiba failed to support King Hassan's military incursion into the Western Sahara (known as the "Green March") in 1975, the implication was unambiguous: this was a movement that dared to oppose the monarchy.[42] Mouti's far-reaching indictment accused him of "forming an association of criminals, plotting the overthrow of King Hassan, and creating an Islamic republic."[43]

THE BUILDING

By the early eighties, Islamism in Morocco appeared to be at a standstill. Mouti was under indictment. Yassine was in an asylum. Groups formally aligned with, or even inspired by, the Muslim Brotherhood were facing bans and crackdowns across the region. The tacit support of authoritarian leaders such as Hassan II was souring. The specter of Iranian-type Islamic revolutions at home was more disquieting than leftist oppositions.

Still, what would become the two major Islamist movements in Morocco found ways to continue to grow and to build their organizations. For its part, Al Adl was not diminished by Yassine's confinement; in many ways, it was bolstered by it. With Yassine unable to travel (in an asylum until 1989 and then under house arrest), his admirers learned to exploit new formats and forums for mobilization, such as magazines, cassette tapes, and (much) later the Internet. As was the case with Islamist movements across the region, repression also forced it to become resilient and even creative: discovering ways to operate beyond the purview of the state, in mosques and in local associations committed to social work, education, and health care.

Even Yassine's refusal to call for violent action was part of a wider growth strategy. Violence, he said, was the sign of "impatient activism," for it could lead to a precipitous end to a movement's lifespan and be used as a pretext for all-out state clampdowns (just as it had with Shabiba).[44]

The incarceration of Yassine and the frequent arrests of other leaders also compelled less visible members to rise and assume responsibility. This often left the task of recruiting to individuals, including high school teachers, peers, pupils, and university students. Aziz, a future Al Adl member, recounts his own recruitment around this time, one typical of those early years—when teachers led the way, members were initiated largely through Qur'anic study, and secrecy was of the essence.

In 1986, Aziz was thirteen. The schoolteacher who recruited him told him only that he wanted him to join some of his fellow classmates in outside learning about the Qur'an. It felt like extra credit for the best and the brightest, he said, and he heartily agreed. The teacher told him that they would meet at a specific mosque every Sunday, and then make their way to a nearby garage. He should expect to see other young people at the mosque, the teacher said, but he also warned Aziz not to congregate with them.

"Do not go to the garage together, as a group. Do not walk with them. Do not act like you are all together." Instead, the teacher said that they should travel in pairs, each following a specific path that he would lay out, taking only certain sets of roads, no two pairs entering the garage the same way. And, thus, every Sunday, seven or eight boys would spend three hours in the garage, listening to "religious, educational and advocacy lessons."

Still, during these years, Yassine continued to disseminate material: sermons, articles, and a dizzying array of books. He sought inspiration from multiple sources, including Sufism, Islamism elsewhere (Qutb, al-Banna, and the Iranian revolution), and even Marxism. Overall, between 1973 and 1989, Yassine's intellectual wanderings resulted in the publication of fifteen major works.[45]

Standing out among more theoretical tomes, *al-Minhaj al-Nabawi* (The Prophetic Way) is the most pragmatic of all his works.[46] Written in 1981, it spelled out, even before the actual creation of his organization, an outline of its organizational structure. It represented a practical blueprint and has been called a "handbook." It has also been called the group's *petit livre rouge*.[47]

Minhaj outlined a configuration with an elected Emir-type figure leading the movement (Yassine beginning in 1981) accompanied by "outreach and guidance councils" at the regional, provincial, and family levels. The Guidance Council of the movement—Majlis al-Irshad (sometimes referred to as al-Majlis al-Rabbani)—began as seven members when the movement was created, and it would later grow to fourteen. The Majlis al-Shura, called the "Consultative" or "General Assembly," is responsible for all its governing decisions and was founded in 1992. It has been called the movement's "internal parliament" by members and is comprised of individuals from throughout the movement's regions; at least 30 percent reportedly are women.[48]

The overall organizational structure is divided meticulously, from the bottom up. The first rung is the individual member, then the "family" (usra), then branch (shu'ba), region (jiha), province (iqlīm) and, finally, nation (qutr). There are also local and regional councils: first at the level of the branch, which usually includes around seven elected members, and then at the level of the province. The head of an usra, which usually composes up to twelve individuals, is referred to as a "naqīb al-usra," and is appointed by the branch council.

Al Adl takes Morocco and its cities as a starting point for its organizational composition—its geographic division of responsibilities—but then repossesses it, forging its own map. The country was initially broken up into four provinces: North, South, East, and Central. (It now encompasses nine.) It carves out pieces of cities, combining neighborhoods and towns to form its own "regions." Only members know where their precise borders begin and end. (They cite security concerns as the reason for this secrecy.)

The composition of the regions determines membership in the Majlis al-Shura or General Assembly. The assembly is population- not geographic-dependent (it also includes reserved spaces for heads of thematic units within the movement). A geographically small part of the country with many members would have more representatives than a large area with few residents. In the city of Casablanca, for example, because there are so many members concentrated there, the movement has delineated multiple "regions" within one city. The densely populated Casa suburb of Ain Sebaa encompasses at least two regions within the movement.

In many ways, the tightly knit organization was a product of a repression that forced the group to close its ranks. Moreover, even though authorities severely limited the group's abilities to mobilize openly, Yassine's arrest often helped boost his fame and standing. A current Al Adl activist named Mehdi, for example, told me of the first time he encountered Yassine's name in the early nineties. He was in high school when a friend of his stumbled upon a magazine one day (*al-Jama'a*). It was lying on the top of a trash bin, and there was something that immediately caught his attention. He rushed over to Mehdi's house to show it to him. He told his friend that he simply would not believe what he had found: a magazine that sharply criticized the Moroccan regime. When the two young Moroccans first read the magazine, they assumed that Yassine was an Egyptian thinker. "We didn't know who he was," Mehdi said. And they could not have imagined, he said, that a Moroccan had the courage to write something like that. When they found out that he was, in fact, from their country, it was almost "impossible to comprehend." His "courage"—and prowess in surviving in a place where the king's opponents often seem to "disappear"—apparently was, for them, overwhelming.

A thirty-something teacher in Casablanca named Abdou also fondly remembers Al Adl underground magazines. "Before I was a member," he said, "I got hold of a magazine called *al-Jama'a*. I loved to read and these magazines were very interesting for what they said about Morocco, for the problems they pointed out in our country." But Abdou became increasingly concerned by the fact that the magazines were so hard to come by. "The magazine was banned, and I had to collect them secretly. I collected more than seven or eight issues. I wondered often why they were illegal. Now, looking back, I know that the *makhzen* was showing its real face in banning these magazines."

Confrontational, resilient, and patient, Al Adl was growing. In fact, it was quickly becoming the largest opposition—and Islamist—group in the country. Yet, once again, it would not go unchallenged. The regime was becoming open to countering the rising Al Adl threat, and its Islamist competitors were ready to exploit this openness for their own gain. Al Adl's very success, it turned out, would lay the foundation for the rise of the other main Islamist stream in the country: the future PJD.

There is no more instructive way to understand PJD's methodical, pragmatic path than to look closely at one of its earliest activists. In the wake of the Arab Spring in 2011, a greying Abdelilah Benkirane became the first democratically elected Islamist prime minister in the Arab world. But in 1981, he was a twenty-seven-year-old Shabiba activist trying to figure out his next move.

Like the future Islamist party he would one day help form (and later lead), Benkirane proved a savvy responder to the winds of political change—and the vicissitudes of competition. Throughout his tenure, his timing has been tactically sage, following the initiatives of rivals and a powerful and reactionary monarchy.

When he was young, he first experimented with leftists, but in the late 1960s, when Shabiba was being formed, authorities were said to have been open to Islamism to challenge a rising leftist opposition, and Benkirane joined their ranks. Ten years later, in light of the Iranian revolution and rising Islamist strength globally and nationally, the political chessboard looked different, and Benkirane's choices shifted accordingly.

By the early eighties, if Benkirane wanted Islamism (and his own ambitions) to develop, there was only way forward. He would curry favor with the state and offer something no other major Islamist movement in the country ever could or would: electoral participation.

Even though Shabiba was officially banned and Mouti was banished, the organizations underlying it did not simply disappear. And, in April 1981, Benkirane chose to set out on his own, severing his Rabat section from the movement at large.[49] A year later, he formally broke with Shabiba, publicly denouncing its violent turn and its head at the time, Mouti.[50]

Benkirane was born in 1954, thirty-two years after Sheikh Yassine, thirty years after Sheikh Abbas, and nine years before King Mohammed VI. But in 1981, the movement Benkirane helped found (and that would later give rise to PJD) was around the same age as an incipient Al Adl. In fact, this was the very same year that Yassine published his own blueprint for his movement.

Benkirane's split from his militant roots was crystallized in 1983, when he applied for formal establishment of an entirely new and separate organization, al-Jama'a al-Islamiyya. His new group formed as a mature offshoot of Shabiba—replacing the word for youth with the word for organization. The desired message was clear: Shabiba had lost its way and its members had gone astray. The new group was the grown-up extension ready to take part in politics.[51] Its goals included "renewing the understanding of religion," "advocating the implementation of the Shari'a," and "working to accomplish Muslim unity and condemning violence."[52] The head of its Casablanca wing was another person who would go on to earn national recognition: Saad Eddine El Othmani, the future head of PJD and foreign minister of Morocco.

The new group's license for legalization was denied, but its activism continued. To endure, it began acting a lot like Al Adl during those days, borrowing and competing with it in the realm of social action and intellectual efforts, and particularly in the domain of student mobilization and newsletter publishing. It began producing a monthly newsletter (al-Islah) in February 1987 and gradually and pragmatically lowered its profile as violence began to unfold in neighboring Algeria. It did not want to be tainted by the violence of Islamists in the neighboring country. To avoid this fate, Benkirane would cling to the state, rather than oppose it. "Morocco produced the PJD," he would say later, "and Algeria produced the FIS [the Islamist movement in Algeria that would turn violent]. They are not the same thing."[53]

In 1981—much like it would in 1997 and beyond—Benkirane's promonarchy group hoped to offer a possible "counter" to Yassine's rising movement (just as Shabiba had once been to leftists).[54] And as Yassine continued to face more backlash from the state, Benkirane doubled down on his strategy of currying favor with it.

Benkirane realized that there was a market for this accommodationist approach. The reflections of a young Shabiba sympathizer at the time capture the fluctuations of this era. In the early eighties, Aziz Rabbah recalled how he had just begun experimenting with militancy. But after Shabiba was shuttered, the future looked bleak in Morocco for political Islam: the movement was crumbling, and the people he looked up to had been "disappeared." He soon fled to Canada to study engineering. "When I was younger," Rabbah told me, "I was at first more attached to my religion, and we were in search of a new model because the postcolonial state was failing. There were radical Islamists and even radical Leftists all looking for the same thing."

But Benkirane's new initiatives and the promise of political participation helped lure him back to Morocco. He had new skills and new experiences, and he wanted to put them to formal use. Thanks, in part, to Benkirane, he said, "We were in a process of reform, a time of reform. Now people are attracted more to modern, not radical ideas. We are moving toward a democratic process and there is no turning back."

Morocco's experiment with Islamist political participation came late relative to most of its neighbors, but proceeded swiftly. By the time Islamists first began appearing on the official Moroccan political stage in 1997, their brothers had already been contesting elections in the Arab world for well over a decade. The Muslim Brotherhood in Egypt, for instance, had been dabbling in electoral politics (sporadically and without its own party) since the mid-1980s; its counterpart in Jordan formed the first Islamist party, Islamic Action Front (IAF), in 1992. The Brotherhood latched onto other parties in the Egyptian elections of 1984 and 1987 and boycotted the elections of 1990; the Jordanian Islamists also participated as independents in the elections of 1989, participated again as a party in 1993, and then boycotted in 1997.

Moroccans were also all too familiar with events in neighboring Algeria, where struggles between Islamists and the state had propelled the country into bloody civil war.[55] Benkirane's push for political participation paradoxically stood to gain from this violent turn next door. Best to "manage" Islamists' entrance into the political system, Hassan II reckoned, rather than for it to be sprung on him.[56] Political scientist John Entelis calls the relationship that was developing between the monarchy and what would become PJD one of "complicity."[57]

Before Moroccan authorities would entertain the idea of allowing Islamists to formally participate in elections in 1997, certain ground rules would have to be set. By the summer of 1996, King Hassan II set the specific parameters for Islamist political participation. He tasked his infamous interior minister, Driss Basri, to signal to his former political opponents that the regime was ready to alter its policies—slightly. Up until that point, Basri (who had earned the sobriquet "Butcher Basri") had been best known for quelling political dissent in the country.[58] Yet, after a decade of refusals, Basri's ministry finally granted authorization to segments of the country's Islamist opposition to take part in elections, albeit incrementally, and in the form of an already existing party.[59] Basri's boss, King Hassan II, told reporters that as long as the Islamists stayed clear of "heresy" (by which he meant they should refrain from questioning the monarch's religious authority), "I will not intervene."[60]

If Benkirane's dreams of political inclusion were ever to be realized, he knew that these would be the conditions. Earlier in the decade, his group had renounced political opposition to the monarchy (and it had abandoned violence), but it had not yet gone so far as to give up its religious challenge. Even the semblance of the word "Islam" would have to be dropped. According to authorities, the mere mention of Islam raised the possibility of a lack of respect for the monarch's role as Commander of the Faithful.[61]

Sure enough, the group eventually acquiesced. And, as if to underscore this change, Benkirane even bragged that the new venture would be open to Jews.[62] By varying their name—by dropping Islam—these Islamists were changing their public course. They were slowly signaling that they were ready to cede any formal religious claims to the state.

Leaders from that era did not deny their gradual about-face, from their giving in to regime demands and their malleability to the competitive context. They didn't need to fight for an Islamic state, they claimed, because the regime purportedly offered that possibility. Mohammed Yatim, a senior movement member, noted: "Our problem in Morocco is not in establishing an Islamic state. Theoretically and constitutionally, this state is already one [an Islamic state]."[63] The future Islamist prime minister of Morocco, Benkirane, also reflected on their decision to drop their Islamic challenge in this same way: "We had understood that we were lucky enough to have an Islamic state (in Morocco)."[64]

With its fresh outlook and organization, Benkirane's new group at the time proceeded quickly to take even more concrete steps to engage in the formal political process. In hopes of participating in the local elections of 1992, it spawned a political wing, Hizb al-Tajdid al-Watani (National Renewal Party). Rebuffed again by the authorities, they decided to give it another try. In 1996, Harakat al-Tawhid wa-l-Islah (the Movement of Unity and Reform) or "haraka" for short, was formed by merging their earlier group with two smaller ones.[65]

This was the movement that would finally give rise to the country's first official Islamist party, PJD.

In light of their continued failures to secure a formal electoral role, the newly structured group chose a new path. Representatives opted to attach themselves to the small but established Mouvement Populaire Démocratique et Constitutionnel (MPDC).[66] Suddenly, national electoral participation was close. And Benkirane was soon triumphant. "We now have a political party," he declared, "and we expect to participate in a limited way in the next general election."[67]

Sure enough, in the national elections of 1997, their hopes of national political participation, the contours of which were first articulated as early as 1981, were realized when it won nine seats in parliament. There was no turning back. A year later, PJD was officially formed.

THE EXPANSION

The unprecedented electoral inclusion of PJD begged two immediate questions: What would happen to the religious movement from which PJD sprang—the haraka? And, what would happen to the new party's main Islamist competitor: Al Adl? The answers to both questions, it turned out, are interwoven. The fate of PJD and Al Adl would be shaped by a similar desire: to structure their organizations to maximize recruiting, most often at the expense of the other.

Soon after PJD was officially formed, its leaders went out of their way to appear to distance themselves, even separate themselves, from their religious movement. When the haraka began sending its leaders to take part in national electoral politics (via MPDC in 1997), it stopped short of dissolving and instead sought to isolate its activism. The creation of PJD, Ben-kirane said, "does not mean the dissolution of our religious movement [ha-raka], which will continue with its activities, but *without being directly involved in politics*."[68] A division of labor was outlined: the haraka would be responsible for religious affairs, and what would become PJD would be de-voted to "politics."

This stated separation was not a foregone conclusion. When PJD was first formed, members considered blending the original religious preach-ing movement—the haraka—and the party into one unit. But instead, they chose a different path.

Abdelali Hamiddine was present during these debates. He joined the haraka in 1996, and when the party was formed in 1998, like many of the founding members, he simply transitioned over.

"There is almost one reference between the two," the future MP relayed to me. "One reference because we are from the same upbringing, the same origins, the same source and the same school." Yet, they specifically and consciously chose to keep the organizational bodies separate.

"When the party was founded and introduced to political work, there were two options at the time," he recalled about the specific deliberations. What he described as "the first option" was the "integration of the move-ment within the party, so that we would become one unit." But there was also what he called "another option": "to separate between political work and religious advocacy work, so that the party would remain a party, and the movement, a religious advocacy movement." Ultimately, he said, they opted for the latter: "There were very long discussions in 1998 that ended with the decision to separate the movement and the party."

Faced with the decision between "integration" and "separation," they seemed to choose separation. But these developments beg a larger ques-tion: why would individuals who ideologically disparage such separation—who speak fervently about the integration of Islam in all aspects of life—nonetheless be so eager to embrace such an organizational split? After all, members routinely berate secularism for precisely such separations. Ben-kirane even declared in those years that "the one thing we do not accept is secularism."[69]

Yes, there was the matter of the makhzen and abiding by its conditions of entry, but the party could have combined the organizations and still abided by the rules of the game.

Some in the party try to resolve the seeming contradiction by articulat-ing a specific understanding of "religion." Hamiddine declared that "We decided that political work and religious advocacy are different." The ulti-

Salma, an activist from Temara, recounted how she had originally been a member of the haraka. But then, she said, "when PJD became more active, I myself immediately became active with them." Her involvement almost seemed to mirror the organizational evolution of the party. "I wanted to see if I could be as successful contributing to political work with PJD in the same way that I was successful working in the area of social work with the haraka. This desire to succeed in politics is the main reason why I am here."

Thus, when PJD entered the formal political process and then intentionally kept its allied religious movement separate, how did Al Adl respond? The short answer is: it also quickly transformed itself.

Shortly after the establishment of the country's first Islamist political party, Al Adl brought its top leaders to Marrakesh to put into effect the most dramatic structural change in its own short history. At a special session of its General Assembly (Majlis al-Shura) that summer, the group opted to form a new "Political Circle."[73] This new circle overhauled an organizational framework that had been in place for nearly two decades. Al Adl could not legally form a political party (it was not granted permission by the state), but it did do the next best thing: it began a political party in waiting. Even though the movement would still not take part in elections, its new organizational structure, priorities, and initiatives, as we will see, could now offer opportunities for what it called "political activism."

Al Adl not only mirrored PJD by creating its own political wing; it also imitated its competitor's broad form. When both groups spawned these new "political" entities in 1998, both kept their allied and so-called religious movements intact. The founding treatise of Al Adl's Political Circle laid out this arrangement. The new circle would handle all "affairs of the State (that is, addressing the social, economic, political, cultural issues of the society)." It would, in sum, be "entrusted" with the "management of the commonwealth."[74] By contrast, what it termed the "other missions of education, training and teaching" would instead "fall within the competence of the Religious Circle." This now separate or "other" Religious Circle (first created in 1987) would include, for example, the Commission on the Qur'an and the Committee on Education and Advice.

These transformations would be difficult to explain by looking only at Al Adl's ideological texts, treatises, or doctrines. There was no mention of a formal "political circle," for example, in Yassine's original blueprints for the movement.[75] While Yassine believed that interaction with society was critical, he also fretted that if Islamists formed parties, they would come to "worship" politics "like Marxists."[76]

If one studied only the relationship between Al Adl and the state, there would be few new developments or overtures to dissect. Al Adl was not obligated to fulfill the conditions set forth for PJD's electoral inclusion: it was not seeking legalization. Al Adl, in short, did not change because it was told it "had" to, or because of a sudden ideological epiphany. It also did not change simply because PJD did. Rather, it transformed in order to continue to compete with PJD for new members.

To help make this point, let's return to the young PJD activist named Itimad Zahidi, whom we met at the beginning of this chapter. When Itimad went to the PJD office in her hometown to sign up, there were no other avenues of Islamist political participation available to her. She likely only heard about PJD because of the attention it received in the media.[77] This was indicative of the new resources PJD had at its disposal, or what I call the spoils of inclusion: state election funding, official party headquarters, legal newspapers, even access to coveted government jobs. Around the same time as Itimad joined PJD, a future Al Adl activist named Bashir recalled PJD members selling themselves in this way. "We offer politics," he was told, "and Al Adl doesn't. We are a modern party, and Al Adl isn't."

It is for these reasons that most scholars, analysts, and journalists predicted that, once PJD was formed, other Islamist movements would be hard pressed to compete with it.[78] After its electoral inclusion, most assumed that the newly legal and newly minted Islamist political party would soon siphon support away from Al Adl. There was near unanimity in Morocco on this point. There would, most seemed to suggest, be many Itimad Zahidis.

But these predictions assumed that Al Adl would remain static, that the group and its members would stand back and watch events unfold, that they would observe their own demise from afar, rather than struggle for their own survival. Yet, movements are made up of members—in this case mostly young people—and these members saw the writing on the wall, on the streets, on university campuses. They saw what was happening. "We could not just let PJD's message win," one current activist named Ali later reflected. "Our cause is too important."

When Al Adl formed its Political Circle in 1998, Yassine's interest in politics was certainly not new, but the formal push to institutionalize these desires was. An opportunity for one movement's success created (perceived) opportunities for other movements. A senior PJD leader realized as much after his party's gains in that first 1997 election. "The fact that nine of our candidates won," he said, "gives something to *all* Islamist currents in

Morocco."[79] An Al Adl spokesman later hesitantly agreed. Perhaps, he said, PJD victories "benefitted Islamism as a whole in Morocco."[80]

But just as PJD was a free-rider to the regime's fears of Al Adl, Al Adl was now free-riding on media and popular attention being lavished upon PJD. It quickly seized on increased media and popular attention to Islamism in Morocco.[81] Far from fading away in the midst of PJD's inclusion, Al Adl only increased its political activism, challenging its opponent every step of the way. Not coincidentally, its activism would later heighten during election years when it sought to recapture the limelight from PJD and urge electoral boycotts. In 2002, it mobilized en masse on beaches. In 2007, it launched its "Open Doors" (*beebaan meftuuheen*) recruitment campaign. And in 2011, contra PJD, it joined forces for a time with the newly formed Arab Spring protest group, the "February 20 Movement" (named for a day of unusually large Arab Spring protests in 2011).

Nadia Yassine, a longtime leader in Al Adl (and the daughter of its founder), articulated the stakes involved. If her movement had not moved to form its own political wing, their own activism might have been too easily swallowed by PJD's newfound fame and success. She even noted that, in the wake of PJD's initial electoral victories, many people began congratulating her on the street. They seemed to be mistaking the two movements. "To the masses," she said, smiling, "all the bearded guys look alike."[82]

If the regime believed that it could "disappear" Al Adl simply by incorporating PJD into the political process, Al Adl would seek to prove otherwise. It would do this largely by offering similar kinds of opportunities for activism. In sum, it transformed itself in order to keep up.

The official spokesman, Arslane, who was present in Marrakesh in 1998, is candid about how the new circle helps them compete, how prioritizing politics is a way of "rallying young people." He is aware of how offering both "religious" and "political" opportunities to young people is a way to maximize the movement's mobilizing potential. "The political answer for what allows us to attract people," he said, "and this is the more obvious one, is that Al Adl has stances about rights. It aims at bringing about justice and fighting injustice. It is not satisfied with the actual running of the state and the squandering of money and the mismanagement of financial affairs."

These stances, he believes, attract youth because "they don't have a future after both political parties and the system at large betrayed their trust. These people have lied and lied and lied to young people by giving them false promises. Youth are thus in need of a trustworthy and reliable model that would allow them to set examples in sacrifice and generosity. This is one way of rallying them."

But they are able to offer this without alienating other, perhaps less politically oriented members. Al Adl, he says, is still able to "quench their spiritual needs and their aspirations for their rights—which put them on the side of justice." "This second issue," he said, "is the dimension of spirituality, the cornerstone of our Jama'a. It is this thirst for piousness, for the afterlife and for the supreme humanistic values of love and altruism that prompt young people to participate with us."

Activists often attribute their success to this multitude of opportunities. According to Bilal, a tutor and longtime Al Adl activist in Casablanca, there are "two sides" to the movement: a "political side" and a "spiritual side." "It is like an apple," he would often tell me. "If you cut it in half, you can look at it from two sides." Rachid, from Rabat, explained the compartmentalization in more literal terms—using the name of his group as the guide. "Our organization's name is Al Adl wal Ihsan. Adl means justice, it means that we defend people's rights. For food, for medical care. Human Rights. Ihsan represents the other part of our organization, the spiritual part." This combination, he maintained, helps maximize recruits. "It is why we have members across all parts of society—especially teachers and students."

These new organizational changes had far-reaching ramifications for mobilization. The Political Circle now houses its own avenues to mobilization and membership. Like PJD, it also formed a new youth wing so that new members' participation could be routed and housed largely within the Political Circle. The new wing also includes its own subgroups (most notably the Youth Section, but also the Women's Section, Trade Union Section, and a Bureau of Research, with additional groups dedicated to research). It even maintains its own separate research operations (devoted to economic, social, industrial, technological, agricultural, naval, educational, and communication issues). The Political Circle meets annually; and elections for its guiding council are held every three years. The Circle's guiding council includes fifteen members, with Abdulwahed Moutawakil at the helm.[83] The youth section is further divided into subsections for the university union, arts and crafts, sports, high school, and children. Hassan Bennajah, the longtime head of the movement's youth wing, located within the Political Circle, is also a member of the circle's guiding council. The movement's general assembly was also amended to make room for representatives from all new departments and divisions, such as the heads of youth and women.

CHAPTER 2

As PJD reorganized toward formal political participation, geographically congregating around the capital, so too did Al Adl's senior staff. How else could they compete? PJD would come to maintain its national headquarters in a leafy suburb of the capital Rabat, and its parliamentarians would work out of offices downtown. Al Adl's base of operations, though obviously more diffuse and concealed, would also have to be housed in this area. For decades, the movement's de facto headquarters had been Yassine's home in Salé, just beside Rabat, along the Bou Regreg River. Because of the house arrest imposed upon him by Hassan II, Yassine remained there, and the locale thus became a rallying point for the movement.

Almost all of Al Adl's leaders came to live between Casa and Rabat. Abdelwahed Moutawakil, for example, relocated his entire family from the coastal city of Safi to a suburb of Casablanca to oversee the group's political circle. Fatthalah Arslane, the movement's spokesperson, lives down the street from Moutawakil. To head up youth mobilization and recruitment for the group, Hassan Bennajah initially left his wife and new baby at his boyhood home in the coastal city of El Jadida and moved outside Rabat, to an apartment in Temara, near the head of Al Adl for the Temara region.

It is in these locations, in these towns and cities, that events of Islamist competition would continue to transpire. But were the plans and organizations devised on paper now firmly in place or would they, along with their members, continue to evolve? How would the hopes and ideals of these new organizations mesh with the realities of the new marketplace—with their survival dependent on their ability to continue to recruit members? With the stage now set, the chapters that follow will delve deeper into this emerging competition, beginning with a look at the motivations of the emerging rank and file.

SPIEGEL, AVI, 1975-

YOUNG ISLAM: THE NEW POLITICS OF RELIGION IN
MOROCCO AND THE ARAB WORLD.
                                    Cloth   246 P.
PRINCETON: PRINCETON UNIV PRESS, 2015
SER: PRINCETON STUDIES IN MUSLIM POLITICS.

AUTH: UNIV. OF SAN DIEGO.

LCCN 2014032950
  ISBN 069115984X   **Library PO#** SLIP ORDERS

                                      List   29.95 USD
  6207 UNIV OF TEXAS/SAN ANTONIO   **Disc**   17.0%
  App. Date   8/12/15   REL.APR   6108-09 **Net**   24.86 USD

SUBJ: 1. ISLAM & POLITICS--MOROCCO. 2. ISLAM &
POLITICS--ARAB COUNTRIES.

CLASS BP173.7   DEWEY# 320.5570964   LEVEL GEN-AC

YBP Library Services

SPIEGEL, AVI, 1975-

YOUNG ISLAM: THE NEW POLITICS OF RELIGION IN
MOROCCO AND THE ARAB WORLD.
                                    Cloth   246 P.
PRINCETON: PRINCETON UNIV PRESS, 2015
SER: PRINCETON STUDIES IN MUSLIM POLITICS.

AUTH: UNIV. OF SAN DIEGO.

  LCCN 2014032950
  ISBN 069115984X   **Library PO#** SLIP ORDERS

                                      List   29.95 USD
  6207 UNIV OF TEXAS/SAN ANTONIO   **Disc**   17.0%
  App. Date   8/12/15   REL.APR   6108-09 **Net**   24.86 USD

SUBJ: 1. ISLAM & POLITICS--MOROCCO. 2. ISLAM &
POLITICS--ARAB COUNTRIES.

CLASS BP173.7   DEWEY# 320.5570964   LEVEL GEN-AC

Part II

IDENTITIES

tening" to them articulate their hopes and goals in chapter 4, we will look in this chapter at the multiple contexts from which these ideas are being constructed. We have to understand *who* they are before being able to understand *what* it is they want.

★

Who are the Islamist rank and file? To tackle this initial question, I want to hone in on the experiences of young people just like Brahim, his roommates, and their friends—not because they are anomalous, but because they are decidedly average. These lives are windows into the shared experiences of ordinary young people and an increasingly blurred Islamist base. In this way, they serve as introductions, as springboards, to the stories of citizens, colleagues, peers, confidantes, brothers, and sisters—all seemingly inconspicuous young people of various ages, professions, and backgrounds. To place them in national and regional contexts, the chapter also draws on survey data, census data, and voting results. But it is only from up-close that we can begin to discover critical details that are lost or distorted from afar.

These details reveal a cohort in motion, one that escapes fixed categorizations or reigning expectations, one whose paths are not predetermined or predestined by socioeconomic class, appearance, geography, or even doctrine. I found that over the past decade, the movements' bases have come to inhabit a fluid trail of Islamist collective action, where membership fluctuates across organizations, within neighborhoods, blocks, and even within homes.

Today's young Islamist activists are often experimenters—navigating between and among movements. These are statements I heard repeatedly: "I was curious so I changed groups" or "I wanted to explore." One person named Fadel who migrated from Al Adl to PJD said: "Each group tries to attract followers from other groups because they know we are looking around." Their experimenting is fluid and relational: it can involve testing out one outlet before switching to another or trying both concurrently. Opting for one forum almost always involves opting *against* another.

Even a casual visitor to the Arab world over the last few decades would quickly see how blurred the category of "youth" has become. Young people have been hovering in liminality: an extended, often borderless zone between childhood and adulthood. Youth have been kept in this liminal social condition for somewhere and anywhere between five and twenty years, protracted by family structure, familiar rites of passage, and the imperatives of being "modern." The result is an almost never-ending youth era: young people educated with job skills, but unable to find work; hoping to start families, but powerless to afford the costs of marriage.[1]

The perverse irony, of course, is that those who try the hardest to break free from this condition—by seeking and attaining additional education— seem only to dig themselves an even deeper hole. Today's Islamists are part and parcel of the most educated generation in the history of the Middle East and North Africa, the product largely of mass education drives that began in the late 1950s. Positioning Moroccan schooling trends on a line graph would resemble a shooting star, bolting from just 1,819 students enrolled in higher education in 1957 to approximately a quarter million today.[2] In Morocco, as in almost every other part of the region, getting an education only delays—and even aggravates—the inevitable. Being unemployed with a college degree, I would often hear, stings that much more. "All that schooling . . . for nothing."[3] In many ways, it is the non-poor who are suffering from a new kind of economic strain, for unemployment remains the most acute for young people with intermediate and higher education who are just getting ready to enter the workforce.[4]

Yet, the evidence no longer supports the notion that these socioeconomic realities predetermine young people's choices, that, in other words, certain among these disenfranchised would inevitably flock to particular movements. In a major work in English on Islamism in North Africa written in the late nineties, political scientist Emad Shahin argued that Al Adl appeals to "middle and lower classes, civil servants, peasants and workers"; and PJD, on the other hand, appeals to "intellectual and student elements." During his research in Tangier almost three decades ago, the anthropologist Henry Munson concluded that Al Adl attracted the support of "young people unable to find work, even some with no more than an elementary school education."[5] But today all Islamist movements derive strong support from the whole range of educated young people, especially students.[6] When I would visit Moroccan universities, for example, I would often observe two desks in the main courtyard—and usually *only* two desks: one affiliated with each of the country's major Islamist movements. The country's main student union is even considered Al Adl's de facto student wing.

The hundreds of young Islamists I encountered during my fieldwork, those who go to conventions, protest marches, group meetings, those who sit during long discussions at homes and coffee shops, all cut across a variety of classes and socioeconomic backgrounds. They range from employed intellectuals to over-educated yet under- or unemployed friends to members of a diverse lower-middle working or no-working class.[7] I often heard Moroccans—journalists, university colleagues, government officials—dismiss them as "mere primary school teachers" or "lower middle class politicians" who are "playacting like adults" or who "don't even speak French." Two colloquial terms used to belittle Islamists also convey a lack of sophistication or wealth: "khwanjiyya" (a play on "ikhwan," the shorthand for the Muslim Brotherhood); and "mewaaleen lehhi" (meaning "bearded ones"). Yet, the younger generation simply does not live up to these stigmas and stereotypes. At a typical PJD youth gathering in July 2013, for example, activists were pulling up in fancy Renaults and Fiats, talking on their shiny iPhones and Samsung Galaxies (which often cost even more in Morocco than they do in the United States). The same could be said of Al Adl, including those belonging to the movement whom I met while living in Europe.

Still, those activists who are employed often express how lucky—even blessed—they feel to have found full-time jobs at all, not to mention a place of their own as well. So many of their friends are struggling. Nearly half of their cohort is unemployed; and those who do work in Morocco and across the region increasingly labor part-time, for themselves, or for longer hours with less pay than similarly situated young people anywhere else in the world.[8] It has been estimated, for example, that educated young Egyptians wait on average five years after completing university before they are able to secure any sort of employment.[9]

Even the new king of Morocco had to be married before procuring work—in his case, assuming his official royal duties. He, of course, had it easy. He reportedly wed in the middle of the night following his father's death in 1999. The woman he chose seemed fitting for the coming century: a former clerk at a cybercafé who once spent her days helping young Moroccans find their way onto the Internet.

In Brahim's case, when he saves up enough money, he too hopes to be able to marry. But he still has some time: at twenty-five, he is six years younger than the average age of marriage for Moroccan men. Fifty years ago, in numbers replicated throughout the region, most men were long married by the time they were twenty-four, and women by eighteen. Even in the early 1970s, only around one in five women aged twenty to twenty-four was single; today more than 70 percent are—their mean age for marriage having jumped to twenty-six.[10]

This prolonged liminality not only results in uncertainty for young people; it also produces analytical imprecision for observers, making attempts to limit or proscribe the category of "youth" particularly challenging. Most social scientists and government agencies still rely on overly limiting definitions—and often the one promulgated by the United Nations. In this formulation, the task is simple and straightforward: wherever one lives in the world—regardless of law, religion, culture, ritual, marital status, employment status, student status, educational background, domicile status (living with parents, alone, etc.)—if one is younger than twenty-four and older than fifteen years old, he or she would be considered a "youth."[11] But such strict age barriers would very clearly mislead anyone seeking to understand contemporary youth activism in the Arab world. These parameters do not reflect how youth define themselves. Nor do they explain how the movements who are trying to mobilize them conceive of their largest cohort.

Many self-proclaimed youth activists are considerably older than twenty-four; others are younger than fifteen. For most of the last decade, the most prominent members of Islamist movements' youth wings, for example, have been in their late thirties. At the other end of the spectrum, I saw fourteen- and fifteen-year-old activists charged with leading study sessions within their movements, even tasked with overseeing the training and counseling of older members. A fifteen-year-old named Amin I met would go straight from lycée in the afternoon to facilitate a six-person learning group or usra (literally meaning "family") within Al Adl. At these meetings, usually held at a member's home, young Amin presides over informal and personal discussions about day-to-day life, about the importance of family, about his homework, and about the Qur'an. On occasion he even dispenses, or at least attempts to dispense, marital advice.

Considering "youth," then, requires looking beyond age and, instead, foregrounding identity.[12] What, we should ask, are the social processes that define the boundaries of youth as a category? Puberty signals a beginning, but the ending offers no such biological clarity. One of my academic colleagues once insisted that I afford marriage that mark. But if a young person is derailed from seeking marriage until he is employed, then certainly marriage and employment are co-equally salient. There is a gendered story here as well: female Islamists tend to be slightly younger than men, or are at least less likely to be married. Perhaps because women marry earlier than men, they have less time to commit to their movements before their disproportionate responsibilities of marital and parental life ensue. And now that the number of women working outside the home has quadrupled since the 1960s, married couples are becoming more common in Islamist youth movements.[13]

We should also allow some freedom for self-identification. Who are scholars, after all, to tell someone that she is not technically a "youth" even though she identifies as such? Youth has long been a category of political identification in Morocco and the Arab world—even if some social critics suggest otherwise. The legendary French philosopher Michel Foucault once suggested that the classification of "youth" was simply a Western invention, that the rift between childhood and adulthood was somehow concocted or even manufactured.[14] But the Arab world, and particularly Morocco, complicates such a contention.

When French colonial administrations performed censuses in Morocco—in 1921, 1931, and 1936—they designated just three categories: Child, Adult, and Senior. Officially for the French occupiers, the category of youth did not exist.[15] But upon gaining its independence, the new Arab nation soon lent official recognition to those the colonial powers clearly hoped to gloss over or, taking a more cynical view, to repel.[16] The Youth of the Istiqlal or Independence Party was launched and held its first official meeting in March 1956 in Fez. A competitor, the Democratic Party for Independence, soon followed suit with the Union of Democratic Youth. And the central student union, known as UNEM—Union Nationale des Étudiant(e)s du Maroc, or al-Ittihad al-Watani li-Talabat al-Maghrib—was formed later that same year.[17] Young people, it turned out, *had* been considering themselves as "youth" long before others might have deemed them as such.[18]

★

Most analysts of Islamist youth proceed on the assumption that to understand their lives it is necessary, above all else, to understand their commitment to their faith; that, in other words, what most distinguishes them from everyone else—and even from one another—is an attachment to religious ideology. They believe that the content and interpretation of sermons and scriptures are the primary drivers of their behavior; and that, at the very least, young people are disproportionately swayed by a movement's proselytizing religious call or da'wa.[19]

But, as we will see, young Islamists are constantly shifting how they practice their religion, and even how they situate their own lives in current religious debates. They are expressing for themselves what Islam means to them. No two individuals I met shared identical views, regardless of their choice of movement.

Many young activists find comfort and inspiration, for example, in the sayings of the Prophet—in linking their lives, even in some detached way, to His. Each has their favorite hadiths, and Soufian from PJD liked this one: "The believer who mixes with people and endures the harm they do is better than he who does not mix with them or endure the harm they do."[20] You have to work in the open, he believed, with people, with neighbors. You have to engage them. He admitted that being immersed in society sometimes means being corrupted by it, but he also maintained that one cannot change it without living within it. For an activist from a legal political party like PJD, such a hadith would make sense. The Prophet challenged the world when he lived in the *Jāhiliyyah*, in Arab civilization before the days of Islam, and he was rewarded for it (even though he did so from outside the existing system).[21] The current political process might be imperfect, but one is far better off contesting elections than retreating and boycotting them altogether like many of his Islamist competitors.

For his part, Mohammed, an activist in Al Adl, preferred this hadith: "Islam began as something strange and will return as something strange, so blessed are the strangers."[22] In a corrupt world, Mohammed said, sometimes being an outsider is something to be proud of. In the Prophet's case, He did not change; the society around Him eventually did. Thus, for Mohammed, strangers should not be feared; they should be respected, even considered righteous. And it is not hard to imagine why this hadith would be pleasing for someone from an illegal Islamist movement, for someone who often feels detached from society, even ostracized. Islam itself began in Mecca as something new, something different, something "strange." If one is patient and continues believing and practicing Islam, Mohammed said, society around him will eventually come around.

Yet, just because they enjoy hadiths does not mean that everything in their lives is dictated by them. Put another way, simply because their lives are imbued with Islam, and their political beliefs are influenced by Islam, does not mean that everything in their ever-changing lives revolve entirely around Islam.

On numerous occasions, I heard several analogies that sought to make a similar point: that not everything about their life is captured by their religious belief; and that if they were not Muslim, then few would even attempt to ascribe their behavior as such. One accusation went like this: "Look at how frequently America employs the death penalty. But if I praised capital punishment as much as Arnold Schwarzenegger once did in California, people would say I was a crazy Islamist. Instead, they just say, 'Oh Arnold, he's so heroic.'" Another invokes the example of ritual animal slaughter: "When we slaughter our sheep for l'eed, we are called barbaric. When Spaniards taunt their bulls in Pamplona, they are called adventurous." "What about Castro?" another asks. "He's got a beard, but no one criticizes him for it. When our leaders have beards, they're called religious fundamentalists." As anthropologist Homa Hoodfar once observed, it is often as though "Muslims, and in particular Middle Eastern people, live in the realm of ideology and religion while the rest of the world lives within the economic structure."[23]

Besides, to the naked eye, the Islamist activists I met live their lives a lot like most other young people in the country. And, contrary to stereotypes that frequently foretell the coming wave of religious devotion in the Middle East and North Africa, Arab Muslims under the age of thirty-five pray less than those who are older than thirty-five.[24]

The roommates attend mosque at approximately the same regularity—as often as they can, but definitely every Friday. Just like the vast majority of Moroccans, they own multiple copies of the Qur'an at home, overwhelmingly approve of the *hijab* or veil, and believe Ramadan fasting to be compulsory.[25] They all try to pray as much as they can, hopefully five times a day, but sometimes, despite lighthearted harangues from their friends or roommates, some of them don't get up in time for the early morning, pre-dawn *Fajr* prayer. With a rush-hour commute and an early school day, sleep is often too valuable a commodity to give up, even for Allah. They quote from the Qur'an when they need to, when they really have to make a point or stop an argument in its tracks or show off their pedigree. But step into any classroom or into any ongoing dispute on any street corner in the country, and one will hear the same fleeting exegesis.

Brahim and his friends take particular pleasure from the month of Ramadan, when they try to work harder, and exercise more, sweating as much as they can to remind themselves of the suffering of fasting. They get additional satisfaction when the holy month falls during the middle of summer, as it did in 2014, when the days are longer, the sun is stronger, and the pain from not eating or drinking all day is even more acute. Soon after twilight, after the sound of the muezzin's call to prayer, they break the fast with their *fetuur*, the word used for breakfast during the rest of the year. But they try not to rush into it. They start with sweets, maybe a few dates or perhaps an almond cookie, and then move slowly onto a warm bowl of *harira*, a tomato and lentil soup with cumin, cilantro, turmeric, and (for the wealthier) small chunks of lamb meat. They will then wait a few hours for dinner, as if to replicate the separation between proper meals, as if to make the night feel as normal as possible.

During the rest of the year, like all their friends, they spend a lot of time on long strolls and sitting outside at cafés. They all feel they must represent their respective movements—to dress and present themselves respect-fully; to attend study sessions; to live a life befitting a valued member of society. They refrain from catcalling women on the street ("ça va, ma ga-zelle?"). When they speak about dating and women and sex, they do so privately. An avowed Leftist once told me that he could never share a flat with an Islamist for only one reason: "they don't allow girls over," he said remorsefully.

Brahim and his friends have all seen their peers experiment with online pornography. A classmate, they knew, would invariably walk into the cy-bercafé, usually after ten at night, utter "Ssalam u'likum" to the male or female clerk, take a seat in the back with the other men, young and old, and put on clunky headphones, the kind that cover one's entire ear and look like black rubber earmuffs. He'd start slowly, first by checking out football scores and fan sites, moving on to social networking sites and chat rooms, then music sites, and then, finally, "sex sites," keeping a few divert-ing windows open at the same time, even though every guy in the back row was doing the same thing. He preferred to look at French sites featur-ing foreign women, the same way that he preferred prostitutes to sleeping with a proper Muslim woman from the neighborhood. At least, a friend once joked, Arab porn stars were to be cherished and honored. But it wasn't really the porn that gave Brahim and his friends pause, it was the public nature of it all. "You wouldn't have sex in public," Brahim said.

Many of their fellow activists also took issue with films or plays featur-ing nudity or obscenities that were sometimes shown on university cam-puses. They often waged sit-ins and protests to voice their objections. "Not everything can be considered 'art,'" Hassan from Al Adl said. "There should, instead, be objective standards through which to judge such matters. "Art," he said, "is something I can watch with my wife and kids."

All of their lives, regardless of their movement affiliations, are rife with elasticity, even incongruity. Despite any of their own personal vices, they are able to distinguish what they do at home or in private or among friends with how the state itself should behave.[26] "Listen," an Al Adl activist named Younes said to me, "people have the right to drink alcohol if they choose to, in their home, but they should not have that same right in public spaces." His friend Mohammed chimed in before he was finished with his own thought: "The state cannot remain neutral to this type of moral disre-gard," he said. "The problem in the West is that people view public spaces as man-made." Another young activist with Al Adl named Hicham once made a similar point about extra-marital sex. "I don't believe in adultery," he said, "but, let's be honest, people do it. Even so, a state should not be building brothels, inviting people in to have sex, and then sending in doctors to supervise." People stray, it seemed, but states should not.

★

Still, for many outsiders, it is difficult to analyze these varied lives without segmenting them along the frames of faith. In this way, the distinctiveness of theological labels is particularly alluring. Why can't young people's paths simply be understood as straightforward attachments to specific doctrines, as part of a story in which, to put it another way, some join one movement because it is more "Sufi" and others join another movement because it is more "Salafi"? Such a view, alas, assumes a straight line between doctrine and action where none exists and assumes that complex individuals can be divided by mere labels. Not only are young people constantly reinterpreting for themselves what religion means, but doctrinal specificities of their so-called leaders are also difficult to pin down.[27] Divining a single ideological marker for their individual movements is thus neither straightforward nor salient.

Take, for example, the writings of Al Adl's founder, Abdessalam Yassine. They are often weaving and desultory, combining—often incongruously at times—elements of Sufism, Qutbism, Salafism, Marxism and, more recently, democratic theory. Yet, some analysts still insist on assigning the movement the label of Islamic puritanism (Salafi) based largely on its political strategy: its boycott of elections.[28] Yassine has certainly cited Salafi writers, but so have PJD leaders and current parliamentarians from other parties and even the Moroccan monarchy itself. In fact, a past (non-Islamist) Moroccan prime minister, Abbas El Fassi, hailed from a party, Istiqlal, that was deeply influenced by early strains of Salafism. Conversely, the former PJD secretary general, Saad Eddine El Othmani, was once labeled "Salafi" by an American think tank after he wrote a paper invoking a Salafi thinker—even though in his case he was offering a re-reading of his texts in order to *criticize* Salafism.[29]

Still others attempt to categorize Al Adl as "spiritualist" or "Sufi." In a masterful work on political opposition in the Arab world, one political scientist cites as specific evidence of this label that Yassine is referred to, within Al Adl, as a "*Murshid* or Guide."[30] Yet, so was the head of PJD's forerunner organization, Shabiba. And, most recently, this was the title given by the regime to female *murshidat*—often called Morocco's first female imams. It is also worth noting that *Murshid al-'Am* was the title favored by the founder of the Egyptian Muslim Brotherhood, Hassan al-Banna.[31]

For their part, Al Adl members often dispute that they joined their movement simply because it was Sufi, even bristling at the suggestion of being "Sufi-like." As one activist told me, in sentiments I heard regularly: "We are not Sufi. We are not Sufi *at all.* We are different from Sufis. Sufi means only that one goes to the marabout [shrine]. That he only says his prayers. All his life he is devoted to prayers, and that's all. And he is only concerned with the well being of his soul. That's all. We believe that this is just one aspect of Islam and not the whole picture."[32]

It is true that Al Adl gatherings often incorporate more of a "spiritual component," including chanting, devotional rhythmic movements, and even discussions of dreams. Some nights, for example, Al Adl friends perform *dhikr*—literally "remembrance"—where they gather to celebrate God, chanting and repeating the name of Allah. But just because they incorporate Sufi rituals did not mean their decisions translate into a wholesale acceptance of them.[33]

There is another reason single markers can be misleading: people dabble, and identities intersect. Parts of their life could be labeled one thing, others another. Local traditions and doctrinal directives converge.[34] Formal Salafi teachings, for example, liken visits to marabouts or shrines to idol worship. But I encountered young women who considered themselves Salafi and who nonetheless made regular visits to shrines to cure ills ranging from infertility to acne. The most devout person I knew, who endlessly extolled the virtues of Salafism, also believed that she could cure splinters by rubbing her hands over the wedged object and chanting. Neighbors believed she had special healing powers.

The Facebook pages of young Moroccans (even those who call themselves "Leftists") are rife with myriad quotes from the Qur'an, hadiths, and even Salafi preachers. Take the case of Aqil, an aspiring musician, who sports dreadlocks, enjoys recreational drug use, relishes reggae music and the words of Bob Marley, and yet also finds inspiration in the unlikeliest of places: the Salafi Sheikh Abi Hicham Yahya El Madghiri, whose quotes and sermons are plastered on his Facebook wall.

Or Ghali, a university student who devours German, French, and American literature (mostly classics), enjoys reading studies in comparative religion, and also has an affinity for heavy metal (Iron Maiden, Judas Priest, and Black Sabbath are among his favorites). At the same time, he also looks up to the words of the Salafi Sheikh Mohammed Zohal. In July 2014, for example, he quoted favorably the preacher's entreaties to youth to ignore images and programs in the media and instead to "please God, and make us one of those touched by its blessings. . . . to fill your time with prayers, recitation, worship, teaching and learning, and especially seeking the legitimate science of Islam."[35]

Many government offices around the world still promote policies based around the notion that there exists a clear connection between doctrine and action in the Arab world. The U.S. Department of Defense, for example, is studying how to use Sufism as an antidote to Salafism, as if doctrine could be weaponized, bottled up, or made static.[36]

Just because young people believe one thing does not mean that they practice accordingly; and just because they practice does not always mean they believe. There is the teacher who drinks alcohol every night, but whose faith is unquestionable, who hopes for nothing more than Allah's forgiveness. Or the young woman who wants to veil, but for a million reasons cannot bring herself to do so. "I wish I could veil," she answers when asked whether she ever would.

The example of veiling, while often over-invoked, is nonetheless instructive here. One study by Moroccan sociologists sought to quantify the attitudes concerning veiling among the country's youth.[37] The headline from a news report appeared to tell the whole story: 84 percent of young people believed women should veil. The findings were compelling not just for this single descriptive statistic, but also for the underlying explanations given. While close to two-thirds of respondents supported the veil for religious reasons, still one-third supported it for purely professional purposes: the idea being that veiled women would be bothered less in the workplace. Any casual conversation with a young Muslim Moroccan woman would supply even more explanations beyond piety: social factors, fashion trends, family tradition, even empowerment.[38] "Growing up, it was cool among my group of friends," is one comment I heard often. One young woman I met, who was unaffiliated with any movement, wore a veil as an antidote to disciplinary action—after being caught out with a boy on a Sunday afternoon. (She had been sure to meet him at a faraway spot outside of town, but a friend of the family had spotted them talking.)

To complicate matters even further, most women within both movements do veil, but not all veiled women are Islamists; and not all women who join Islamist movements are veiled when they join. One activist in Al Adl's women's group, for example, began to veil only after joining the movement. In fact, she suggested that she actually joined despite the veil, not because of it. The ubiquity of veiled women initially had alarmed her. Yet, there were other parts of the movement that were attractive for her, and she was able to disaggregate these. "I saw young people who protested, who formed circles to protest against the exclusion and oppression of Islamist students. I was intrigued by this and I later learned that these students were Islamist members of the student union (UNEM)." Soon, she said, "I found that I had a lot in common with their goals for students." "But," she also noted, "I chose not to veil because I thought that a veiled woman did not speak to boys and was locked up in the house! By observing these Islamist students, I soon realized that this was false." Ultimately, she opted to wear the veil, but, in her case, she did so because she wanted to show common cause with students who were protesting on students' behalf. The veil was a sign of support, of solidarity—and even a ticket of admission.

★

Can appearances, then, tell us anything? A *New York Times* reporter once concluded that a demonstration in Egypt in 2013 was not "Islamist" because a lot of the protesters "do not look like Islamists"—and then he linked to a photo of a clean-shaven, curly haired young man.[39] During a presentation at an academic conference, a fellow panelist suggested that I employ "creative proxies" in my efforts to disentangle the new Islamist base. And by creative proxies, he meant attire. He was certain that in order to determine what "type" of an Islamist one is or even who *is* an Islamist that I should first look at the "clothes they are wearing."

But, today, more than a decade since both movements became more politically active, since both spawned political wings and parties, such proxies would be next to meaningless. The Islamists I encountered—across protests, meetings, conventions, and personal encounters in a variety of settings—mirrored each other in most external ways. And they certainly all wore similar varieties of clothes, or at least they changed their attire so often as to make it next to impossible to establish any clear patterns. Young people live in a complex, multilayered globalized world, where some Leftists I met with were bearded, and Islamists were clean-shaven. Attendees at Islamist youth conventions were just as likely to be wearing wool djellabas as they were crisp denim jeans and new trainers.

Regardless of their attire, the daily lives of young Islamists are surprisingly similar. Most usually devote at least one night a week to a meeting with their Islamist group of choice. Most often, it is Tuesday, Wednesday, or Thursday night, depending on others' schedules. "Leftists have a cell," Brahim said. "He has an usra"—pointing to his friend from Al Adl, using that group's term meaning "family." "We have a *jalsa tarbawiyya* (educational lesson)." Then he paused, almost to reflect, "I guess they're all really similar: just a way to get together at a set time, like a book club. But for us, that book is the Qur'an."

73

They meet to discuss how to pray, how to worship Allah, how to behave toward people and act around them. "We talk about Shari'a, which instructs us how to treat those who make mistakes," Brahim said. "We talk about education, about virtues, about how to live honestly and love." His friend Mohammed chimed in: "We try, of course, to be close to Allah and hope to end up in paradise."

Sometimes a lecturer comes and talks about a specific religious topic; sometimes there is a documentary shown or a regular film or movie. Sometimes there is specific educational material or syllabi provided by the movement about specific topics. On some weeks, one of their friends fast on Monday or Thursday or both.

Even though many activists work during the week, their weekends tend to be busier. On Saturdays and Sundays, they find time to spend with their Islamist group of choice, almost always waking up at dawn to pray, and then going back to bed for a bit, starting their days at around nine in the morning. They go to protest marches, demonstrations, campaign events, interesting lectures, or they volunteer their time with a local council or with one of the hundreds of associations affiliated with their groups: be it those that work with youth, with women, or children. One enjoyed helping an affiliated theatre group—"a classy theater," he said.

Both groups also offer similar opportunities to march and rally for Palestinian rights. In March 2012, to use but one example, Al Adl brought tens of thousands to the streets to mark "Land Day," leading crowds in chants in support of Palestinians. And, in a speech at the sixth annual PJD Youth Conference in Agadir in August 2008, a PJD MP accused his government of not doing enough to help Hamas and what he called the "option of resistance." PJD and Al Adl were both outspoken against Israel in the Gaza war of 2014. PJD Youth of Casablanca, for example, gathered together in September 2014 to rally in favor Hamas.[40]

The schedules of those in both groups are similar in other ways. Those in Al Adl go on "retreats" (*ribaat*); their PJD friends have what they called "camps." The retreats are sometimes overnight, sometimes for three days, and even once a year, usually in the summer, they can last up to forty days, during which they "spend time worshipping God and praising Him." They also attend camps and retreats in other cities, which provides an opportunity to meet new people, an opportunity that they have come to relish.

The assumption is that their groups are so eager to grow that they would take anyone off the streets. But both make it challenging, or at least appear to make it look challenging, to join. Applications to attend some of the camps, for example, are intense, with only the "most brilliant" selected.

The intent of the selectivity is not primarily to shut out new members, but rather to make future ones feel even better about joining.

Regular recruitment drives are also competitive. Friends joke with each other about how many people they can get to join. As soon as a "cell" nears twelve people, it splits into two. The goal, in the words of one PJD activist, is for them to grow "like bacteria." It is often a sociable competition, like peers vying with each other to see who could sell more magazine subscriptions or Girl Scout cookies. And they are rewarded for their talents. Rising within the organization relies on attendance, discipline, talent, but most of all on how good they are in bringing others on board, on recruitment, on salesmanship.

Weekdays are also busy. During a typical week, Brahim and his roommates, for example, all wake up around the same time, and share a light, brief breakfast, of bread, jam, and tea. They take turns in the bathroom, sprinkling water over their feet, cupping their hands in front of the sink, filling them with water and swishing back and forth in their mouths. Two or three spits and they are out the door. When going to work, they usually wear dark, baggy wool polyester blend suit separates, with no tie and brown or black Oxfords, which they saved up to buy at the Bata shoe store in the old medina.

Most nights, they return from school by early evening, stroll leisurely through the streets, meet friends, sit at a café, relax over tea or fruit juice (usually bananas blended in milk) and perhaps a *casse-croûte* or a snack. Some days, one or two will stay late at work and meet the others directly at the café. They eat dinner together at home at around nine. They take turns preparing the meal the night before, normally a version of a tagine. The vegetables—potatoes, carrots, and onions—largely remain the same, but the meat changes with the days. Chicken is served earlier in the week; the more expensive red meat is reserved for later in the week. On weekends, they mostly eat out or sneak in a home-cooked meal with their friends' families. The restaurants they frequent are not the eateries that tourists visit, that feature high-priced, diverse cuisine or have menus in multiple languages. Instead, theirs are the cafés with a single item (usually a tagine), or rotisserie chicken, or even a *haanuut* or shop, where they buy bread and cheese sold by the gram.

Their twice daily commute begins with a fifteen- to twenty-minute ride in a grand taxi that transports the young men from the taxi station near their home to the central bus station near their work. The cost of the ride is fourteen dirhams, almost two dollars. When they are not in a rush, they take a local bus, which costs four dirhams, or around fifty cents. The busiest time of the day to travel is rush hour, when traffic is worst, when thousands are coming and going from work or entering the city center in search of employment or for appointments or even just for leisure. The shared, aging Mercedes taxis (three people in the front, four in the back) only depart when they're full and eventually make stops along the way at surrounding blocks of apartment buildings, originally painted white, but turned light brown from the gradual coating of sand and wind. Before these buildings were built, forty years ago, there was nothing but hard sand.

★

To further understand the fluidity of their lives, we cannot look past these buildings—at where young Islamists live. Even though Islamism is largely an urban phenomenon, I found no specific spatial patterns of recruitment within such areas. To the contrary, one could be forgiven for asking what even constitutes "urban life" anymore in a major Arab capital, when rural life is fading, and when urbanization is so profound and so multilayered.

The land between Casablanca and Rabat, for example, has produced so many new micro-towns and neighborhoods that the space between the respective commercial and political capitals is shrinking rapidly. Empty lots have largely been filled with building projects; new structures spring up yearly, and seemingly cloned developments rise rapidly from the earth. The landscape is also littered with half-built structures, products perhaps of a yet to be completed construction job or a location whose time has not yet come, or perhaps more troublesome, of a permit expired, a legal roadblock, a bribe that went unpaid, money run dry, problems with local authorities, or perhaps simply overeager and overambitious builders. The tallest and most lavish of these works-in-progress are very likely the ventures of the mounting numbers of Moroccans living abroad, mostly expatriates from France and Spain, who often long for a place back home—for status or convenience—and whose collective remittances now contribute more than $2 billion a year to the local economy. (In the entire Arab world, only Lebanon receives more remittances per capita.[41]) At the other extreme, many of the most abject of the remnants are likely signposts of a government eager to appear serious about combating the rise of shantytowns. In 2012, the government redoubled its efforts to raze these illegally built homes, bulldozing close to 44,000 structures in the process. It had long promised to eliminate the need for shantytowns, but it ended up simply eliminating many of the shantytowns themselves.[42]

The remaining scattered empty lots and crevices still manage to find use as temporary outdoor markets, as pastures for the occasional sheep grazing, or even as makeshift soccer stadiums, with sticks and trees as goal posts, and tin cans as balls. The diffuse developments remain bookended by industrial plants: factories for canning food and sewing clothing (toward Casa) and for processing chemicals and electronic parts (toward Rabat). All stand as not-so-subtle landmarks to those with jobs and to those without.

There is only one reason why these areas have seen higher rates of population growth than anywhere else in the country. One suburb in the area, for example, grew from less than 50,000 in the 1980s to almost a quarter million at present. It is also one of the reasons for the massive rural outmigration unfolding throughout the region: the lure of more stable economic prospects. Even though fertility rates across the region are slowly leveling, urbanization rates are skyrocketing. While only a quarter of the country in the middle of the last century lived in so-called urban areas, by 2030 around 75 percent will. For at least the next fifty years, the Arab world's swelling cities will be composed largely of citizens under the age of thirty. The urban population will soon become *the* national population.[43]

Take the example of a town near Rabat called Temara. There are now two separate places called Temara. There is Temara *Wahid* and Temara *Ithnayn*. Temara One and Two. The generic names connote both the towns' newness (it is almost as if there is not enough time between the appearance of new neighborhoods to devise new names) and their similarities (they are differentiated most notably by the order of the stops for public transportation and not by any clear landmarks or great distinctions in their appearance). Those who live in Temara Ithnayn, for instance, live in a suburb within a suburb, or more accurately an extension of an extension of an extension of a major downtown (Rabat). This homogeny is often disorienting. The first two times I visited Temara I accidentally got off at the wrong grand taxi stop.

In a nearby town or suburb, the mosque might date to the twelfth-century Sultan 'Abd al-Mu'min, but most everything else surrounding it will have emerged more than eight centuries later. Here, apartment buildings are indistinguishable from one another, parts of groups of units in larger developments of new homes, all erected only in the last three decades. The buildings were constructed by blocks, not by home: whole neighborhoods cropping up almost overnight, the tiny distance between them mimicking the close living of homes in nearby ancient medinas. And, yet, their generalized interiors reveal nothing of the individualized décor of the old *deyuur* or medina homes. Waterproof, factory-made plastic (*meeka*) mats cover floors in place of hand-woven wool carpets (*zeraabi*); the mass-produced ceramic tiles on the bottom half of most walls reference the meticulously placed *zeleej beldee* of a different era. These are mechanized, routinized, and mirrored suburban spaces—outside of cities, but small cities of their own. A frequent visitor to any one of these environs could likely map the landmarks by heart: the téléboutique, the café, the pâtisserie, the cybercafé, the haanuut and so forth.

The apartments, like the buildings themselves, are almost standardized in their layout. Two bedrooms of similar sizes, one large salon, a bathroom, and a sink outside. The bathroom is equipped with a simple squat toilet or *twalet beldee*, a traditional latrine with a hole in the ground accessed by squatting and flushed with a bucket of water; as opposed to a *twalet ruumee* or a Western/"Roman" toilet used by sitting and flushed by a lever or handle. There is a small kitchen toward the back.

Young people live like this all over the country, if not in their own apartment (only a fractional percent have this luxury), then on their parent's *ponge*, or long, soft sofa cushions placed on wood benches.[44] Their neighborhoods, usually called *sha'bee* neighborhoods, have swallowed cities and towns, as populations and workforces needed to sustain the spreading metropolises continue to grow. If cities across the Arab world were once a place for the well to do, they are now occupied just as much by the poor and the growing middle class—or what sociologist Asef Bayat calls the "middle class poor."[45] The term sha'bee (meaning popular, familiar, even accessible) suggests this uniformity. The word itself connotes this commonness, this generic quality: the blocks of similarly situated young non-elites of varying socioeconomic classes living side by side.

When Islamist parties contest elections, when they run voting registration drives (or, in Al Adl's case, campaigns to convince citizens *not* to vote), when they construct meeting spaces or group headquarters or set up associations in youth centers, these are the areas they head to first. Any analysis of voting data from recent Moroccan elections would quickly expose the obvious: Islamist support comes overwhelmingly from within these scattered urban districts.[46] But, as we will see, a bird's eye view of these areas can only tell us so much about the personalities and profiles of the people who actually live within them.

★

Most young urbanites have only lived in their current locations for a short while. Have they come to assimilate wholly to their new surroundings?

What of their relationships to their families, to the people and places they had (not so long ago) grown up around? Many have sought to understand their lives by looking at these changing relationships, at these growing social separations or breaks from often-rural origins. This line of argument supposes that new urban migrants—lost, lonely, and isolated in their new surroundings—would be particularly open to the camaraderie, companionship, social support, and even routinized order that Islamist networks could offer.[47]

It is true that if it were up to Brahim, for one, he would probably marry and then pray for a transfer back to his hometown in the southeast of the country. It is his fantasy to return to home, an outpost town five hundred kilometers away, toward the Sahara, just west of the Algerian border. Except how likely will it be, he often wonders while lying in bed at night, for him to meet a woman in his new city, marry her, and then move back home? He also believes that many women, even the most conservative or family-friendly, would not be too fond of life there: the sun is much hotter, the people, he says, "are darker," and amenities are farther away.

It is also true that his employer, the ministry of education, does not make his dreams of marriage any easier. The ministry has been known to assign teachers to places far away from where they were born; the teachers, in turn, have long been promised that this policy will change. He heard once, but never could verify, that the right amount of money paid to the right bureaucrat could buy him such a transfer, but he doesn't feel comfortable engaging in bribery. "Why," he says, "should I have to pay someone to do what they have said they would do many times? Why should I pay someone much older than me to do what's right?"

He also heard that he could do what is sometimes referred to as "pulling a switch." After a few years of teaching, he could get lucky enough to find someone to change places with him. If Brahim were a woman, there might have been one last option. If a female teacher gets married to a male teacher, and the couple is posted in different locations, she could likely apply for a transfer to be with him. But no one had ever heard of this happening the other way around.[48]

Brahim is not shy about the fact that in his new surroundings there are moments when he feels like a migrant in his own country. Living closer to home would mean better meals and less housework. It would also mean being nearer to loved ones. He returns home only three times a year: for the major Muslim national holidays of Eid al-Adha and Eid al-Fitr (known colloquially as l'eed elkebeer and l'eed sseghreer) and for a month during the summer. Growing up, his home overflowed with visitors. There were so many people around so much of the time that as a child he could barely tell who his blood relatives were, could barely tell who was a cousin and who was a neighbor, who was an aunt and who was just a friend of his mother's. Their names were almost purposely concealing: every contemporary of his parents was called aunt or uncle, and every elder was called grandmother or grandfather. During major holidays, there were so many houses to visit in his village, so many people to pay respect to, that in the afternoons he and his sisters split up and fanned out across the neighborhood, covering more ground that way.

Theirs was a home ready for hospitality, ready at any moment to entertain: the tablecloth was always left on the low, round wooden table in the salon; the tea set was always left out, stocked with large cones of sugar and fresh mint. Boxes of homemade almond cookies were almost always to be found in a sealed plastic container under the table, just in case. It was only when he was older and living on his own that he realized that those things did not appear there by themselves, that they did not materialize like magic. It was his mother and his sisters who put them there, who prepared the house for guests *and* for him, and who not only did his laundry, making his clothes cleaner than he ever could, but also did the painstaking work of baking, cleaning, preparing, scrubbing, and cooking. They often did this long after he fell asleep at night or before he woke up in the morning. He could come and go, but they would stay and work, and work, and work.

But now, even with the passage of time, even with the geographical distance between them, even with the recognition that keeping up a home can be grueling, and even with the occasional longing for his sister's homemade *amlu* (an argan oil and almond paste), Brahim is not forlorn. To the contrary: the feeling Brahim and his friends experience by living independently sparks a sensation far closer to elation than to what Émile Durkheim famously imagined as "anomie."[49]

In fact, some first year university students in Casablanca once told me that they were simply "too busy" to join an Islamist organization—even though they wanted to. They would wait until they were more settled with their studies before they made a commitment. It was not that feeling alone drove them to join; it was that being busy in a new location prevented them from doing so.

Brahim does not feel groundless in the absence of social cliques and norms; he feels almost light without their constrictions. He relishes the freedom to explore himself and his beliefs, and to plot his way in the world; it is a freedom for what sociologists call ideational change.[50] And it is a freedom he never had: never at home, with his family's firm social controls, with people and expectations constantly surrounding him; and never at school, where cheating was widespread and where memorizing terms, even entire passages, was often rewarded over synthesizing concepts. As much as it sometimes pains him to admit, he likes the city, even likes being away from family. It gives him confidence, gives him faith that he will one day be a better husband and father. He has, after all, grown to relish a certain anonymity that comes only from being far from home; he doesn't know everyone and he likes it that way. He likes sitting at a café by himself sometimes, reading the paper, alone with his thoughts, watching whatever match is on, and not having to worry about who he will see or who will stop by his table or who he will offend by not greeting.

Technology has also eliminated many of the least agreeable parts of living far from family. His predecessors would have only called home as often as they could afford, relying on the rows of pay phones—and the heavy pockets full of coins that accompany them—at the neighborhood téléboutique. Activists today instead cherish their téléphone portable (or "portable" for short). For the majority of the last decade, three quarters of Moroccans have owned a prepaid mobile phone; cellular phone lines have become more than ten times more common than fixed ones. Phone users have grown so rapidly that twice in the 2000s the country had to add additional digits to phone numbers to make room for new lines. Young people once frequented the neighborhood cybercafé, where they are still able to chat and email and even occasionally use the webcam to communicate with loved ones and new friends. But economic realities now dictate that they sign up for Internet in their home. For 150 dirhams ($15) per month, they can have unlimited Internet access—an amount that can be shared among roommates and friends. Cybercafés still charge between twenty to thirty dirhams an hour per person per computer. When I first went to Morocco in 1997, less than 1 percent of the population was on the Internet; today over half are. (This is still less than the Gulf countries of Bahrain and Qatar, but more than regional neighbors Egypt and Tunisia.[51])

Much is often written about the importance of the Internet to contemporary Islamist mobilization. But this attention is often overstated. Al Adl's youth wing, for example, only joined Twitter in 2014, and, as of December 2014, had a meager 724 tweets and twenty-eight followers.[52] Yet, all this time, the movement still managed, at almost a moment's notice (largely through the use of person-to-person contacts), to mobilize tens of thousands onto the streets. Their movement's websites largely became spaces to broadcast information or even to lend a veneer of professionalism. They were places to disseminate and not necessarily to discuss material. Indeed, many of these young activists were friends without even being Facebook friends.

The Internet is certainly offering the possibility of new modes of activism, and even new avenues of authority. But despite the exponential rise in Internet usage, young Moroccans, like their counterparts throughout the Middle East and North Africa, still cling to their televisions, and still claim to receive the majority of their religious and political news from their TVs.[53] In the main room of most Moroccan households, low, cushioned ponges are arranged in a t-shape, hugging three of the four walls of the room, and opening up to the room's—and thus, the apartment's—showpiece: the television. For young people like Brahim and his roommates, time indoors, for example, is still spent right here. When guests come over, this is where they are seated, the television immediately switched on upon arrival. On most nights, this is also where they fall asleep, in front of their beloved *telfaaza*, marking their living room as their de facto collective bedroom. They take full advantage of the second item often purchased for a newly rented apartment (after the TV, but before the pots and pans): a *parabuul* or satellite dish. Depending on how late it is or how tired they are or even their mood that night, they might alternate between shows they can all agree on: a debate program on Al Jazeera, a match from Spain's La Liga if it is on, or maybe a subtitled Hindi film.

Part of young people's attachment to their television is cultural: shows, serials, live sport, news programs still dominate conversations; and local shows on state-owned television channels (particularly Channel 1 and Channel 2) offer programming not found anywhere else. Television might also still be a preferred medium because of the perceived poor quality of the Internet. As is, they often complain about slow connections and frequently paused pages. The quality of their web surfing is largely subject to the rates and services of the corporate behemoth Maroc Telecom, one of the country's largest and fastest growing companies. Bandwidth for the whole country, as they are acutely aware, is still principally supplied from afar: via a 200-kilometer-long submarine cable from Spain.

★

No doubt there will be those who will maintain that a look at the daily lives of Islamists glosses over the thrust of their existence: that a focus on the mundane neglects or even normalizes something more sinister; that, in other words, these youth organizations are repositories for radicalism. Indeed, among more cynical onlookers, there has long been the belief, especially pronounced in the ten years between 9/11 and the Arab Spring, that young Islamists in general were simply more "radical" than everyone else. Once, at a lecture I gave at an American university prior to the Arab Spring, a faculty member in the audience interrupted me with a question masquerading as a statement: "But young Arabs are always angry." This notion—that these young people will always rebel, and that Islamism is simply the outgrowth of this rage—represents what I call the "theory of inevitable Arab youth radicalism."[54] But such a theory, in addition to grossly demonizing the diverse Islamist base, would over-determine the membership of groups that were perceived to be more radical. It would assume that young Arabs would be more attracted to groups such as Al Adl that reject electoral participation, and it would fail to account for the strength of mainstream Islamist political parties in the first place.[55] Such a theory would also mischaracterize the nature of Islamist competition itself, one that is not necessarily violent—as demonstrated by the not uncommon living arrangements of young people such as Brahim and his roommates.

For much of the first decade of the twentieth century, many painted a picture of Arab youth, when they bothered to paint one at all, simply as sources of terror. Thomas Friedman once blamed 9/11 on what he called "sitting around guys" or unemployed young people.[56] The bloody civil war in Algeria was attributed to similar culprits. But while unemployment forecasts are certainly daunting—the region will likely continue to produce half a million unemployed individuals each year—the responses to them are not necessarily predestined.[57] Yet, ever since 9/11, foreign policy experts at respected think tanks have been sounding warnings about the violence to come. One wrote of "The Mideast 'Bomb' No One Talks About."[58] Another forecasted a coming "youthquake." Joblessness, she said, would "leave an entire generation ripe for radicalization."[59] In this description, unemployed Arab youth would inevitably become "radicalized" Arab youth. Population growth and, with it, the increased presence of young Arabs—indeed, their mere birth—was conceptualized as troubling and even threatening.[60]

These tropes endure. In the midst of anti-American protests that overtook the region in September 2012, the image of young Arabs-as-human bombs was routinely employed. In the pages of *Foreign Policy*, for example, one well-known analyst declared: "The frustration and embitterment of tens of millions of unemployed and currently unemployable young people" unavoidably leads to what he called, "insidious danger."[61]

There is no denying that many young Arabs have long expressed feelings of hopelessness, of being trapped. But only a limited number of citizens in the Middle East and North Africa, a statistically small figure, ever choose the route of terror.[62] In focus groups with Moroccan university students, I often asked respondents to imagine their future by using metaphors. The responses I heard were unabashedly dark, depressing, and at times even unsettling. Many compared their government to "blood suckers," "vampires," "ghosts," "dark castles," and even "smog." In one typical answer, a student described a white room that resembled a prison cell, with white walls on all sides. Every citizen in the country (from all ethnicities, religions, and political views) had been squeezed into that small cell. Once a day, a large, "fat man" draped in a Moroccan flag would enter the room and take everyone's belongings. On his way out, he would leave one red apple in the center of the room. The implication was unmistakable. Everyone around them—and the bloated, embezzling central government in particular—was seen as squeezing, impoverishing, even robbing the citizenry, and then starving them all, leaving only a single piece of fruit to be shared among the masses.[63]

Still, the responses to this discontent have been far from obvious. Countless more, for example, have opted to flee than to fight. The late King Hassan II used to describe his country as a date palm rooted in Africa and rustled by the winds of Europe.[64] And, yet, surveys increasingly suggest that many want to uproot that tree. One poll found that more than 90 percent of young people expressed a desire to emigrate from Morocco, and more than 70 percent of university graduates hoped to settle abroad.[65] A joke I occasionally heard morphs the country's Arabic name "al-Maghreb" with the phonetically similar word "al-Mekhrib"—meaning the "ruined."

Too often, young people grew up taunted by their surroundings, by the idea that life elsewhere must somehow be better. The most well-to-do neighborhoods in most Moroccan cities are often named after foreign countries (like *Souissi* in Rabat). Even the poorest districts feature street names like Milano or Florence. The nicest avenue in Rabat is named after France. In Sidi Ifni, a small outpost in the south, locals still look longingly at the Spanish-built hospitals of the 1950s, telling me more than once: "those were better than the ones we have today."[66]

One Al Adl activist I met named Khalid once visited Tangier at the northern tip of Morocco, and from the city's promenade on a clear day, he said, Europe looked so near he could almost touch it. Not a week goes by, it seems, that news does not emerge of someone being turned back, or even dying, attempting to brave the rough waters between Morocco and Europe—either through passing the Strait of Gibraltar or by tackling the cold Atlantic waters off the west coast of Morocco, where Spain's Canary Islands also appear deceptively close. During one typical year in the 2000s, 100,000 attempted to cross illegally into Spain.[67] Local television airs documentaries on the hazards and dangers of clandestine immigration; young people watch them to get pointers on how to do it.

In August 2012, Spanish police arrested 120 Moroccans when they tried to storm the border fence separating the Spanish enclave of Melilla and the Moroccan town of Nador in northeast Morocco. The strategy was simple: overwhelm the guards with their sheer masses, and perhaps, it was hoped, a few would not get caught. Some making it was better than none, they must have figured, and if they weren't among the lucky ones, they could always try again at a later date.[68]

I particularly remember an encounter with Reda from the small town of Tiznit in southern Morocco. Aged twenty-two, with a high school education, and living with his parents, he too opted for escape. He saved up for a spot on a creaky fishing boat, ready to brave the rough waters to the Canary Islands. But he and his shipmates were lost at sea for weeks. He relayed to me how he subsisted on scraps—a dead bird and anything he could forage from the sea—while he watched his friends beside him die one by one. It turns out that he had been duped: the man they had all paid to captain the ship knew even less about boats than he did. After Reda miraculously managed to make it ashore, his suffering was almost for naught. He was turned over to Spanish authorities and immediately placed on an airplane back to Morocco. I asked him if he would make another attempt. I feared I knew the answer. "Of course," he said, "I have no future here." Besides, he later told me, he was able to gloat to his friends about the flight home: none of them had ever experienced airplane travel before.[69]

In addition to illegal immigration, this decade has seen another source of youth mortality: suicide—not from terrorism, but from depression. There have been nearly a hundred self-immolations among young people since the Arab Spring came to Morocco in February 2011. Some copycat, no doubt, but some much more. Publicly setting oneself on fire is altogether so much more public and more political than any other form of suicide. In the words of one Moroccan sociologist, killing oneself in this way has become for young people the "last mode of speaking in a society that does not allow for listening."[70]

In this chapter, we have seen how the growing and multilayered Islamist base often follows no clear divisible patterns—how multiple movements draw their memberships from largely educated young urbanites who seem to look and act a lot like one another. But if the Islamist base is so blurred—and if there is an absence of any striking external characteristics segmenting them—what then differentiates young Islamists from each other and what determines their decision to join one movement over another?

Before he found his movement, Brahim once told me, he was a "nobody." He still is, he says, but what is different now is that he has the potential someday not to be. Like his fellow activists, he didn't necessarily come for the friends, the theology, the order, or even just for the struggle. He came for something bigger and even more elusive. In the next chapter, we will look deeper into the lives of wider numbers of young Islamists to explore what that *something* might be.

Chapter 4

WHAT YOUTH WANT

For much of the 2000s, before he became a government minister, Aziz Rabbah was the person charged with overseeing the recruitment of young people into PJD, the largest Islamist party in Morocco. He traveled around the country, toured its cities, led conferences and rallies—all to try to convince young people to join his organization. And, as it turned out, even his family was not immune from his efforts.

In the middle of one of our discussions, his attention turned to his own teenage daughter. She was, he admitted, still "searching for her group of choice." He was biased, of course: because his daughter "believes in her country." Because she is "intelligent," he added, she would most likely follow in his own footsteps. But, he was sure to point out, it was up to her.

"So she hasn't made up her mind yet?" I prodded. "No," he said, "Everyone has the freedom to choose whichever group they want." And then he paused as if to underscore his point: "Even my own daughter."

Sometimes when you interview someone, when you listen to them speak, listen to them ramble and go off on tangents, as everyone does when they talk casually, there are certain points that stand out only later, that only seem to resonate in retrospect, that jump off the page when reviewing your notes or transcripts, but go almost unnoticed when listening to them for the first time. This was one of those moments. What was remarkable here was not that a politician was invoking a family member to drive home a point (they do that all the time, the world over). It also was not that he seemed unsure where his daughter would end up (his comments may have even been hyperbolic).

What struck me was that his daughter even had a choice at all—and that he took this for granted. I could not count how many people tried to explain to me young Islamists' decisions by simply saying: "kids just do what their parents do." Yet, even for the daughter of the man tasked with recruiting every young person in the country, he recognized that there was work to do. That even his daughter would have to decide for herself between movements. And this very choice, it turned out, was the predicament—and power—facing young people across the country.

But my surprises did not stop there. In order to understand the multiple paths of diverse young activists, I proceeded to expand my research, to look beyond certain individual cases such as Rabbah's daughter. And, as I did this, I came to be struck not only by the fact that a choice of movement existed, but also at what was motivating these choices. My goal in this chapter is to unearth these motivations: why youth now join the Islamist movement in general, and why they join one specific group over another.

When I coded and analyzed the trove of data I had uncovered—culled from first-person narratives and life histories, transcripts, and extended participant observation—I did not find evidence that supported reigning explanations of Islamist activism. I did not find that young people were simply being enticed by the prospects of religious salvation or that they were being bought off, lured wholly by the potential of social services or even solidarity—or even that they were engaging in the kind of detached cost-benefit analyses often presumed by economists and political scientists.

Instead, I uncovered something more intricate and, at the same time, harder to condense: I found that they were looking for nothing less than a new sense of self. Their decisions are multiple, multilayered, and constantly renegotiated, but they can only be understood by making sense of the new identities that are sustained by their collective action. Islamism, I argue, is not simply ideological; it is instrumental—an avenue to a new identity, to new ways of seeing and thinking about themselves. Call it the *new politics of personal empowerment*, where Islamist movements are reimagined as individual improvement factories: places to go not simply to become better Muslims, but to better their lot in life or the perception of that lot.

The data also revealed another layer of decision making. The pursuit of self-betterment was not understood in one singular, overarching way. Rather, it encompassed a combination of material and non-material needs—and it is this distinction that paves the way to understanding the divergent paths of individual activists.

All youth are interested in improving themselves, but they differ in how they go about it. Those who join PJD are looking to equip themselves with specific skills to better their lot in life: to gain practical experience, training, leadership opportunities, to improve their resumes and professional connections. Those, on the other hand, who join Al Adl are seeking more expressive benefits from their participation—specifically, the perception of bettering their lot in life: to feel empowered, to feel like they are contributing to society or even feel like they are someone who could contribute to society. In sum, youth who are attracted to self-advancement in *tangible* ways steer toward PJD; those who seek the same thing via more *emotional* means find a home with Al Adl.

In the pages that follow, I will develop these points at length: first, by grappling with popular explanations of young people's participation in Islamist movements, and then by illuminating ideal typical identities forged through Islamist activism.

★

Social scientists have long questioned what drives individuals to activism when sitting on the sidelines often affords them the same benefit. When one can profit from a movement's activities without participating—when one can get something for free—why pay for it with time, energy, and, in some cases, physical security? What drives individuals—especially the continued activism of committed members—in the face of a multitude of obligations to the movement, a variety of demands on their personal life, or even the specter of repression or social alienation?

In the case of Islamist movements, four broad explanations have often been mustered to solve this puzzle. Yet none alone explains the decisions of the increasingly blurred Islamist rank and file.

First, and most widespread, is the suggestion that young Islamist activists are driven by a specific religious call—by the summoning of the symbolic and ideological resources of the movement. It is religious salvation potential young Islamists are after, this predominant argument goes, and it is thus religious salvation that sustains their commitment. Such an assumption is ingrained in common understandings of religious movements, including sects or even cults. Scholars have found, for example, in the case of the Hare Krishna movement, that prospective members are seeking what has been called a "genuine conversion."[1] Islamist movements are sometimes referred to as "cults," suggesting this correlation.[2]

As a result, many also assume that the strongest religious believers become the most committed activists, and vice versa. According to the CIA's former "point man on Islam"—the person who spent two decades researching and meeting with Islamists around the world—this is certainly the case. Islamists, he says, follow a linear path to activism. He outlines a "six stage" process, beginning with recognition of one's "Islamic identity" and climaxing in a desire to change the system based on this identity ("stage four").[3] A clear and positive relationship emerges between Islam and activism: as an activist's religiosity and interest in Islam increase, so too does his or her commitment to the movement.

It is tempting to consider that, since they are *Islamists*, it must be, above all, Islam driving their decisions—*that their complex choices can be encapsu-*

lated by a single, overarching explanatory variable known as "Islam." But social movement theorists doing research elsewhere have shown the limitation of such a model. Pre-existing values and cultural orientations alone are usually not enough to compel activism. Strong believers in environmentalism, to use but one example, were not shown to be any more likely to join environmental organizations.[4] Moreover, much of our understanding about the way religion influences young people still follows a perception of religious teaching as something handed down to them, as if they are taught or instructed or inculcated by their elders *to be* Islamic, rather than figuring out for themselves what such a construct might mean.

In rare and pathbreaking field research among young Muslim Brotherhood activists in Egypt in the late nineties and early 2000s, political scientist Carrie Wickham found that what drives young activists is what she calls a "religious obligation."[5] Certain incentives might lure young people initially, she argues, but these interests alone could not possibly account for their long-term commitment, especially in instances of high-risk activism, the kind that involves personal risk. Instead, Wickham maintains that what drives their continued activism is a belief that their involvement is compelled by God, compelled by the need for service to the da'wa, or the Islamic call. Such an ideological attraction only worked, she noted, when the message fit the life experiences of young people.

But, in general, such theories no longer address the changing dynamics of youth recruitment. Religious obligations simply are no longer enough to explain continued loyalty to any Islamist movement in the contemporary context. Ongoing commitment to any movement, of course, requires that the collective identity of the movement "fit the life experiences of young people." But the life experiences of young people have changed, and their choices have expanded significantly. And, more and more, Islamist groups tailor their recruitment strategies to meet the new, lived realities and experiences of this emerging generation of Muslim youth.

This is not surprising, nor is it in any way an indictment of important prior research: earlier theories were largely devised more than a decade before the Brotherhood in Egypt, for one, even began formally participating in politics. While such groups were, of course, dabbling in the political sphere, they were still largely religious movements, operating under the direction of clerics and without formal political parties—and without significant competition from fellow movements.

Beyond ideology, the second argument as to what might propel sustained activism with Islamist movements is rooted in the half-century-old writings of economist Mancur Olson. In the absence of coercion, Olson claimed, individuals will be moved to act by the lure of selective incentives.[6] Potential activists will calculate for themselves whether joining social movements is in their best interest, engaging in rational cost-benefit analyses.

But can the rational actor model truly explain Islamists' diverse behavior? For as long as Islamism has existed, scholars have debated whether it was really in an individual's pure self-interest to be a part of such movements.[7] After all, at least until the Arab Spring, joining the Islamist movement seemed, if anything, largely irrational. In some cases, membership required sacrifice, long hours, and intricate training practices. On the surface, membership very often seemed to incur more costs than benefits: including potential arrest, loss of personal freedoms, and regular house searches. This is especially the case with illegal movements such as Al Adl in Morocco or the Muslim Brotherhood in Egypt. Even for legal Islamist political parties, for whom repression was more limited, their chances of success in the midst of the harsh grip of authoritarian rule—the notion that the fruits of their labor, their significant investments of time and energy, would someday pay off—seemed remote, at best. And yet all of these movements—legal and illegal Islamist groups alike—seemed not just to survive, but also to thrive.[8]

A third, and related, school of thought suggests that Islamist movements entice activists with the promise of free, well-organized, and omnipresent social services. This is a promise that such movements have become famous for in second-hand accounts: free health care, extra class instruction, childcare, and so on.[9]

When the postcolonial, Arab nationalist commitment to social support failed to materialize or faded away, Islamists purportedly benefitted from stepping in to fill the void.[10] In the midst of neoliberal economic transitions, as Arab socialism waned and state-supported sectors (health and education, in particular) suffered, Islamist movements were happy to take advantage. Or so the argument goes.

But, upon closer inspection, this reasoning, especially in the twenty-first century, begins to lose its persuasiveness. Individuals' interests are not static; they evolve. Perhaps a specific social service might attract someone at first, but it would be difficult to explain one's extended activism based on a specific provision, especially once he or she is no longer the recipient of such services.[11]

Discussions over social service procurement also tend to paint young people in particular as simply pawns to the whims of material gain. The director of an NGO committed to women's rights in Morocco reflected this view, explaining away Islamist activism due simply to an addiction to "welfare programs." Islamists, the director said, are "used to receiving assistance, and have become passive people who refuse change, lack the capacity to defend their rights, and accept their destiny."[12] Not only is this a convenient explanation for secular competitors (Islamists have more money, thus they are more successful), but it is also ultimately misleading: there is little that is "passive" among young people—women and men alike.

Such overly simplistic (even ad hominem) characterizations fail to probe activists' complex lives and motivations. Students I encountered certainly appreciated how Al Adl, in particular, offered help with housing, study materials, and even the procurement of textbooks. But, of course, not only were some young people already employed or capable of affording such services before they signed up with their Islamist group of choice (though many were not), it would, I found, take more to convince them to join a movement than, in one student leader's words, "someone offering tutoring to my sister." In short, young people cannot simply be bought.

A fourth main argument suggests that what motivates Islamists is actually the promise of something different: solidarity.[13] Here, obligations to the collective—to friends, prior bonds, even new cohorts—matter more than duty to self. It is true that the name of the world's first formal Islamist movement—the Muslim *Brotherhood*—suggests this fraternal bond. One might also note that Al Adl's bottom rung, the initial placement of an individual upon joining, is called the *usra* or family, suggesting a potential connection that is both potent and unbreakable. Even the secular militants of Italy's extreme left, for example, reportedly relished camaraderie, the filial feeling that "every moment of the day" was transformed.[14]

For this line of argument, the power of social networks is extolled, largely because young people supposedly are propelled to support the work of their friends even in the absence of any personal reward. In an oft-cited study of Dutch environmentalist movements, for example, sociologists found that close to a majority of activists were recruited through personal contacts.[15]

But if young Islamists are driven purely by a commitment to community, why would they be so willing to move from one group to another? Such discussions of "brotherhood" would suggest that young people would or could never leave their movement: after all, a family is something that one is part of forever. But one can migrate from a movement at any time—and many I encountered often did. Why, also, if social networks were singularly significant, did so many of the activists I spoke to claim not to have known anyone from the movement before joining?

Instead, my findings reveal a broader understanding of the benefits attained through Islamist activism: they are neither wholly material nor non-material, but rather *both*. Moreover, the dynamics of these particular benefits are more far-reaching and textured than is normally suggested.

★

Activism, I found, allows young people to construct new identities, to build better versions of themselves—and it does so in multiple ways.[16]

If social movement theorists are correct that "identity" can be understood as one's "place in society," then joining a movement, *choosing* a movement, involves individuals negotiating a new place—and a new perception of that place—in the world around them.[17] Within movements, activist identities begin to become "collective" when they are shared by other members, when, to use one formulation, the "I" turns into a "we."[18] But, contrary to typecast, it is not as if young people are indoctrinated into assuming a single overarching identity.

How, then, do these new identities emerge? Are they constructed purely through activism or are they preexisting? This is what research from other contexts tells us: that collective identities tend to be both ascribed and asserted—formed through activism, while nonetheless being informed by preexisting aspects of individual identities.[19] We know that recruitment itself is rarely a top-down process (despite how it is often portrayed for young Islamists); it is not simply about movements framing messages to persuade potential members. Rather, recruitment is a relationship—between outreach and agency, of collective and individual identities finding common ground.

I certainly found this to be the case with the activists I encountered. Identity construction is a dialectical process: internal and external to both the individual and the organization. Yet, I also uncovered a unique aspect of this process. In an increasingly competitive marketplace, where Islamist groups vie with one another to mobilize an overlapping base, the undercurrents of recruitment are slowly shifting. As rivalries intensify, organizations compete to align themselves with the (preexisting) experiences and desires of individual recruits, striving more to adapt and respond to young people's needs than to inculcate them into their "master" plans. Indeed, if collective identity formation through mobilization were most salient, activists would *not* be likely to leave a group: their identities would simply shift through activism to reflect the shared identity of the whole organization. Thus, in the midst of alternative choices, Islamist groups cannot simply rely on persuasive marketing of ideological or material benefits because if reality does not meet promise, youth will simply sample other outlets for activism. Nor can they assume that the current pool of young recruits meaningfully resembles previous generations of Islamist activists in terms of their experiences, values, or motivations.

The young people I encountered were seeking what has come to resemble a new Islamist dream—a variation of the famed American dream—an ethos of possibility, of responsibility, a belief that they could remake themselves, that their contribution matters, that *they* matter. In the Middle East and North Africa, these are not conventional ideas—that anyone can succeed, anyone can rise. In societies steeped in patriarchy and drenched in both clientelism and corruption, these notions of personal possibility were nothing short of *revolutionary*. These were possibilities that each movement came to recognize and ultimately to brandish, to go out of their way to prove that they embodied more than the other. And, to the hearts and minds of young recruits, this was often the secret to their success. As an Al Adl activist named Abdelhaq noted: "If a student has a gift—perhaps, in writing or in public speaking, even in art or in drama—it is our responsibility to help him and give him an opportunity to develop it."

To complicate matters further, young people's yearning to construct a desirable new self manifests in different forms. It is not instantiated uniformly. In my research, I found that it is most often fulfilled via a tangible *effect* or an emotional *affect*. Put another way: the search for a new self and the search for a new sense of self are intrinsically interrelated, but often distinct. Islamist groups worked to offer these benefits in the ways they could, the ways they knew how, and the ways they could be most effective: with PJD veering toward the tangible and Al Adl toward the emotional.

The fact that both groups contend to make room for similar new identities to flourish confirms that the push for self-help is not merely ideological (say, born simply out of a Sufi ideal of "personal transcendence") or even political (say, a difference between effecting social change from inside or outside existing institutions). Young peoples' identities are also not segmented by groups (i.e., everyone from one movement wants one thing or sees themselves in one way), but rather by individual (i.e., each person is unique and desires something specific to them).

While these emerging identities are diverse, multiple, and fluid—even within a single group—I want to isolate three ideal typical Islamist identities that emerged from my fieldwork: the "Autonomous," "Ascending," and "Altruistic" Islamist.[20]

In the case of the "Autonomous Islamist," activism is understood as the prospect of living as an independent, autonomous person, of exercising agency, of the simple yet persuasive act of choosing for themselves the lives they want to lead. In particular, PJD activists relish earning specific skills in order to gain control over their lives. Those in Al Adl, on the other hand, seek out the feeling of being valued—that they are and can be taken seriously as autonomous individuals.

For the Ascending Islamist, activism offers the prospect of self-empowerment: to ascend to new levels, to become a better version of themselves. For PJD members, self-empowerment translates into upward mobility: the potential for new jobs and limitless ascent within a nonhierarchical organization. In Al Adl, ascent becomes something much more intimate: the sensibility of personal empowerment—not upward mobility, but inner strength.

In the case of the Altruistic Islamist, activism represents the opportunity to become someone uniquely attuned to the needs of others, someone who works harder and with more rigor on behalf of their fellow citizens. In Al Adl, members come to experience a certain pride in helping others—as if they possess a special understanding of the lives of others Those who join PJD, on the other hand, appreciate the formal tools, experiences, and training they procure in order to serve citizens.

For both groups, altruism should not be conflated with "moral obligation" or even selflessness.[21] More often than not, young people highlight what working for others does *for* themselves. Al Adl members, for instance, come to feel (even flaunt) a certain cachet, a "coolness" factor, in their professed altruism. For PJD members, their work for others helps their own images and reputations and how they are seen in society.

The remainder of this chapter will elaborate upon each of these ideal types.

THE AUTONOMOUS ISLAMIST

Every Islamist has a story. And, at first glance, many appear only to involve being in the right place at the right time, a fortuitous encounter made possible, in some cases, by the omnipresence of Islamist groups. I heard many such stories: an overachieving middle schooler who wanted extra lessons at the local youth center; the bored custodian who stumbled upon a meeting on an evening stroll; the call center worker who happened to sit next to an Islamist leader on a train; women who wanted to meet husbands; boys who wanted to meet girls.

Others were even seemingly more purposeful: the young woman who used the activities of a local Islamist association as an excuse to get out of the house and out of household chores. For some, it offered a venue to express anger at the United States over its foreign policies and/or the failure of local leaders to speak out against them; for others, it was just plain disgust at the domestic distribution of power. "I joined," Walid from Al Adl told me, "because it was a chance to say—how do you say?—fuck you Morocco; fuck you king. Why does he have all the power and we the people have none?" Once again, the Islamists were there to answer the call, to offer support. They were, at times, even beneficiaries of their own name recognition, of the legwork of an earlier generation.

But when we look more closely, these are not all simply "right place, right time" stories. For those who remained in these movements, who stayed committed, this was more than mere happenstance; there was something else underlying their search. These are often narratives of young people finding and embracing an opportunity to take control over their lives. Choosing among a variety of Islamist activisms provided the opportunity to exercise choice at all—or, as sociologist Alberto Melucci once wrote of global youth in general, "to regain control of their own actions, to reclaim the right to define themselves against criteria of identification imposed from without."[22]

They could be escaping youth, escaping imposed liminality, but what mattered was that they had the ability to escape at all. With their choices, they are actively charting their own futures, or at least feeling like they are—something they had not previously been able to do.

There is often inspiration even in the experimentation itself, even in the simple acts of imagination associated with it. "What I see on American TV," Ayoub from Al Adl told me, "people are always sticking out their middle finger to their bosses. I laugh when I see that, but that's how I feel."

When young people choose between multiple Islamist groups—when they ask themselves, as they often do: why should I join one over the other?—they would not necessarily engage in a battle over whose beliefs were more authentic. When young people tried to recruit them into these movements, they would not hear them say: if you want "real Islam, true Islam, come with us." Instead, they would hear other reasons. They would hear: if you really want to work for your country, if you really want to give yourself to others, if you really want to change who you are, you should join us. When I asked one leading recruiter for Al Adl why someone would join his movement over PJD, his answer was telling: "We are working harder than they are; we offer more opportunities for personal growth than they do."

For Al Adl, this takes the form of *feeling* independent. Amina, for one, came to Al Adl after working at a small Leftist organization committed to human rights.[23] When she first joined that group, she was excited about the work that lay ahead. Except, over time, she grew increasingly disenchanted. The tasks assigned to her were menial. The work was unchallenging and generally lacked substance. In short, she was being ignored. The director reported, wryly, and in French, that youth must be *encadré*—that is, monitored, or looked after. They were, in this regard, like schoolchildren or foot soldiers: nonsubstantive, non-essential personnel, who were not to be taken seriously as sentient beings and not to be treated as significant actors in their own right.

Amina began to voice her concerns, and community members soon learned of her frustration. Shortly thereafter, Amina was approached by someone in town who asked her if she would like to work instead with the Al Adl association. She was assured that her duties would be dramatically different. Perhaps she might have to make some personal adjustments, maybe dress more conservatively, or even be looked upon with suspicion by others. But she would also be given real responsibility. Sure enough, she soon began to play an important role in its work. She did not shirk from these obligations; she relished them. But it was also, it seemed, the feeling she relished: that she was being treated like a real person, someone with agency and autonomy, who could make her own choices.

These sentiments also pervade the discourses of PJD members, but often in more concrete ways. Take the example of Mohsine. At first, it seemed, he came just for the Islamic books. He was sixteen at the time, just a "bored student" in Casablanca when he first encountered PJD. It all happened, he said, "because he loved to read." Around his seventeenth birthday, his father had told him that he would no longer buy him novels unless his grades improved. But school was not capturing his attention and he craved outside reading. So he settled for the only books he could find, the only ones available for free: books about Islam at the local library.

One day, after about a year of visiting the library and reading the books, a young woman approached him and asked him which *jalsa tarbawiyya* (educational lesson) group he was in. He did not know what that was, so she explained them to him and told him he should join one, especially since he wanted to read more books about Islam.

This interaction, this opportunity, initially captured his attention, but upon joining, he came to remain for another reason. Because of his time in the library, his classical Arabic skills were better than the other kids and that was useful to the group. "I was good at reporting," he said. The others in the group kept telling him that young people could get ahead if they were "hardworking and disciplined"—and he was getting ahead. Thus, he came for the books, but he stayed, he said, because for the first time in his life, he was really gaining "valuable" practical skills.

An activist named Zouhir migrated from PJD to Al Adl because he no longer felt like he stood to gain anything more from the work he was doing with PJD. He had recruited so many young people, gained so many important skills, that it seemed he had reached the pinnacle. When someone from Al Adl approached him one day at a mosque, telling him of the possibilities that lay ahead if he came to a meeting, he agreed. He could experience something bigger than himself. His old PJD friends, he said, were disappointed, but he didn't really mind. In the end, he said, he relished having this choice, carving his own path. Choosing between movements gave him a certain satisfaction. "I had a choice to leave," he said, and "I did." A new, more fitting path for his self-improvement lay ahead.

Even Qur'anic study is understood in these terms. Both groups construct such study as paths toward self-betterment: not simply as study for the sake of studying. For Al Adl, meeting to learn about the Qur'an helps make one a better, more independent person. While these attributes could surely help members become more employable, that pursuit is secondary. For PJD, on the other hand, Qur'anic study sessions explicitly aid career advancement, within and outside the party, offering opportunities for promotion and job contacts.

An Al Adl member named Jalil who landed a coveted job at a Spanish Internet firm in Casablanca told me how useful his weekly Qur'anic study had been for his personal development. First, Jalil said, studying the Qur'an regularly gave him "discipline." Second, it helped him develop "a logical process, including thinking and reasoning skills." Third, it helped him with "decision-making." And, fourth, it aided his ability to engage in what he called "big-picture thinking."

His activism helped him feel like a new person. "We all realize," he said, "that such study can be very helpful with our professional lives." When a job interviewer is looking at candidates, he said, they can "see a difference" with those candidates who have studied the Qur'an. Even if they do not know the candidate is from Al Adl (a fact most would likely not advertise in a job interview), "it is as if they are looking," he said, "at someone who went to a very prestigious private school."

Praying itself, even attending retreats, is often understood not only in terms of religious duty, but also self-worth. "It's all very corporeal," one former Al Adl member named Ashraf told me. "Why do you think we learn about fasting, hunger, and even patience? It helps our bodies, helps us gain strength and self-confidence."

Mohammed from PJD enjoyed attending educational sessions to learn about the Qur'an, but he also valued the professional contacts he was gaining from them. "It was like gaining entry into a new world of helpful connections. I knew where to go to ask for a job, who to ask for advice." In some cases, it was almost as if they took Islam for granted. They took these movements' religious foundations as assumed; some were even looking for what one activist expressed to me as "more than Islam."

A fellow PJD activist named Anas went even further, describing membership as life preparation—bypassing family, school, even the mosque: "You learn nothing in school or anywhere else; you have to come to the party to learn about the world." He loved this idea of learning; it made him smarter—not simply more pious, but more intelligent. "The difference between us and other Islamist movements," he said, "is the *level* of understanding of the issues."

New PJD members, for example, are trained not necessarily to be better people or better Muslims, but to be independent individuals. PJD activists at a typical training seminar heard tips, for example, on how to work better to get their point across in the midst of debates. These included:

"Avoid satire and lies."
"Avoid over-confidence."
"Never interrupt others during a debate."
"Never use obscenity or bad jokes or vulgar language."
"Formulate your requests directly to those in charge of an organization."

For young activists from both groups, they might already have a job, or have a job they aren't proud of, or have five small part-time jobs that barely earn any money, or have no job at all, but their work for their movement gave them something to be proud of: an ability to create a path for themselves that they would have control of, that they could determine. They weren't fleeing their country; they weren't blowing themselves up; they weren't even sitting back and watching events unfold.

"If you go to a coffeehouse and ask people what they believe, what their worldview is," Zakaria, 32, from Al Adl bemoaned, "they will tell you they don't have a worldview. That they don't have a reason to live. They will say that they just want to get through the day. Or that they want to leave— to go abroad." He then pointed his index finger at his chest. "I am different," he said. And "different," in this case, was code for "more independent." But, as we will see in the following sections, it was also often code for "more powerful" and even "more aware of the needs of others."

THE ASCENDING ISLAMIST

To relay how the dynamics of personal ascent and empowerment operate in Al Adl, I want to recount an experience from a typical group meeting.

I grabbed a spot on a cushion toward the back of the room. I was late, and the Al Adl gathering was about to begin. But first, a young man, we'll call him Wasim, needed to show the group something. He had a police summons that had just been delivered to his home, slipped under the door. Someone else, a young guy named Abderrahman, also dressed in a button down shirt and slacks, immediately popped up from his chair. "You got one too?" he asked excitedly. And then, like teammates following a great play, Wasim ran over to Abderrahman, grabbed his lower arm, turned his palm outward, and smacked his hand to give him five. They were partners in opposition. The room cheered.

The oldest man in the group, a lightly greying professor in his mid-forties, then stepped in. He sternly brought the group to order. He looked upset. I suspected that he would chide them for their revelry, for taking pride in legal infraction. But what he really wanted was their undivided attention. When everyone was looking his way, he gently reached into his back pocket, and fumbled for a moment as if to stir up anticipation. And, in a single rapid motion, he pulled out his own police summons and held it up high for everyone to see. He then broke into a huge grin. "I have one too!" he squealed, and the crowd roared with laughter.

That scene long perplexed me. What was funny, I would wonder, about three people getting summoned to the police station? Would not hesitation or concern or even fear have been the more appropriate reaction? After all, at the time, I recall feeling a bit anxious. Were the police going to barge through the door at *any* moment?

But there was a method to their merriment. Their perverse humor was found in the ostensible charade that would soon follow. They would not actually be arrested. Their lives would not be altered in any significant way. They would proceed to the police station, answer some questions, and return home that much stronger. The intended goal of their summons was intimidation; the unintended result was empowerment.

Many of their friends had also gone through similar experiences. And even if the summons did ultimately lead to arrest or even jail, the police action would likely validate their own accusations of unfair treatment against the regime. They would become living proof of, and for, their cause—evidence that the state represented a tyrannical system. In this way, there was power in this ridicule. The tables had been turned. These young people told themselves that they were now even more powerful than the all-powerful makhzen. An old Moroccan proverb reflected this milieu: "Three things cannot be overcome," the saying goes, "fire, flood and the makhzen (or the governing elite)."[24] But, to that mythic list, they could now not only add the name of their own organization, they could add their *own* names.

A few months after the incident with the police cards, some of the friends of those who had originally been summoned by the police were, in fact, arrested. One night, Hassan Bennajah, Al Adl youth leader, was presiding over a small youth wing meeting at a home in Mohammedia. As relayed by those present, eleven were congregating when seven police cars surrounded the house. They were rounded up and immediately taken to the police station, where they were reportedly held for twelve hours, and interrogated for six. To speak more to police excess, members made a point of noting that the sixteen-year-old son of the host, who was uninvolved with the meeting, was also arrested.

Upon their release from police custody, the group of twelve sent around a photo taken outside the police station. They even posted it on their website. It was an image of both triumph and resolve. The head of the youth section, Bennajah, stood in the center with a wide smile on his face and a self-congratulatory finger wagging high in the air. Others appeared cheerfully unfazed. One was even too busy texting to look up for the photo. They fought the law, and *they* won—at least for the day.

Theorists of mobilization have often found that experiencing a confrontation with authority (police, military, etc.)—witnessing abuse or injustice up close—can move individuals to act.[25] But the small, quotidian encounters such as the one described involve much more than that. More than confirming their own worldviews ("the government is corrupt"), it validates their own personal contribution to the movement, and, by extension, the world. Such encounters, as interpreted, render them as important, powerful people, a feeling one Al Adl member named Abdoul described as the "best feeling in the world."

The notion that personal courage can be culled from standing up to the regime is an idea that runs throughout the narratives of many Al Adl activists. The background of one in Casablanca, Moulham, is particularly telling—and dramatic: his family is made up of police officers and intelligence agents. In his narrative, activists attain individual courage and power from standing up to the police. And his sense of personal fulfillment comes not simply from Islam, but from having the power to oppose those in charge.

"My story is unique," Moulham began. "My father was a policeman. My brother-in-law works for the Moroccan Intelligence Services. My cousin is a top ranking police officer in Casablanca." It took him some time to join Al Adl, he said, because it required him to "give up fear." But even after he joined, "My brothers were always protecting me, watching after me. They would always warn me not to tell my father about my involvement. They would tell me that if I told my father, then something could happen to me or even to him."

After a while, "it became too much for me to handle, really. Too much pressure." So he opted to leave Al Adl for a few years. But he soon changed his mind. Given his family background, he was particularly worried about what they might think. "I was concerned that my family would find out about my involvement." But Al Adl, he said, gave him the courage to come clean. "Now, thanks to Allah, my family knows everything. Everybody knows. They come to my house and find books by Abdessalam Yassine. But now no one will utter a word because now *I am powerful*."

These are themes that are widespread among activists. One university leader recalled that when he witnessed a protest march near his university campus, he saw police approaching him. "When I saw that huge number of police, I was afraid." He then turned to me and said: "You previously asked about fear, well, yes I was afraid. It is a natural instinct." But his time with Al Adl has changed that—his time has changed him. "What we learn through our involvement," he said, "is avoiding cowardice."

Members of the cross-ideological "February 20 Movement"—Morocco's Arab Spring protest group—once told me that during their very first meetings, when young people would stand up in front of the room to rail against the regime or to talk about how corrupt the system is, those from Al Adl would often just sit in the back of the room quietly, and not say much. Yet, the other attendees did not want to stop talking. Those "February 20" meetings would often start at 6 pm and last until 6 am, ending only when "everyone got tired."

Some deduced from this that those in Al Adl were shy or socially awkward. I take a different view: what was a unique opportunity for many youth—an opportunity to criticize the state in public and the feeling that came from doing that in an open meeting—was old news to those in Al Adl. They had received a rush from doing this for years.

How, then, did new identities of personal empowerment and ascent come to be forged through PJD activism?

★

I once noticed the PJD youth leader Aziz Rabbah in the lobby of the party headquarters in Rabat. He was sitting in an oversized leather chair in a room off the main courtyard, with his feet resting comfortably on a table. He was holding court—office hours of sorts—and young PJD members were stopping by for his counsel. He offered them advice on whatever questions they had: on life, politics, even uncompleted roadwork in front of their house. Everyone was drinking tea and eating cookies. He wore a black suit with a black tie. The young activists who want to be just like him were swooning at their own potential future.

Rabbah's path to success is now the stuff of legend—at least, for young activists in PJD. From a low-ranking party member, he rose to the position of head of the youth wing, acquiring at the same time a coveted desk job at the prime minister's office. From there, he was placed on the party's national voting list, became an MP, was elected the mayor of the city of Kenitra, just north of Rabat, and then, almost by design, became a cabinet member himself, after being appointed minister of transportation in 2012. Most members would not be surprised if he rises to the position of party head, and even prime minister.

When I once visited the headquarters of Morocco's main Islamist party, I was greeted by the unexpected sounds of laughter, as three young activists sat in the corner of the courtyard poking fun at a more senior member. "If you could have any ministerial position in government," one asked him, "which one would you choose?" Before he could answer, a voice from the distance shouted, "Why not minister of tourism!" And then the chuckles began. It was funny for them because back then it seemed so farfetched—farfetched that the king would ever deign to ask them to serve as the public face of the country, especially overseas. They would, another joked, more likely scare away visitors than beckon them.

They were enjoying themselves, enjoying fantasizing not only about what jobs they could have, but also about the people they could become—all by virtue of their activism. At all formal party events, Rabbah, for his part, was treated as a minor celebrity. At youth conferences, his picture was plastered alongside the secretary general's. Young people asked to have their picture taken with him. On the final night of one conference, after the official activities had concluded, Rabbah made the rounds among the crowd, sharing kisses and shaking men's hands, and thanking them for coming. He had changed into a brand new, loose-fitting white gown, not the traditional djellaba, but a *gendora*, a luxurious, hoodless variation. It was the kind of garment one would wear in the comfort of one's home.

They had reason to look up to him. He was living their dream. He was not just an active PJD member, he was also—and largely as a result—a government employee, with a substantial government salary and a higher status in society. He was their inspiration, because by looking at him, they could see themselves; by looking at him, they saw the palpable potential of their activism, the potential contours of their futures. At the party's eighth annual youth conference in 2012, Rabbah returned—now as minister—to receive a special award for his service to the party. They presented him with a gold-framed painted portrait of himself. Rabbah stood on stage, listening to the endless applause, watching the standing ovation, taking it all in, continually kissing his wife and grasping his daughters. His wife began to tear up. The party faithful looked at him with awe.[26]

At one of our earliest meetings, when he was still just the head of the youth wing, I visited Rabbah at the prime minister's office, where he worked as a paid staff member. I got lost on my way there—all the white government buildings looked almost identical. I was late, and Aziz did little to hide his displeasure. He waited for me at a table in the outdoor office cafeteria. He had already ordered for me, and the personal sized tagines were waiting for us to open their clay lids. Aziz's annoyance was perhaps also partially caused by hunger. After a few questions, he interrupted me: "I suggest we eat," he said with a tinge of impatience, "so I can concentrate better." He paid for lunch. We then retired to his upstairs office where he ordered us a fresh *berrad* (kettle) of tea; he said that he wanted to be sure to show me his office. He seemed to take pleasure in being able to summon the maid to bring us more tea. He seemed to relish being in a position to be served.

At the end of our meeting, he stood up and handed me his business card. He had given me his *carte de visite* before, and was obviously quite proud of it. His position—in truth, his life—was a siren call for young people across the whole country to see the possible rewards of Islamist activism. His future was intricately and positively tied to his party. Emblazoned on his pristine white business card in all capital letters were the words: ROYAUME DU MAROC LE PREMIER MINISTRE. In the center of the card, his position was stated even more clearly: Chargé de mission auprès du PM, Conseiller en TIC du Ministre des Affaires Economiques et Générales.

These words on a business card were icons of power: written evidence of party ascent after years of service.

Let's look also at a group of young PJD members discuss why they became active. Two related notions quickly become synonymous: the role of the party in their own futures, and their own futures in the role of the party. Taha, an engineering student, declared: "We are the future of the party. Our leaders are not eternal. The only criterion that matters is ability. Most of the leaders of this party are young people." But could one of them even become leader of the party one day? Hamza, a party activist, was resolute: "Why not? Thanks to our internal democracy, anything is possible."[27]

In these two simple statements, Taha and Hamza captured a recurring theme heard among activists: that by joining the party, young people manage to procure a future they never had in Moroccan society. The party is a space—an opportunity—for them to become someone important, even a place to fulfill their personal ambitions.

In this way, young people can come with nothing, knowing nothing or no one, and they could rise to the top. Only in PJD, members claim, is this type of rapid ascent possible. One oft-heard statement reflects this claim: "There is no bureaucracy in PJD"—or, put another way, there are no barriers in place to stifle ascension and personal ambition.

To begin with, there is the simple but nonetheless revolutionary notion that they would possess a future at all. A familiar refrain among young people in Morocco (and the frequency and prevalence of this belief is backed up by survey data discussed in earlier chapters) is that there is "no future in Morocco." The presence of opportunity in, and with, PJD is a direct refutation of this widespread idea. The statement that *we are the future of the party* is both advertisement and affirmation.

To make this point, another activist, Omar, posed a question to me: "PJD knows that youth are the future of this country, and its leaders want to pass responsibilities onto the next generation. And if you notice: during our forums that we organize, all our senior leaders were present." "Why is this?" he asked.

He then offered his own answer: "To train the future young leaders. This is what they are telling us: 'We have started and you should finish and continue on the same path.' When we work in this context, this safe and familiar atmosphere, we find that our leaders are interested and caring. It is normal to want to come here and participate and work for the common welfare."

Notice the contours of their criticism of Al Adl. They reject joining their rival not because of theological differences, but because of its structural deficiencies, for its lack of potential upward mobility. It is not a group in which they can see themselves rising to the top, as being powerful or important enough. "How can they," one PJD activist named Bachir asked of his Al Adl friends, "join a movement that is led by someone like Yassine? He is a big boss man. Everything leads to him." An activist named Ahmed also invoked the "big boss" epithet. "PJD doesn't believe in glorifying its leader. If someone is the leader today, after four years another leader will take power and continue the work. In Al Adl, they have their big boss who governs. But one person cannot manage everything! Their movement lacks openness."

PJD, they claim, is avowedly inclusive, making room for youth and for people of all backgrounds. According to Badr, "people don't participate in politics because Moroccan parties—except for us—are old! Their members are old and they do not care about youth." Or, in Khadija's words: "The average age of a party secretary general is seventy! Someone that old can no longer think about young people and their needs. He's too old even to drive a car!" By contrast, PJD "gives youth a chance to express themselves, to participate and produce change. Even if they do not become members, they just want to know more about us."

Within PJD, they believe that they can be and do anything. They are able to strive even for leadership positions. And, in their minds, this is what makes their party unique—different from those such as Al Adl with seemingly eternal leaders (Yassine) or even in Morocco writ large, with the king and his hereditary claims to rule. To ascend in PJD, they need not be members of a particular family, descendants of the Prophet, or even possessors of profound religious knowledge or training. All that matters is their ability to perform—and excel—at the tasks of the party. All that matters, in sum, is that they learn how to become effective politicians, good bureaucrats.

THE ALTRUISTIC ISLAMIST

I once asked a university Al Adl leader named Youssef an obvious question: Why, in the face of personal hardship, would anyone join an outlawed group such as Al Adl? Would not the prospect of arrests deter recruits?[28]

"It is not easy to be a member of our organization," he said, "it is not easy at all." He began answering these questions by chronicling the rigor of his own labors—always being sure to compare them to the ostensible ease of his competitors. "I was in jail for seven months when I was in university for my role in protests. It then took five years for the university to let me back in. My parents always tell me to leave Al Adl. They wonder why I am putting my safety in jeopardy. We suffer so much."

His friends in PJD do not experience any of this, he said. "For them, it is simple. I could go to PJD and have everything. I could have money, newspapers, the open support of many people." So why, then, does he remain active in Al Adl? "It is our responsibility to choose what is difficult." "What is difficult," he said, "is true."

But there were rewards in the perception of working harder than they ever imagined: they saw this self-sacrifice as proof that they were more attuned to the needs of others. I often heard how those in Al Adl might not have been offered the possibility of employment, but they were still reaping the benefits of their perceived public service. A familiar rhetorical question asked by activists usually takes one of these forms: What would the state do *without* us? Or: where would Moroccans be *without* us? Or: where would I be *without* Al Adl? The questions reflect the overarching significance they place in their work: they see it as essential to Morocco. The elevation of their anti-regime protests reflects this new dedication: without Al Adl, Moroccan society would disintegrate. Young people, I would often hear, would crumble, their personal health would worsen, their futures would be ruined, or they might even choose the path of terrorism. Their work could change other people's lives—but it could also change their own.

When those in Al Adl seek to recruit potential members, they do not diminish these hardships; they highlight them. And when they explain their choice of Al Adl over PJD, they often point to the challenges they suffer relative to their competitors. Here, PJD becomes the lazy couch potato to Al Adl's sweating laborer. As Jabr from Al Adl noted: "Other parties like PJD have surrendered. They have given in. This is a sign of weakness. They chose the easy but wrong path. But the views of the people are on the other side. And we are on the side of the people."

"Think of the bees," thirty-two-year-old Zouheir whispered to me. Zouheir helps organize Al Adl events outside Rabat. "When they go on a long journey, one might die or get hurt, but do they stop? No! They keep going because if the destination is important enough, the journey will be difficult." Why would they be watched by the authorities or even face arrest, they would ponder, if they were not making a difference in the lives of the citizenry? Why ban a book if no one wanted to read it in the first place?

"We organize camps and offer activities for young people," Zouheir once told me. "But the state shut down our camps beginning in 1999. They were too popular!"

As another activist named Karim put it: "Our goals are so big that resistance is sure to be as big. It's obvious that when you propose something so huge, there will of course be huge opposition. To do something difficult always requires suffering." This is a sentiment I heard often from young Al Adl activists: "For something to be true it must be difficult." Phrased another way: "Makayensh sheehaaja mezyaana we sahla!" ("There is nothing that is great and easy!")

There is also a certain cachet gained from this feeling of self-sacrifice. The ways young people come to convince one other to become active in the organization are embedded, counterintuitively, within this nexus: join us *because* of our political protest, *because* of the rigor of our daily lives. Significantly, such traits come not simply from daily prayer or religious ritual. Repression, arrests, and crackdowns are not viewed as reasons to avoid membership: prospective recruits are not told that life is easier than it might seem. In fact, the opposite occurs. Evidence of police harassment is conspicuous in promotional materials, pamphlets, DVDs, and on their website. In their biographical DVDs—burned on computers by youth and disseminated to those wishing to learn more about the movement—the cover images often highlight both a police van *and* people being arrested and beaten with their faces blocked out.

This suffering is cited as evidence of their commitment to others. According to Bennajah, students join the movement because: "Kankhedmu bessah" (We work seriously). He then immediately went on, in the next sentence, to relay tales of incarceration. "We are serious," he said, "we go to jail, and all for the sake of students." Jail time or police arrests are not concealed: they feature prominently in the biographies and accounts of members and leaders. It is their badge of honor. Their websites even include a place for postings about recent harassment from the police—a space for members to give testimony of violations or what many call "human rights violations." Photos posted routinely include evidence of beatings and abuse—of bruised bones, black eyes, and streaming blood. The more vile or maudlin, the more popular; tales of cruelty against women and children are particularly well read among their fellow activists.

One student, who preferred not to share his name, told of his "story of my abduction from the security services" which allegedly involved being thrown into a black 4x4, gagged and blindfolded, and then taken to an unknown location, where he sustained injuries and a "barrage of insults and various kinds of mental and physical humiliation." Finally, they dropped him on the side of a road, but not before taking all his money. Injuries to his kidneys from being beaten so hard, he stated, resulted in a thirty-day medical disability certification, forcing him to miss work.[29]

An Al Adl member named Sharif described his story in this way. He began with accounts of famous activists who had been targeted and whose reputations were purposely destroyed by the state. He pointed, in one case, to the authorities' use of "electric shocks to his sex organs." He ended with the accusation that police ("through endless, harassing telephone calls") had caused a fellow female member to suffer a miscarriage.

Once when I saw a young group leader, my first question was intended to be somber: "Are you still having problems with the police?" He laughed at my inquiry: "Without problems with police, something is missing!" "Our members do not feel at ease if they are *not* arrested," he said with a certain conceit. "This kind of sacrifice has been there since the days of the Prophet. With a single phone call, I could organize a million people in front of the parliament tomorrow. The police will beat us and try to persuade us to drop everything and give our allegiance to the king." Yet, they have tried this already, he claims, but it "doesn't work."

The group, I was told by a few members, supposedly maintains a warehouse of evidence of such abuse at an undisclosed location. It is their pilgrimage site (real or imagined): hallowed ground to reference their bravery. In recalling the abuse that he and his friends suffered, one particular interviewee named Issam was forced to stop mid-sentence. The subject matter, he said, was too painful for him to continue talking about it. "You simply cannot bring yourself to watch some of the videotapes that are stored in the jama'a (organization) archive. Sometimes what you see is more dangerous than what is happening in Palestine. In the latter, at least, there is a religious conflict between Muslims and Jews. But it is worse here to see a conflict between two sides of the same religion."

Then, his description veered again to the tawdry: "I feel upset and not able to sleep if I watch some of these tapes." "For example," he said, "a student was once detained. They took off his clothes and a girl came to seduce him." At this point, he suddenly stopped talking; his eyes became red. He covered his mouth. Whether he was putting on a show for me, I will never know, but he certainly seemed to believe what he was saying. "I cannot keep on talking about this," he murmured. And our discussion hastily came to an end.

Youssef, a fellow activist, relayed how, in the eastern city of Taza, "they [police] stole furniture from the house that hosted an event." In Rabat, they "stole the medical equipment from a physician, whose house hosted an event." "It is funny," he said, "they also stole the food prepared for the guests." Al Adl members are so effective, or so the narratives go, that even their snacks could be threatening.

★

Even though the circumstances surrounding their activism are quite different, those in PJD make similar arguments about how tuned in they are to the lives of their fellow citizens. But many reject membership in Al Adl because it does not inhabit a formal party and thus cannot possibly offer them an opportunity to work hard enough for others. Its illegality makes it almost impotent.

When I once asked a group of party activists how they compared with their peers in Al Adl, the moans that arose in the room were telling. A young woman named Samira spoke out: "You really can't compare us with them. We have a party. They are just an organization." If they changed their course, she continued, then perhaps they might be worthy of analogy: "To be compared with us, they should get involved in politics and form their own party. Perhaps then we could compare them with us."

Everyone in the room nodded approvingly. Her message was evident: PJD's legal status affords it respect. In possession of a political party, they occupy higher ground. In this light, to be compared to Al Adl is viewed as an insult. Yet, it is not that only formal political parties can work more effectively for political and economic development. Rather, it is that only parties can offer opportunities for self-advancement.

In these formulations, youth can change peoples' lives (and their own) only through the training offered by PJD. They talk about the political system the way they used to talk about Islam itself as a mechanism for societal transformation. In the words of Zineb: "Our main objective is to develop our country. Young people distrust political parties because they know that they will do nothing for them. The Moroccan educational system does nothing to offer relevant training for young people to cope with the demands of the job market. The Moroccan economy is unable to absorb university graduates. Therefore, most young people seek opportunities elsewhere, even outside Morocco."

Another friend added yet a different analogy to explain his activism with PJD. He relishes work with PJD because he begins to feel like he is helping others, working for others—in addition to working for himself. He noted that problems with the status quo are inevitable in any political system, but that at a certain point, if they want to help young people, they need to participate: "Some people like to talk in terms of a cup. Is the cup half empty or half full? Is the political system more good than bad? But I believe that at the end of the day you need to drink to get water. You can spend all day debating these things, but if you want to drink—unless you want to die—you will have to drink from the cup."

The problems for PJD are not structural: the system is not broken. Instead, the people inhabiting it are. In Rabbah's words, it is up to the individual politician to work to make politics more honest and corruption-free: "Our main value is that we don't support the party; we support the person. So if the person is good, then people will support him. It is a question of person, not of party." The individual member here is elevated above all—anyone is capable of anything.

"I was raised in a family that loves work," Namir said, "I was taught to give back to the community and to participate as best you can in helping to better society. I was raised with a strong work ethic—if you do something, you should do it well. Of all the political groups, we work the hardest."

They wanted to help in some way, and PJD was the best outlet they could find. "I was originally with the Istiqlal (centrist Independence) party," one new member named Nabil noted. "I joined up with them when I was in high school because they seemed like the best party. But when I went to university, I began encountering Islamists and I was attracted to them because they engaged in intellectual debates. With Istiqlal, young people joined just for the possibility of employment. With PJD, you have the possibility of employment *and* intellectual debates." It is true, he noted, that Istiqlal has more resources because "it is an older party and young people can benefit more financially from activism in their party." But, he quickly noted, PJD is growing quickly. It was, he calculated, a good investment for his future.

One activist, Ahmed, affirmed these themes by describing his parents' first reaction to hearing about his association with PJD. They were so nervous about politics in general that they were "skeptical." But he was eager to demonstrate otherwise. "My parents," he said, "don't trust any political endeavor. They have had many experiences and all have showed that those in power do not fulfill their promises. Nobody experiences any change. Unemployment, recessions . . . these remain the major problems and no party has been able to find a solution." No one, that is, until PJD came along.

Rabbah has echoed these sentiments, pointing out that hard work is part and parcel of PJD life. It is easy *not* to work, he said, but PJD members sacrifice their time and effort for the good of the country. "If we win," he said, "the winner will be Morocco."

Activists' daily lives become entangled around an identity as someone laboring to help others. And, contrary to Al Adl's claims, for them, being in PJD is not the "easy way." They believe—and relish—how they have chosen the far more difficult path. As one member named Mounir recalled from personal experience, "I used to be a member of a more radical group, but I decided that my country needs to have a real political movement. More human rights. More competence in politics. And more transparency!" I asked him which group he had previously been a member of. "Al Adl," he replied.

According to his colleague, Abdelfatih, "It is hard to work within the system. You need to have courage. You need to be a courageous person." But, he said, it also took something else: "You need to hold many workshops, meetings, and conferences. This takes work. You need to build an organization. You need to travel throughout the country. You need to engage in dialogue."

Al Adl may face arrests and other costs, but PJD members see themselves as the ones who are truly sacrificing. "We were taught to be afraid of politics," said Amine, an activist in Rabat. "Our parents were afraid of politics. There was corruption. There was violence." Participating in the political system, for Amine, means giving up this fear, and moving beyond it. "We are no longer afraid of politics. We are free to participate. So why would we not want to take this opportunity?"

In the words of Jalal, boycotting, not embracing, elections is a sign of trepidation: "Besides the distrust people have, there is also a kind of fear too. Most people equate politics with oppression and prison." "But," he said, "we are not afraid."

For them, activism is about becoming someone new, someone more generous. "Young people in Morocco have all sorts of distractions," Soufian said. "They can listen to hip-hop or even emigrate illegally, to sneak away on ships." But he and his friends were distinctive: "We choose to stay and fight in the realm of politics. It is not always fun or easy; it is hard work. But we choose to do this."

He concluded his thought with perhaps the most cogent articulation of the identity that attracts someone to political Islam: "We are young people," he said, "who choose to work for others instead of going to the disco."

Part III

SHADOWS

Chapter 5

UNHEARD VOICES OF DISSENT

I want to begin this chapter—an exploration into how young Islamists relate to the authority of the state—by peering inside a discussion in Morocco that could only take place privately behind closed doors. The discussion occurred on the outskirts of Casablanca in a home with more than two dozen Al Adl members, ranging in age from eighteen to thirty-eight. The night was different from any of my prior encounters with the movement.

A typical meeting of mine with an Al Adl activist would often proceed as follows. To meet Youssef, for example, I would arrive at the train station at a pre-assigned time. We had a routine: I would call ahead and we would pick a train arrival, usually late afternoon or early evening, late enough (in this case) for Youssef to leave work. At the given hour we would meet at Casa Port—the train station in Casablanca equidistant to his home in the old medina and to his work downtown. The Casa Port station handles mostly local commuter lines, composing six separate routes, the most popular of which begins in Kenitra, just north of Rabat, and then makes its way through Rabat, Temara, Mohammedia, and finally Casablanca. It is one of five stations in the greater Casablanca metropolitan area and the second most used after Casa Voyageurs (Kasa Musaafireen). Trains have been traveling on this line since 1907.

After locating each other at the station, Youssef and I would then go to a nearby café. The first time we met, he was alone. The second time, he brought a friend, a fellow Al Adl member. The next time, he brought two fellow members. And this continued. He slowly increased my access to other members incrementally, allowing me to talk to as many of his associates as possible. But he was still cautious. My exposure grew only as time passed and only as I increased my knowledge of the movement.

This time, for our fifth meeting, Youssef greeted me, as he always did, at the train station. He apologized for being late; he had been fasting all day for religious purposes. But then he immediately grabbed hold of my hand and led me across the street, through the buzzing, winding traffic of a congested Casablanca boulevard. Our usual meeting place, the café, was behind us, on the other side of the street.

But before we reached the sidewalk, Youssef paused at a black sedan stopped at the traffic light. The two of us stood in the middle of the street.

Then someone from inside suddenly opened the backseat door and told me to get inside the car. I asked where we were going. He said we were going to see someone—and he mentioned a man's name. I did not recognize the name.

Seconds felt like minutes as we sped off out of town, into the distance, away from the train station, in a direction I had never been. Where were we going and why had I simply gotten in the car without more circumspection? Nobody knew about my meeting that day, not even my wife, who had asked me to check in with her every night. Was I being swept away by the excitement, by the prospect of new material? Why did I, at that very moment, think of the journalists who risk their lives for the story?

It was dark. It felt like we were heading north, but I was not sure where. Off in the distance, on the right hand of the vehicle, the men in the car pointed out Derb Moulay Cherif, Morocco's most infamous prison. For them, like for most Moroccans, the landmark is a lingering symbol of the cruelty of past rule, a "torture center" of yesteryear that once housed the regime's most prominent opponents, Marxists and Islamists alike.[1] A French newspaper once called it "Hassan II's secret dungeon."[2]

About ten minutes later, we entered a nondescript district of Casablanca. We took a back route to the house, weaving through identical block buildings. We parked and entered the home. We took off our shoes and went upstairs to the house's main salon, an unusually large version of the typical Moroccan salon. I was told it was someone named Mounir's home, but he was not there. There were four of us inside—the same ones who were in the car. We began to make small talk. Sa'id, our driver, soon left. I wondered how I would get home.

Soon, young Al Adl members began to trickle into the home. They came individually, and also in groups of two, three, and even four. They stayed for a few minutes or a few hours. They were often quick to point out that as soon as the fourth person entered, we were officially breaking the law, violating the official ordinance preventing the congregating of a banned movement.

We had first filled up two rows of cushions, but we soon filled almost six, taking up most of the room. When each person entered, he slipped off his shoes, uttered "Ssalam u'likum"—may peace be upon you—under his breath, and, from left to right, made the rounds of the crowd, kissing each man on each side of their cheeks, twice over. Every time a new person entered the room, we re-initiated the complete round of greetings.

The young men who gathered at Mounir's house were the picture of Islamist diversity. A few wore djellabas. Most wore slacks and patterned, untucked, button-down shirts. Some wore jeans and a t-shirt. Some sported sneakers; most had some semblance of a slip-on shoe. Their facial hair was equally mixed. Some had full beards, others goatees, even mustaches. Still others were clean-shaven. One would not have been able to identify these young people as Al Adl members or even "Islamists" simply by glancing at them on the street.

We talked about a number of issues that night, but one was particularly telling. Hamid, in his mid-twenties, began this exchange by posing a rhetorical question. "The question we need to ask the Moroccan regime is this," he paused. "What kind of Islam do you want?" It was a seemingly simple question, but the assumptions underlying it were significant. Hamid and his friends recognized that, contrary to the expectations of Habermasian or democratic theory, there was never any doubt that religion would be present in Moroccan rule—as it is in most Arab states. The question, therefore, was whether *other* competing expressions of Islam could also be allowed to influence such rule. Could their voices—and those of their fellow Islamists—be heard? In this chapter, I will first explore the contexts of these voices vis-à-vis the state, and then, in the next chapter, I will examine the varied attempts to regulate them.

★

Relative to prior generations, this group might seem uniquely well positioned to oppose the state, poised to penetrate even the thickest of state defenses. The dawn of the twenty-first century brought new opportunities for Islamist activists, especially ones from illegal movements, to resist authority and to flourish—beneficiaries of the globalizing world around them.[3] To begin with, their funding sources cannot easily be cut off. Al Adl, for one, profits from the growth of foreign remittances to North Africa and, with it, newly sophisticated tools for the movement of money, such as Western Union and its imitators on the Internet. Al Adl's funding is membership based, coming in small batches, sometimes electronically or, even harder to track, in incremental hand-to-hand contributions—and not from Qatar or Saudi Arabia, but from the grassroots.

In addition, their overall ability to communicate is less easily disrupted. Every time, for example, the government tries to shutter Al Adl's myriad websites, as they sometimes do, young people across Europe, in Spain, France, and Belgium, create mirror sites. As one activist told me with an air of confidence and technical savvy, "Every time they shut our site down, we're up again in a matter of minutes."[4]

Finally, and perhaps most significantly, combating the dissemination of propaganda and publicity is nowhere near as straightforward as it once was. Authorities can outlaw the publication of materials or even confiscate books or clamp down on frightened booksellers, but banned movements can simply print more—and elsewhere. Al Adl even set up its own publishing house—in a place that is perhaps farthest from the reaches of the Moroccan regime: Cedar Rapids, Iowa.[5] On one occasion in 2000, authorities ordered printing presses in the country to halt the production of two newspapers associated with the group.[6] The following year, when youth in the movement clandestinely managed to print thousands of their newsletters, police quickly confiscated the copies.[7] Yet young members also proceeded as youth most everywhere did: they moved on to a new format. They simply began posting the documents online as early as 2000.

Indeed, when it became necessary to keep Abdessalam Yassine from preaching to his followers, the current king's father had it easy: secure the sheikh's house, board up the doors, post officers around the perimeter, and make sure no one got in or out. Yes, the errant audiocassette or CD might make its way past the guards, but far-reaching communication was limited. Now, the tables have turned: Yassine's successors have it easy. From the comfort of their home, even alone in a room, today's Islamists can broadcast sermons to individuals anywhere in the world with the simple touch of a cell phone button (as Yassine began to do online on most Fridays before he died). House arrests have largely outlived their usefulness.[8]

In any city or town in the country, authorities can close illicit mosques—colloquially called "garage mosques"—but another can open up next door or down the street or across town within days. They can control sermon writing at official mosques, but young people can look up another sermon on the Internet when they get home. "I watch respectfully when I'm at the mosque, but I don't really listen," one Al Adl activist admitted about his local imam. The state can regulate what websites young people surf at cybercafés, but young people, in turn, can simply avoid cybercafés altogether. They can monitor cell phone calls, but a new SIM card for a cell phone can be purchased for pennies. Because of intense competition between mobile phone companies for subscribers, SIM cards are readily available, even given away on street corners by representatives of companies—Meditel, Maroc Telecom, INWI—with the hope of hooking new customers. Contraband ones are also openly on sale at souks next to pastries, spices, tagines, and baby clothes.

An authoritarian state cannot even control the circulation or the production of incendiary videos. When Al Qaeda of the Islamic Maghreb posted on the Internet a seething attack on the Moroccan king in September 2013, the Moroccan regime had no way of stopping it. (The video called on Morocco's youth to launch a jihad against their king.) In frustration, authorities arrested a respected journalist, Ali Anouzla, who had simply reported on the video. In an online posting, Anouzla did not link directly to the video or even embed it; rather, he linked to a story in the Spanish newspaper *El País* about the video (and that story then linked to the video). Even under international pressure, the regime held firm: it was trying to give the impression that it could actually control the video. (Mustapha Khalfi, the PJD minister of communications, claimed that terrorism threats demanded the journalist's detention.) But the arrest, in all its urgency, also made clear the obvious: that the regime simply did not have the power to stop the dissemination of the video in the first place. Its only recourse was displacement: it could not precisely target Al Qaeda so it redirected its wrath onto a lone, nonthreatening editor.[9]

In this context, it remains almost farcical that Arab authoritarian leaders still pursue another tactic: the practice of banning books. What use is prohibiting a specific volume in Morocco, for instance, if it can still be sold in France? From there, copies can be mailed back to Morocco or carried home by visiting expatriates or scanned and emailed to friends thousands of miles away or even ordered on Amazon.fr and shipped directly to Morocco.[10] Purchasing the e-book version online from a computer in Morocco would be even faster.

That the books once outlawed by Tunisia's dictator, Ben Ali, appeared in bookstores in that country so quickly after his fall (in 2011) were evidence of this charade: such books were already well known.[11] They were being purchased in the aftermath of the Arab Spring by citizens and tourists alike, not to read (for they had already been read), but to cherish. They were bought in the same way that pieces of the old Berlin Wall were bought in a newly unified Germany: as souvenirs of antiquated forms of rule, vestiges of a different era of total top-down control. It was as if those procuring the printed volumes were proudly exclaiming: Banning books! Building walls! That is *so* twentieth century. The once-banned books had become totalitarian kitsch.

Arab universities are another site where outdated modes of oversight are on display. College campuses in Morocco were long monitored by secret police, or what students playfully dubbed "AWACS," named after the American surveillance planes that detect enemy aircraft (the Airborne

Warning and Control System). But their systems of scrutiny, unlike the airplanes' radars, have failed to evolve. As early as the turn of the century, in the pre-Facebook or Twitter days, students easily possessed more sophisticated means of mobilization. Even when they were not yet fully exploiting the tools of the Internet that would later become available to them, they still embraced strategies like text messages or simple web forums that gave them new outlets through which to discuss and to organize. One SMS message sent to dozens of activists could arrange an off-campus meeting at an undisclosed site within minutes.

Television itself also offers room for new voices to emerge. In the midst of what political scientist Marc Lynch has termed "new Arab publics," the state cannot even control access to airwaves.[12] It has the *paraabul* or satellite dish to thank for that—the silvery metallic half moons nestled on rooftops across the poorest villages in the countryside and across even the most dilapidated shacks or shantyowns, powered oftentimes by generators, and often at the expense of bare necessities such as refrigerators or heaters. State TV faces competition from myriad satellite networks: a Moroccan citizen who at one time would only have been exposed to Moroccan preachers on one of two state television networks, can now, within an instant, and on that same television set, switch between preachers from Egypt, Saudi Arabia, Lebanon, or Qatar, to name just a few.

★

Yet, even with these numerous emerging outlets and strategies available to them, young activists, especially from illegal movements such as Al Adl, still manage to feel constrained. When I sat with them that night in Casablanca, and with other activists on other nights, they did not sound invincible. They did not sound like they were in the driver's seat. They did not passively submit to the power of the state, but they also did not operate with impunity.

Immediately after posing his initial question that night, Hamid took a stab at his own answer. "It is OK according to the state to have Islam with a long beard like this one." He then pulled slowly at his own beard. "It is even OK to pray often and seriously." "But," he then paused for dramatic effect, "this is true only if you support the status quo." By way of proof, he offered the example of many of the king's advisors—men, he said, "who have long beards and who pray often and seriously." This group included activists and leaders from PJD. There were beards everywhere, he said, just not *their* beards.

But just then, a friend interjected, scolding Hamid. He wanted to make the point that those religious leaders who support the regime should not be considered "religious" men—because they are inescapably complicit in its "oppressive" political project. It was as if their religiosity was disingenuous. "The king's religious advisors propagate tyranny," he said. "They support the fact that the king should stand above the law. That is their Islam: Islam in support of the king." What matters to the regime, he and his friends concluded, is not piety, but politics. You can have a long beard, they concluded, but "if you oppose the regime for any reason, then there is a problem." To them, Islam is accepted only if it bolsters the status quo.

Another activist named Farid pressed the point even further: "We believe that, in Islam, there should be a contract between the ruler and those over whom he rules. But the king's Islam says that the ruler—only the ruler—derives his power *from* Allah." He then instructed everyone to listen closely to the king's speeches from the throne. "The king," he noted, "says that 'Allah appointed us over this *umma* [nation].' Let me repeat what he says: 'Allah appointed us over this umma!' "

Farid then paused for us to consider this statement. "What does this mean?" he asked. "This means that it is Allah who made him king! If you attend Friday prayer, you will hear the imam of the mosque ask: 'May you protect the One who has been appointed over your people and the land.' Think about what that means: they are implying that Allah is behind the king!" "This," he said, "is a problem." According to this reading, because Al Adl rejects the divine right of the monarchy as un-Islamic, the king, and by extension PJD, are simply too presumptuous and in violation of Islam.

Paradoxically, Farid then cited the West as a prototypical model. "People in the West wonder why we mix religion and politics. It is true that mixing it in the way this king does is an issue."

"Why," I asked, surprised by this seeming denunciation of a core tenet of the Islamist project.

"Because the political power in Islam should be a civilian power," Farid said. "In the West," he continued, "the church and the state agree that each has its place. That the latter has its affairs and will not interfere with the other. They agree on that. In Morocco, what is dangerous is that the state is in control of *everything*."

Another attendee named Amin inched forward on his seat cushion and pointed out what he and his friends see as a double standard. "The state," he said, "tells us [in Al Adl] not to mix religion and politics. But during Friday prayers, they mix them! The state schedules national feasts to coincide with religious ones. When King Mohammed V died, the state pretended that it was the 10th of Ramadan because only righteous people die then. They use Islam to endow their politics with sanctity, with meaning."

Mustapha explained it this way, drawing tacitly on Sunni classical political theory. "In the history of Islam," he said, "it is the umma [the nation], that elects the governor and then watches over him. The ruler should say to the people: I am governing you because you elected me." For Mustapha and his friends, "Those who support this king support neither Islam nor democracy."

Amin continued: "The problem is when a ruler pretends that he is the *only* one who decides the fate of himself and the fate of his people. The ego of such a ruler becomes dangerously large when we as citizens are not allowed to question him."

Mustapha interjected again—suggesting that since Islam should play a role in the lives of all Muslims, then perhaps it need not even enter explicitly into formulations of political rule. Muslim politicians—like all Muslims—should be guided by the moral codes and laws of Islam, whether in office or not. "I am not saying that religion should not guide what we do," he demurred. "For a good Muslim, Islam, of course, does. Islamic law is clear. We know not to support gay marriage or abortion because Islam teaches us these things. Christianity says the same thing, by the way." But if you believe these things, he said, and "you don't have a beard—which is my way of saying that you don't belong to an Islamist movement—then it somehow doesn't seem to be a problem for the world."

Amin then returned to the subject of the West, and invoked the surprising example of an abortion protester in order to reiterate the point regarding the problematic relationship between Allah and the king—a relationship that he views as undercutting the power of the citizenry. "I once saw on satellite TV a woman protesting anti-abortion laws in America," he said. "A journalist asked her why she was protesting. And she said that she did not believe that God should be able to make decisions for people. And you know what: she was right!"

He then pivoted back to his own country. "This is the real problem in Morocco," he continued, "the king is acting like he *is* God and dictating to everyone what is haram (forbidden) and what is halal (allowed). No one in the world would want a ruler who says that he is ruling in the name of Allah. He should rule in the name of the people because it is the people—the umma, the nation—who chose him."

Moreover, when politics is promulgated in the name of Islam, he said, it risks alienating Muslims. Politics, here, takes on a corrupting character: if practiced wrongly or undemocratically, it has the power to turn people away from Islam. As Hamid, who began this discussion, later remarked: "A leader who speaks in the name of Islam is only as good as his policies." Another member expressed a corollary: "If Islam is too wrapped up with your political work, if you then fail, people will say that Islam is a failure. But it shouldn't be Islam that was a failure, it should be your political program." I heard similar concerns from Al Adl in the wake of the Muslim Brotherhood's fall from power in Egypt in 2013—that they tarnished Islam because they governed so appallingly.

A young activist named Rashid even noted that he wished that the king were more like an unlikely figure: the American president in recent memory that he despised the most, George W. Bush. Even though this activist took issue with Bush's policies, especially the Iraq war, he admired the way Bush seemed to tolerate protest. Beware, he said, of leaders who stamp out dissent entirely. Beware of what he called, "the high holy man."

"We are not allowed to be legal here," Rashid said, "because Morocco is not democratic. What he really admired was not Bush, but the freedom of speech promised by the First Amendment. In America, you can even wear a t-shirt that says "Fuck George Bush!" But in Morocco, he said, they don't have that same luxury. "Here," he went on, "you have no right to express yourself. You have no right to think for yourself, to make up your own mind about things. Whatever the king says is the right thing. What he says should not even be analyzed. His words are *the* law and cannot even be discussed. It's just not like that in America."

But, perhaps above all else, what most troubled these young activists is that their opinions, their beliefs, are not allowed into the public consciousness—and that even their fellow citizens are complicit with the regime's use of religion to bolster "tyrannical" rule. "What we are really talking about here is *consciousness*," an activist seated behind me named Tariq chimed in. "Look at the history of the Christian church. When they discovered that the Church was helping to support tyranny in Europe, they turned their back on it. Christians asked themselves a serious question: what is the source of knowledge? Is it revelation? Or is it the mind? From their history, they concluded that at least their mind protects them against the tyranny that the church embodied and supported."

In the days and weeks that followed, I would dissect this dialogue and others like it, contextualizing each one and examining their significance.

rial and ideological integrity of his country. Even in the midst of the Arab Spring, amidst much-heralded news that the king would be decentralizing his power through constitutional reform, the new constitution of 2011 still enshrined the king as "inviolable" (instead of being both "sacred and inviolable," as older versions proclaimed).[15] The new constitution also maintained the king's sole power to appoint the critical ministers of defense and Islamic Affairs, among others. Consider that the only other people in the modern era to claim the title Commander of the Faithful have been Mullah Omar, the head of the Taliban in Afghanistan, and Abu Bakr al-Baghdadi of ISIS.[16]

Scholars also point to the supposed spiritual power of the king. The modern Moroccan monarch has been called the "spiritual link between his people and God."[17] Past kings have been described as "untouchable," "omnipresent," and "towering above all."[18] King Hassan's minister of Islamic Affairs used to refer to his boss as the "shadow of God on earth," equating criticism of the king with criticism of God.[19] More generally, the modern Moroccan monarch has also been compared to a father figure.[20] Others have suggested that the monarchy instills in its followers a kind of "psychological contract" that demands loyalty.[21] Such devotion has also been equated with that of a master-disciple relationship prevalent in Sufi brotherhoods.[22]

Other scholars point to history. The modern Moroccan monarchy has long used and manipulated its religious underpinning as a tool of control. It has been marshaled to counter, among others, Nasserism and Arab nationalism, Wahabism, Socialism, Shi'ism, internal Islamist opposition, tribal and ethnic divides, and even internal religious divisions.[23] The anthropologist Clifford Geertz once reflected that the twentieth-century Moroccan monarchy, instigated by Mohammed V, Mohammed VI's grandfather and Hassan II's father, was itself a resolution of a national tension between what he called "Scripturalist" and "Sufistic" Islams.[24] Even leaders of the Sa'di Dynasty of 1548–1641 used the Prophet's birthday to ritualize support of the monarchy.[25]

Still others look to custom.[26] To observe a state visit, even in the twenty-first century, is to watch rituals that remain unchanged for hundreds of years: citizens lining up to kiss the king's hands, touching his hand only for an instant, as if their skin was not worthy of contact with his, as if they receive a blessing or *baraka* merely by being in his presence. The annual *bay'a* or allegiance ceremony still takes place in Morocco as it does in different forms in Saudi Arabia and Jordan. The ceremony in Morocco—where citizens prostrate themselves to the king and repeat the words "Our Lord bestows his blessing on you"—has deep origins in Islamic history, inspired by pacts given to the Prophet Mohammed.[27]

Yet, despite all of these oft-cited examples, I will show in the next chapter that the king's authority does not simply materialize or happen by itself. Rather, it is carefully manufactured, implemented, and negotiated. And to understand how Islamists relate to the authority of the state, we have to look beyond official roles, rituals, or proclamations.

Chapter 6

REGULATING ISLAM

How does an authoritarian Arab state enable or encumber Islamist mobilization? Conventional wisdom has long maintained that the authoritarian leaders of the Arab world controlled opposition movements largely by pitting them against one another. To ensure that no single force was ever strong enough to challenge their rule, they displayed an acute and pitiless ability to marginalize any viable resistance. They did so, at times, by banning groups outright, banning certain kinds of groups, balancing existing groups against each other, and even by artificially bolstering shadow parties themselves, such as former Egyptian President Mubarak's long involvement with the incongruously named "National Democratic Party."[1] During his thirty-eight-year reign, King Hassan II of Morocco imprisoned or "disappeared" countless challengers who stood in his way. Across the region, oppositions were seemingly held, to use historian Theodore Friend's term, on an "implicit leash"—there to be yoked or strangled as the leader sought fit.[2] Scholars have long put forth these notions, often invoking the language of warfare and the theory of "divide and conquer."[3]

In this chapter, I elucidate a different model of state action—different in both content and form: in what policies are pursued and in how they are implemented. I suggest that the Moroccan state under King Mohammed VI has not simply elevated one Islamist group at the expense of the other, but rather, it has aimed to impede and impel distinct forms of activism *within* groups—in this case, attempting to draw new divides between religious and political modes of activism. These are policies that can be understood not simply by the old theory of divide and conquer, but by one more aptly conceptualized as *selective suppression*.

The prevailing terminology employed by journalists and scholars alike usually declares Al Adl, for example, to be "banned yet tolerated."[4] The oft-used aphorism is meant to suggest that while the group is technically illegal, its activities have been crushed only partially and not systematically by the state. This is accurate, but imprecise. The crackdown of Al Adl has tended to follow specific forms. It is not the entire organization that is tolerated; rather, it is aspects of what is perceived as "political" protest. Yet, on the other hand, the state has banned altogether any public (and even increasingly private) protest in the name of Islam. In this way, state action against Al Adl is compartmentalized: political opposition is sometimes *tol-*

erated; religious opposition is altogether *banned*. For its part, even though PJD is allowed to participate in elections, its activism must also follow these very same guidelines.

These rules are implemented not by coercive force or even the force of a "holy" aura, but rather by formal and informal modes of social control. To block new and inchoate ideological "threats" from public consciousness, the state employs the aid of others in society (informal social controls) and enacts specific top-down rules and incentives to regulate passage to the public sphere (formal controls)—together making entry or non-entry either too socially challenging or too cost-prohibitive.

These modes of implementation are a function less of personality than of circumstance and efficacy. It has often been said, for example, that Mohammed VI lacks the treachery and sheer brutality of his father, Hassan II, a man who survived multiple coup attempts and routinely resorted to torturing political opponents.[5] It has also been remarked that Mohammed VI lacks the desire—or perhaps even ability—to talk publicly about religion. During Ramadan Qur'anic lectures, for example, he does not engage religious scholars as his father famously did. He prefers to be a silent observer, adopting an approach of "present absence."[6]

But these character traits are far less significant than one might assume. The policies outlined here reflect realpolitik, not restraint. They earn geopolitical dividends for the Moroccan state: subtly allowing the king to delegate enforcement while inhabiting the mantle of reform and capturing accolades abroad as someone who permits dissent. They also recognize, and keenly adapt to, the substantial limitations on authoritarianism in the twenty-first century discussed in the last chapter. In the midst of globalization—in the midst of increased information flows—the game has changed. A globalized gatekeeper needs help.

Informally, the state attempts to construct social norms surrounding what constitutes "good" or "bad" Islam. Contrary to secular notions of the state, it is not the role of Islam itself in the public sphere that is considered aberrant. Rather, manifestations of religious expression outside of or different from the state—outside an imagined "Royal Islam"—are deemed deviant. A "good" Islam becomes a "national" Islam—one embodied and policed by the monarch. Regardless of citizenship, nationality, or background, those at odds or different from the state's notions of Islam—be it Al Qaeda, Shi'i Muslims from Iran, Christian evangelicals, Al Adl, or even anomalous PJD members—are construed as dangerous "others," as intruders, as "questionable," heretics, illogical, lawbreakers, and even as "foreign agents" or "terrorists." And, thus, these constructions of Islam begin to represent some-

thing that needs to be hidden away from public view—demanding ostraciz-
ing, shaming, and surveillance.

More formally, the state remakes the rules of collective action, enacting
diverse regulations to govern Islamists' abilities to mobilize on the basis of
independent religious claims. Such regulation has included bureaucratic
maneuvers, varied financial incentives, and the diverse tools of administrative law. Together, these work to positively and negatively adjust transaction costs: the everyday costs of doing business. Like park exclusion orders
or trespass laws protecting private land, the state tries to carve out space
for itself—in this case, to privatize a sacralized public sphere. Some forms
of activism (say, neutral political protests with no overt religious displays)
are rewarded for compliance; others (say, campaigns that might implicate
religion) are penalized, often financially, for infractions.

For PJD, the spoils of submission have simply become too great. Like a
young law firm associate who buys an expensive house and then has to
keep a job she dislikes in order to pay for a mortgage, PJD, from the moment it began participating in elections in 1997, came to rely on, and grow
dependent upon, the millions of dollars in electoral funding offered by way
of state assistance. It could no longer afford *not* to get these rewards. The
freedom to maintain their own newspaper, to continue holding and promising the prospect of government jobs, and to mobilize in public meeting
spaces—from soccer stadiums to city halls to youth centers—have all become too critical to their recruiting efforts. And those are not the only rewards offered: in return for their compliance, PJD members are officially
accepted by the state as good Muslims, as patriots, as citizens.

But, just as PJD has been positively incentivized toward acquiescence,
so too has Al Adl been negatively incentivized toward acquiescence. Simply put: as we saw that night outside Casablanca (in chapter 5), Al Adl
activists largely refrain from public religious displays. When the state
bans their public prayers, for example, they relent. Of course, activists
still experiment with new forms of opposition, always testing the waters,
but they also almost always eventually surrender to authorities. It is true
that they don't want to risk arrest. But they also talk frequently (as we
saw in chapter 4) about how such arrests empower them. They also recognize that much police action is only for show: they are taken to the
station, but not always actually arrested. Young Al Adl activists, in sum,
superficially submit to the state in order to continue to do the business of
subverting it.

In this way, Al Adl's relationship with the state (indeed, just like PJD's)
serves to push its own religious activism to the private domain (outside of

mosques and places of public worship). For the illegal movement, the safest, easiest, quickest, and most effective means of expression has also become the most public: political and economic protests that do not directly engage Islam.[7] More likely than not, an Al Adl demonstration will take the form of an anodyne march on local economic issues—say, unemployment in the southern town of Sidi Ifni or bread prices in the central city of Taza— or popular global issues relating to Palestine in any city in the country.

These evolving relationships belie reigning dualistic portraits of these movements' relationships with the state. If, for example, one were to ask scholars, onlookers, or analysts—for that matter anyone familiar with the country—how Islamists in Morocco relate to the king's authority, the question would likely be answered with little hesitation or doubt. It has long been argued, even stated as obvious, that the two major Islamist movements diverge most dramatically when it comes to acceding to the king's vast power.[8] One wholly submits to it. One altogether rejects it. But the realities on the ground cannot be understood in such wholesale terms. Rather, both groups abide by the same rules of "selective suppression." While PJD's support for the king's religious policies are tacit, Al Adl's is more implicit and, of course, begrudging. Yet, by merely abiding by these rules, Al Adl accedes to their legitimacy.

Members of PJD have been called the "Palace Islamists"—and, more bluntly by opponents in Al Adl, the "puppets of the King."[9] Members routinely declare how the king is an important component to reform. Aziz Rabbah, the man tasked with recruiting future PJD members throughout the country, once told me: "We need to help the king who has a lot of major projects planned." One party leader spoke admiringly of his movement's "rich history of forty years of serious work in favor of our national unity, the nation's fundamental principles, the constitutional monarchy led by the Commander of the Faithful."

But party faithful also often speak out against the political policies of the king. They did so, most notably, in the 2000s with calls for constitutional reform, and then again during the Arab Spring, when some among them voiced support for anti-regime protests.[10] One party official, Mustapha Ramid, was outspoken in his support for curtailing the constitutional powers of the monarchy; he was later appointed minister of justice.[11]

Thus, members can criticize the king's politics and endure. But what they cannot do is question the state's religious foundations. (We will see in the next chapter what happens if one does.) Recall that when first gaining approval to join a political party in 1997, future PJD leaders willingly gave up any religious challenge.

As for Al Adl, its founder, Abdessalam Yassine, used his first public act, the 1974 letter, to attack the king. Al Adl activists routinely speak dismissively and disparagingly of the king. In one representative formation, a high-ranking representative of the group told me that "the king is a liar and a thief and everyone knows it." A young activist named Rachid put it more comically: "Our view of the king differs with PJD. Their starting point is that the Moroccan regime will last forever, till the end of time. Even when Jesus Christ is resurrected, the same monarchy will continue to exist! We believe in the utter opposite."

Yet, despite this impassioned and controversial rhetoric, Al Adl's daily activism tends to adapt to the same forms of state action as PJD. To be sure, Islamists, regardless of their organizational affiliation, do not accept state power reflexively. Instead, they have all come to relate to it, even oppose it, in ways that preserve their ability to exist, to function at all. They comply, in the end, to compete—not because they are told to, but in order to be able to recruit new members it makes sense for them to do so.

All youth are subjects of the state in both forms of the word: *subjects* as citizens living under the king's rule and *subjects* in the grammatical sense: not as passive objects, but instead as active subjects—opting to engage the new rules of the game, to dissect them, and, yet ultimately, to play by them. Contrary to their own renunciations, this is true even for those who claim to cast off such authority entirely. Even within Al Adl's rejection of the regime, the shadow of the regime, to borrow Freud's language, still "falls on" Al Adl and "obscures it."[12]

In the remainder of this chapter, we will uncover the silhouettes of these shadows, by looking first at informal and then formal modes of social control.

★

Like most field researchers, every time I returned home from abroad, I eagerly embraced family and old friends. But I also always faced a less endearing prospect: hundreds and hundreds of pages of field notes that required deciphering. When I began this wondrous and agonizing task one summer afternoon, I sent an email with a small linguistic inquiry to a friend of mine in Rabat, a question about a phrase I did not recognize from some Al Adl materials. This was his response:

Dear Avi,

Everything is OK. It's just the nature of the subject that makes me worried. We are in a situation in Morocco in which even the question of having a beard may direct doubts towards you. A colleague of mine related a strange incident that took place a couple of days ago in Fez. A follower of an illegal Islamist movement was in a cybercafé. He asked the woman in charge for a website of a hadith. She showed it to him. From that site, he moved to others. He then asked the woman to print a page for him.

Can you imagine that the woman was arrested for that? After that happened, the owner hung up a sign (one that was signed and officially stamped by the local authorities). It stated that any person may be taken in for questioning "IF THEY ACCESS RELIGIOUSLY QUESTIONABLE MATERIAL" and will be forbidden access to the cybercafé.

Thus, if you have a question like the one you have [about Al Adl], we had better wait until I see you next in person. I hope you understand.

Yours fondly,
Hammidou

The letter offers expression to the efforts employed to stop those viewed as challenging the new normal.[13] Note the fragments of Hammidou's fear: they were *bearded* men, looking at a website for a *hadith*. He seemed to feel—and that was, after all, the intent—that it was their *religion* that was being policed. With a mere makeshift sign, authorities could not actually control what young people surf on the Internet—even at the cybercafé—but they could influence them informally, setting norms around what is considered "religiously questionable religious material."

This widespread perception that religious "otherness" is punishable is also captured in a joke or *nukta* among Moroccan youth.[14] The joke, versions of which I heard often, goes like this: Two men are standing in front of a shop, browsing the wares. One of the men has a long beard and is dressed in traditional garb. The other, a young hippie in casual clothes, is not just smoking hashish, but is ostentatiously holding in his hands a large, noticeable plastic bag filled with drugs. When the two men suddenly see the police coming toward them, only one of them runs to flee. The man holding the drugs stands nonchalantly where he is, unfazed by the police. But the bearded man runs away in fear. The message behind the humor is that having a beard—practicing one's own form of Islam—is perceived as even more threatening by the authorities than the committal of a formal crime: the possession of illegal drugs. An abridged version is even more direct: "if you have a beard, they will arrest you."[15]

In another instance, I was speaking on the phone with another Moroccan friend as he was riding a bus in Casa. We were talking about Al Adl. Instead of saying the group's name, he would just call it the "association" (jamaʿa). And when I asked him a question about Yassine, he would say: "The leader, I don't want to say his name." "Why?" I asked him. "I don't want people to look at me the wrong way," he replied.

In these cases, as per the sign at the cyber, "religiously questionable material" came to mean anything other than official government sites or forms of worship. And, in these cases and others, the signs, the jokes, the social mores, the peer pressure, all had the desired effect: young people all construed Al Adl's religious practices as constituting a "bad" form of Islam.

None of this was the product of coincidence, but rather of specific endeavors by the Moroccan state. To begin with, Mohammed VI has introduced the largest ever restructuring of Islamic affairs in state history. He created a new religious council, and assumed control of all fatwa making and religious education and instruction. In his first announcement of these initiatives, on the anniversary of the 2003 Casablanca bombings, the king said that he sought to draw away young supporters from religious competitors of all stripes. He aimed explicitly, he said, to guard the "domain of the religious" from the influence of "intruders."[16] "Lest others," he warned, "resort to expedient ploys or seek to spread confusion and chaos." The most threatening among these potential intruders were not simply terrorist groups like Al Qaeda but also Islamists, namely Al Adl, and even potentially PJD—anyone, in short, who perpetuated alternative readings of Islam from the palace.

The king ordered a complete overhaul of the Islamic affairs ministry, making room for a directorate in charge of mosques and one in charge of religious education. The palace sought to regulate how mosques would be designed, how they would be financed ("in a transparent, legal manner"), and how prayer would proceed inside their walls ("in a quiet, peaceful atmosphere"). All Qurʾanic schools would also be carefully overhauled and monitored. The aim was not to enhance education, but to sway it: "to preserve it from misuse or deviation which might impair the Moroccan identity."[17]

Even the unlikely choice of Islamic affairs minister was strategic. Before being appointed in 2002, Ahmed Toufiq had worked as a professor, librarian, novelist, and a trained archaeologist. But, most important, he was also a leading member of the largest Sufi brotherhood in the country: the Boutchichiya. And his appointment was part of an effort to co-opt and bolster the Boutchichiya by explicitly bringing it into the fold of a Royal Islam. Despite its claims of distance from, even apathy to, politics, the Boutchichiya has become, in the words of one scholar, the "de facto official brotherhood of the Moroccan monarchy."[18] In the runup to the vote over a new constitution in 2011, for example, Boutchichiya descended onto the capital to march in its favor. When I asked one member about the seeming contradiction, his response was telling: "That's not politics," he said, "it's just supporting the king."

The new Islamic affairs ministry would be almost as tightly controlled as the country's infamous ministry of interior: a national 'ulama council (of Islamic scholars) would be appointed; and regional delegates would then be chosen. All religious personnel were instructed to take a "close-proximity approach," which was a euphemism for local surveillance (or what the ministry termed "proper supervision"). The king made no effort to hide the necessary qualifications: "loyalty" to nation was as important as "erudition." Even individual imams would serve as the regime's eyes and ears on the front lines. A former government official, Ahmed Abbadi, told me in his office within the Islamic affairs ministry that the state would be physically "closing the doors" to extremism.[19]

Contrary to popular usage, "radicalism" or "extremism" here did not by definition mean the use of violence. Rather, it simply meant anyone who dared question the regime's religious legitimacy. Such constructions skillfully manipulated popular, especially Western, stereotypes. Take for example a rare blurb from the *New York Times* regarding Al Adl. The headline proclaimed: "Morocco: 330 Arrested in Crackdown on Islamists." The first line of the article read in part: "The police in several cities arrested and later released 330 members of an outlawed Muslim fundamentalist group, Al Adl wal Ihsan."[20] Because illegality is often invariably embedded with radicalism, and the term "fundamentalist" hews closely to radical in common usage, the effect is illusory: when broad signifiers are used interchangeably and loosely, Al Adl appears here to assume all characteristics of radicalism. In short, the average reader likely assumes Al Adl to be illegal, violent, and certainly divorced from the realm of the political system.

Their illegality even came to affect my own perceptions: when I entered the activist's car in the episode described in the last chapter, I conjured up images of slain journalists—images I would likely not have contemplated with PJD members.

For their part, I often heard those in PJD brandishing their role as "proud citizens" and as "moderates." "I believe," a senior member once told me, "that Al Adl should change their political stance on the king. They need to become active in the political sphere. They should start a party. We are moderate. And the population thinks that we can bring people together, that we can offer solutions to political, economic and social problems. They do not like Al Adl because they are radical, and people don't want radicals."

The makings—and promulgation—of this new "moderate" "Royal Islam" have gone even further. It also includes steps to extend social control through a variety of mechanisms, including a new official website that allows ordinary Moroccans to converse with "official" scholars at more than a thousand mosques; the launching of radio and television stations devoted to Islamic learning that comprised daily programs of Qur'anic commentary; increased public debates on current issues like secularism, modernity, and the role of women; the publishing of an instruction manual of sorts by the ministry of Islamic affairs for the nation's Imams, a so-called Bulletin for Imams and Preachers; plans to set up libraries in annexes of hundreds of mosques (offering religious as well as scientific and cultural works); and special telephone lines for the public to ask questions of religious authorities.[21]

Mohammed VI's reign has also witnessed the most dramatic increase in the construction and oversight of state-run mosques in the country's history. By way of comparison, in 1991 there were approximately 21,000 registered mosques in Morocco. That number rose to at least 35,000 by the end of the first decade of the twenty-first century.[22] And today, that number stands at around 50,000.[23]

To make sure that theirs was the dominant message reaching young people, the ministry initially connected 2,000 of the country's largest mosques under a program (reaching 80 percent of the population), colloquially called "Mosque TV," which disseminated sermons and religious guidance produced by the ministry of Islamic affairs. Religious guidance and sermon-making were now being nationalized. The palace was watching. The goal according to the minister of Islamic affairs was "to spread noble discourse" and "to protect mosques from weak and deviant speeches"— and by "deviant," he meant straying from official royal positions.[24] By 2014, the ministry reportedly was able to "monitor virtually" all 50,000 official mosques, even those in more rural areas.[25]

In addition, beginning in June 2009, the Islamic affairs ministry undertook what it claimed was "a major operation, which has no equal in the world."[26] By committing $200 million to re-train—or what the minister termed "upgrade"—the 45,000 state-employed Imams, he set up nearly 1,500 centers around the country to educate those "responsible for the supervision of (religious) belief and practice."[27] As part of these efforts to control and police Islam, the ministry has also begun sending 1,500 state-trained religious supervisors into more rural areas "to make sure that imams are preaching the moderate local version of Islam and respect for King Mohammed in his role as leader of Morocco's Muslims."[28] In late 2008, the regime even sought to extend its control beyond their borders: they ordered one hundred state-sponsored Imams in Spain and an additional forty in the Netherlands to return to Morocco for additional training.[29] In 2014, the ministry even extended their reach south, promising to begin training imams in Mali and Nigeria.[30]

The late King Hassan II had once warned his Islamic affairs minister when he first appointed him: "Be careful, be careful! Do not intervene in what does not concern you, like a rise in the price of gasoline or cigarettes."[31] But Mohammed VI sought to extend his own religious ministry into the far reaches of public life. In one of its annual reports, the council boasted that it had "organized thousands of training and orientation sessions for preachers and muezzins [those who lead the call to prayer] both in rural and urban areas"; and that it conducted "other initiatives in universities, professional organizations, orphanages, prisons and public and private institutions to include development issues, such as the fight against illiteracy, family, and childhood promotion."[32]

One celebrated component of these new reforms, especially in the West, included the introduction of women into Rabat's imam training program in the Dar al-Hadith al-Hassania. The women would not be called imams, but rather *murshidat* (or guides, the same titles, interestingly enough, bestowed upon Sheikhs Yassine and Hamza and the Shabiba's Mouti). The program was announced in the first annual report of the new 'Ulama Councils. Almost fifty years after Moroccan independence, in May 2006, the minister of Islamic affairs presided over the appointment of these female *murshidat*. He made certain to clarify that their responsibility was preaching but also loyalty to the king; they could not diverge from this new official ministry-organized version. Their twofold mission was not only to keep extremism at bay, but also to work to support the Islam of the regime—and, thus, the longevity of the regime itself. "You must," he said to them, "be committed to the faith and politics of the state which the people have chosen. This choice includes the policies of the *Amīr al-Muʾminīn* (Commander of the Faithful), who runs deep in our veins." "Your duty," he ordered the packed room of veiled women, "is to prevent intrusion by *foreign agents* trying to violate our values and traditions" (emphasis added).[33]

The move was liberalizing, while simultaneously de-liberalizing: allowing women to participate in the process, but policing what they said and how they acted. The head of Al Adl's political circle noted this paradox: "If you take the idea in the abstract, I must say that it's an excellent idea, because it gives an opportunity for women to participate in an area that has been monopolized by men." But, he added, "if you look a little deeper and analyze the motives, you will find out that it is part of a strategy adopted by the regime to control the religious field and not to leave that field open for their opponents—the Islamists. So they want to control that area and convey their official view of Islam."[34]

In July 2014, the ministry expanded on the notion of the "official" murshid when it announced the formation of yet another program: this time, the creation of a kind of *super* imam. These 1,300 individuals will go by the title "imams-mourchidines" (or imam-guides) and, according to Toufiq, will assist regular imams around the country with "preserving the fundamentals of Islam in Morocco." The concern, he said at the official event, was that "contrary" ideas are "invading the minds of young people."[35]

State action on a national level has reflected these fixations. In July 2013, for example, authorities closed a large number of Qur'anic schools in the city of Marrakesh.[36] Earlier, in September 2008, they sealed thirty-three of Morocco's 113 Qur'anic schools that it deemed as "agitators."[37] They shut down sixty additional schools run by a prominent sheikh after he issued a fatwa declaring that marriage could be undertaken by girls as young as nine. Around the same time, they also boarded up religious schools run by Shi'i Muslims that were "contrary to . . . the Kingdom of Morocco."[38] The government then severed diplomatic ties with Iran for what it claimed were steps the Shi'i majority country was taking (including sending missionaries and setting up schools) to "alter the religious fundamentals of the kingdom."[39] Morocco's foreign minister accused Iran of attempting to "implant the Shiite Muslim ideology" in what constituted a "cultural infiltration" of his country.[40] Authorities also expelled sixteen Christian missionaries, much to the chagrin of the U.S. State Department.[41]

Contrary to some interpretations, these were not moves intended to signal Morocco's independence on the international stage. Rather, these steps were largely about religious conservation at home. The goals were so critical to the regime that it even risked alienating powerful states such as Iran and the United States. It was not simply that a particular fatwa or school or even a single missionary was offensive; it was that these individuals dared to issue a fatwa or run a school or preach a religion in the first place. Competing authorities (even those from within Shi'i Islam and Christianity) were intruding the regime's religious airspace, infiltrating its religious monopoly.

★

As it turned out, more was required than flooding the airwaves with the king's own version of Islam to wrestle away threats from competitors or to guard against "intruders." It would also require formal new regulations—not physical force, but original, often administrative oversight.

A typical PJD gathering elucidates this dynamic. The annual PJD youth conference was about to start, and I moved about the crowd looking for a spot in the back of the auditorium. The 1,400 young activists gathered in a room built for 400. Men were seated on the left side; women, with their heads covered, sat in almost equal numbers on the right. It was approximately one hundred degrees (Fahrenheit) outside and around fifteen degrees hotter inside.

There was a reason the party once considered holding the five-day August event in coastal Casablanca—the same reason why all the passengers on the train were heading away from Meknes, the imperial city, just southwest of Fez. But the party decided that it was worth bearing the extreme heat to show support for their locally elected brethren who controlled the city council. (The city's popular mayor was a longtime PJD member.) One youth quoted the Moroccan version of "no pain, no gain." And you could easily see and smell the pain: men packed in two, three to a seat, sweat pouring through their normally airy djellabas, and a number of young women being whisked away to the hospital for heat stroke and dehydration.

On my way out the first night, I stopped by the souvenir stand and leafed through the selection of policy platforms and biographies of party leaders. I even picked up a new pale blue party hat. I could look like them, but I could hardly keep up with them. The sixteen-hour days were awash in power point presentations on micro-credit, voter turnout operations, and lectures on local governance: young people excited more about the prospect of receiving World Bank loans than by discussing Qur'anic recitation.

At the end of four days, the conference eventually ended the way all PJD conferences do—and the way all official conferences of all legal groups in Morocco do: with the singing of the national anthem. The last stanza reads:

Nushīd al-dunyā
Anna hunā nahyā
Bi-shi'ār
Allāh, al-Watan, al-Malek.

We call to the world
that we are here present.
We salute as our symbols:
God, Homeland, King.

For the final line, the language of the crowd slowed to a staccato, the fists of the young people pumping in the air with each consecutive word: "Allah!"—"al-Watan!"—"al-Malek!" or "God!"—"Homeland!"—"King!" The order was resolute: the king and all those who follow him are the accepted heirs to God. The anthem reflected, in musical terms, PJD's new religious and political realities: in the wake of its inclusion into the political system, their religious claims would have to be ceded entirely to the state. As the last stanza makes clear, they could now only publicly reach God by way of the king.

This is the price for legality. The party is permitted to host recruiting and mobilizing events in official venues—at city hall, or at soccer stadiums, for example—but at a price: they would have to surrender any independent religious entitlement to the state. Their political party is generously funded by the state, and they are allowed to campaign for national and local elections, but again, at a price: not in the mosque, not as an official "Islamist party," and not in a way that would contravene, or be perceived to be contravening, the official religious authority of the palace.

A Moroccan citizen walking casually past the PJD youth conference that week would have immediately noticed a number of things from the calm of the street. He or she would have seen a large banner draped over the front of the off-white building that normally serves as City Hall. The banner was emblazoned with the words: Youth of Justice and Development (in Arabic and French). It was hung just below the permanent sign that read Hôtel de Ville (City Hall) as if to suggest that the two—the city and PJD—were one.

Onlookers also could not have missed a massive photo (covering almost the entire front portion of the city hall building) of the Egyptian cleric, Yusuf al-Qaradawi. Again, the signage and location were symbolic: Qaradawi, by virtue of the fact that the event was taking place at an official city building, would be speaking at a government-sanctioned event, not an *Islamist* event. It was also covered on official state television.

The state took complete possession of the Qaradawi visit: not only were the authorities watching (much of the nation was, indeed, watching the speech on their televisions), but they also assumed sponsorship of the speech. It was acceptable for the state to champion a controversial speaker;

it would have been incendiary had PJD done so on its own. The youth of the movement, whom I accompanied to the speech, had to arrive four hours in advance in order even to be allowed entrance. On the way in, one mumbled to his friend, "I thought this was our event."

If the passerby were to peer inside the hall, the iconography would tell a similar story. Throughout the day, the conference paused for members to pray (as is also often the case even with conferences of non-Islamist parties). When prayer time beckoned, the men would leave the main conference hall and move to the next room to assemble for group prayers. (The women would continue separately to a room on the ground floor.) They would stop en route in the bathroom to perform their ablutions, for which the *balladiyya* (city hall) building was woefully unprepared. Swaths of young people crowded over three sinks and urinals to fill up empty plastic bottles with the light water flow of the trickling toilet flush. They would subsequently step to the side, cleanse themselves with the water, and then pass along the empty water bottle to their friends.

They were then ushered into a narrow but oversized passageway behind the staircase next to the main meeting hall, where they would pray. In this corridor, PJD had placed a massive photo of Mohammed VI. The king was blessing their prayer—as long as they were praying in front of him. By displaying the photo of the king where they prayed (or rather, by praying under where they had placed the photo), their prayer and, inter alia, all expressions of religious worship were literally and figuratively both shadowed and subsumed by the state. They were allowed to hold the event in a public building, but they could express themselves in religious terms only under the auspices of the king. Indeed, in the next room, where they held their political rallies, there were no photos of the king—only a huge banner announcing the event, with pictures of the secretaries general of the party and its youth wing.

The iconography at the conference imparted a larger meaning. PJD's religious message has become a component of the state: their religious symbols have become national symbols—and vice versa. Here, we are increasingly witnessing a case of the nation Islamicizing a movement (in its own image), and no longer a movement seeking to Islamicize the nation.

★

With electoral inclusion and legalization has also come an increase in state-funded PJD party resources—or the spoils of inclusion: money, party headquarters, salaried members, and an enhanced ability to disseminate their message via media, licenses to run newspapers, and websites. One young person I met at the conference named Karim said it was his first time coming to an event like this. I asked why he chose this occasion. "I don't know," he said. So I pressed him further. "It was very cheap," he said, "and it was an opportunity to travel. It's summer, man!"

Karim's fellow attendees had also traveled here from all over the country. Some had taken twenty-hour bus trips from as far south as the coastal city of Dakhla in the Western Sahara, near the Mauritanian border, or from the northern city of Nador, located on the Mediterranean just below the Spanish enclave of Melilla and just beside Morocco's border with Algeria. They paid only around 250 dirhams (twenty-five dollars) for six days—an amount highly subsidized by the party, and thus, the state. It included accommodations, conference events (as well as concerts, speeches, and all seminars), and all food.

The attendees were even offered the rare chance to sleep at the city's famed soccer stadium. If their official activities took over the largest municipal work complex (city hall), their accommodation and leisure commandeered the city's most noted and largest sports complex. During the few moments of free time, they played and even prayed on the main field. They slept, not on the grass, but on cots arranged behind the seats in indoor corridors. Men and women ate and slept on opposite sides of the stadium. Beyond the mere allure of travel and the chance to see a new city, the conference program also included a tour of the old city of Meknes, a rock concert by a noted Moroccan singer, and, as mentioned, the opportunity to hear Qaradawi in person.

If their sleeping arrangements were unassuming, the food they ate was not. When I was invited to join a number of young activists for lunch, we sat at large round tables with formal white tablecloths and full table settings. The waiters wore black slacks and matching black bowties. The catered meals ranged from lamb tagine to chicken couscous on Friday.

These spoils do not appear accidentally. The party's monies come largely from state-granted election resources. This funding—along with the many financial opportunities PJD's legal status offers—is the major financial perk that followed its entry into the political system. This has underwritten the party's headquarters (it now has two separate buildings in Rabat), its staff, and the publications of party materials, such as books and campaign leaflets. The money also helps supplement party meetings, such as its major annual convention and its youth conference and smaller events around the country throughout the year. As their participation in parliament grew, so did the income from the state. The increase in the first five years after their initial entry into politics was most dramatic. Before participating in politics, they received no federal funds. In 1997, they received four million Moroccan dirhams, and by 2002 the number had increased to seventeen million.[42]

The state has also financially incentivized the party toward public displays of politics. While party members often criticize Al Adl's system of collecting portions of its members' salaries for organizational financing, PJD also insists upon a similar scheme, albeit on a smaller scale. (They can afford this lower "tax" due to state monies.) PJD has made it obligatory for its MPs to reapportion parts of their government salaries to the party. And it collects dues from members: approximately 200 dirhams per year (approximately twenty dollars) for employed members.[43]

In the wake of the party's perceived ascendance following the 2002 elections, the regime moved to limit the party's religious activism even more. (During the legislative elections of 2003, following the Casablanca terror attacks, the regime restricted the amount of districts PJD could contest in the first place.) But in 2005, it championed an electoral reform bill, which, among other things, moved to outlaw any explicitly religious or Islamist parties. Thus, to continue to contest elections, the limitations were again set—and PJD again paid the admission fee. "I don't like the term Islamist," Othmani, then party head, later remarked, the way a child chosen last for a team might defensively claim that he didn't even want to play anyway. "I insist on 'with Islamic references,' like the Christian Democrats [in Germany], he said."[44] Nonetheless, I still heard the term "Islamist" employed regularly by young members and even at conferences.

Beginning in the following election cycle, in 2007, PJD's campaigning was further limited. The palace directed it to physically and literally vacate the formal religious sphere. The chair of PJD's election campaign, Jamea Al-Moatasim, declared: "We instructed election campaigners to avoid electioneering at, outside, or even nearby mosques."[45] The party directed its campaign workers, and even members, to remove any evidence of PJD association (shirts, hats, or anything adorned with PJD's emblem) when entering mosques. "We must respect the sanctity of the houses of worship," Al-Moatasim said, by which he also meant to respect the religious authority of the state. PJD's activism was allowed within the domain of the political arena, but not within the domain of the mosque.[46]

Thus, if the legal political party has little choice but to submit to the whims of the state, what happens with the illegal Al Adl—a group that often talks of the overthrow of such a state?

★

I once sat in the home of one of Al Adl's senior leaders. The head of the youth wing had called him to ask him to meet with me. We were discussing the relationship between his group and others like it throughout the region. He told me that he had actually written a paper on the subject for a master's degree in politics that he completed two years earlier. He suggested that I read the paper. I asked him for a copy. He told me that his copy was locked away. I joked with him in Arabic: "Is it that bad?" No, he said. Because of the state crackdown on the movement—including recent home break-ins and confiscation of material—he had stashed all of his prized possessions in a safe. In the paper, he had raised objections to the regime's religious foundations. He was thus compelled to lock away the tenets of the group's religious opposition to the regime. And, he was not alone in this reaction.

Al Adl consistently responds to state action by attempting to cloak its otherness, transforming itself into more palatable forms in public, and assimilating into the king's public space. Thus, the group has largely come to abide by these rules (of enforced liberalism) even though Yassine himself often criticized such an arrangement. The curse of modernity, Yassine once wrote, is that "it wants religion to be confined to the private sphere, while the public sphere is left to politics."[47]

At one point in 2008, for example, the interior minister sent a letter to all regional governors and state workers urging vigilance in preventing Al Adl activism—to "take all necessary action to prevent such activities."[48] But he was specific: Al Adl, he said, "has placed itself outside the logic of law. It preaches an ideology which, as many regard, can be considered subversive."[49] There was a *logic*, if not a method, to these orders and to the application of the law. It was the *preaching*, the religious ideology, that would have to be prevented and banned.

This pattern plays out regularly at the local level. Associations affiliated with Al Adl are permitted to form on the understood condition that they not take part in activities related to religious ritual or observance. Its members formed the al-Mishkat Educational and Cultural Organization, for instance, in Sidi Slimane, a city northeast of Rabat, in July 1999.[50] Local authorities gave the group a permit on the basis that it was dedicated to helping the poor. But when it began, a year later, to engage in activities surrounding religious rituals (including distributing sheep for families to slaughter for Eid al-Adha and offering to pay for circumcision ceremonies) it ran into trouble with the police.[51] The office of the *basha* (prefect) notified the group that it would have to cease operations—that it had run afoul of the law.

From that point on, under these rules, they have been able to operate "with one exception," according to the president, Slawi Benali. The "exception" was a training course the group planned to prepare citizens for the hajj. On that occasion, authorities dispatched an officer to the door, blocking participants (the would-be pilgrims) from attending.

Take also the example of the Assubh Association, which Al Adl members started in nearby Sidi Kassem. It too was granted papers from the local authorities, who also even granted them 3,000 dirhams (approximately 300 dollars). In its early years, it engaged mostly in efforts to help the poor, including offering medical care. It was only when the group began planning Qur'anic chanting events that authorities stepped in. In 2009, the group's leader was called into the basha and legal problems ensued.[52]

Another example occurred in May 2012, when Al Adl students from the northern city of Tetouan wanted to organize a group camping trip—to move their spiritual retreat outdoors in the summer. When they arrived at the campground, they were rounded up by the police. Another time authorities broke up a spiritual retreat (ribaat) outside a home in the central coastal city of El Jadida in August 2008. Movement leaders claimed they were being singled out unjustly in a city that, they said, "like most Moroccan cities, is teeming with all kinds of dancing celebrations and festivals of debauchery and depravity." Their conclusion: "everything is allowed except the devotion of God."[53]

Al Adl's most active mobilization campaign of the last decade offers perhaps the most dramatic example of the emerging compartmentalized nature of the crackdown. In 2000, its members took to the beaches in a bold effort to attract young people where they gather most in the summer: à la plage. They held summer camps, prayed together on the sand in large groups, read the Qur'an at low tide, and even talked to bikini wearers about the virtues of modesty. One newspaper described an ice cream boy on the beach, an Al Adl sympathizer, as "peddling Qur'anic injunction with his *Cornettos.*"[54] Such injunctions were said to have included: "Why debauch yourselves in nudity?" or "Repent and return to Islam!"

It was the explicitly religious nature of their outreach that sparked a particularly harsh response from police. According to Fouad, an Al Adl Casablanca activist, "It was when we wanted to pray on the beaches that the government stepped in and broke up our camps." "The police told them," he alleged, "we could do anything in public except pray. This was our War of the Beaches. Now, everyone prays in public in Morocco—except for us."

The interior ministry called Al Adl's activism at the beaches "ideological pollution."[55] The minister himself, in 2000, appeared on television to decry littering on beaches and quickly transitioned to a wider discussion of various forms of pollution, including the ideological variety. Security forces policed the coastline, set up checkpoints to gain entrance to beaches, and dispatched riot police to arrest those who "sported beards."[56]

The university, the site of Al Adl's loudest presence, offers yet another example. Al Adl is permitted to run in university elections, allowed to maintain a political desk on campus, but their so-called religious activism is banned. As the head of Al Adl at Hassan II University outside Casablanca relayed to me: "Police recently came to the university and they took away our Qur'ans, girls were obliged to take off their veil; prayer is forbidden at the university. We are in a Muslim country and they don't even let us pray."

In analyzing the contours of the crackdown, I also found that authorities often attempted a different tactic to impede Al Adl's ability to mount a religiously based opposition: it sought to embarrass and shame its high-ranking officials with well-publicized arrests—more often than not for crimes of a moral nature, having nothing to do with the group's political protest. These were actions that sought to undermine Al Adl's religious authority and social standing. For example, Mohamed Abbadi, Yassine's successor and the onetime head of the group's "East Region," was accused of immoral business practices when he was indicted and fined heavily for six counts of alleged illegal construction. The trial of Rachid Ghoulam, an up and coming Moroccan singer and loyal Al Adl member (his music was often played for me by young members) was also noteworthy. He was prosecuted and then sentenced to prison in El Jadida based on the atypical, even rococo, charge of "incitement to debauchery."[57] The state leveled the charge against Ghoulam ostensibly for committing (the not uncommon act of) adultery, and more specifically after Ghoulam's wife opted against filing charges of her own against her husband. In a further sign that the trial, like related arrests and threats, was more about asserting social rather than legal control, Gholam was eventually acquitted in April 2011, but the damage to his reputation was already done.

Thus, in this part of the book, we saw how young Islamists relate to the contours of state authority. In the next part, we turn our attention to the power dynamics within their organizations.

Part IV

INDIVIDUALS

Chapter 7
EVERY RECRUITER IS A REINTERPRETER

Who speaks for young Islamists on matters of faith? Who possesses the authority to interpret religious tenets and texts?

The answers might seem obvious at first. Analysts, for example, regularly hone in on the words of clerics or even movement organizers, often summoning quotes from specific individuals. Articles and books about Al Adl dissect the writings of Yassine. To discover how the Muslim Brotherhood "thinks," onlookers routinely mine the words of the well-known Egyptian cleric Yusuf al-Qaradawi, who is sometimes (and too broadly) referred to as "the supreme authority" or "de facto spiritual leader" of the Muslim Brotherhood.[1]

But there are two main problems with this approach—with the periphrastic prop of "but this preacher/cleric/elder/leader said." First, even though contemporary Islamist movements comprise diverse, complex organizations, this approach assumes that a select individual speaks for the masses, that he encompasses the views, goals, intentions, and wishes of the entirety of the organization, and that he possesses some kind of magical, charismatic clout. And, second, even if by chance he did speak for the masses, it assumes that the mostly young members of such movements accept, adopt, and even swallow such words uncritically or in toto.[2]

But do young activists really relate to authority in this way? Do specific individuals even possess this power in modern Islamism, especially in the Middle East and North Africa? In a play on the old saying about a tree falling in an empty forest: What if a cleric yells in a crowded forest of activists and no one listens?

This part of the book is devoted to understanding how young Islamist activists construct religious authority. To engage these questions, I asked and allowed activists to construct for themselves what authority meant to them. On some occasions, in the midst of our discussions about these issues, activists would spontaneously take out a piece of paper and begin drawing for me an evolving organizational chart of their movements. On many other occasions, I asked young members to create such charts for me. This was a methodological technique inspired both by young people themselves and by the political scientist Elisabeth Wood, who once asked peasants (*campesinos*) in El Salvador to draw their own maps of civil war insurgencies.[3] Wood sought to understand how the insurgency redrew the boundaries between class and citizenship. By contrast, I wanted to understand how young Islamists were redrawing the boundaries between religion and authority. Such an endeavor is particular salient in the case of Al Adl, of which few public organizational charts exist (largely because of members' fears of security reprisals). Thus, in addition to ethnographic fieldwork among young activists, this chapter also draws on these charts and on young activists' renderings and interpretations of them.

Yet, employing such methodologies turned out to be easier than analyzing their results. Briefly put, in qualitative research, one pores over data looking for patterns. To analyze what can often be thousands of words and multiple texts, researchers employ techniques such as "ocular scanning" or even search functions in word processors; they also increasingly employ sophisticated software. Usually, and eventually, the moment comes when patterns begin to emerge—the moment that scholars call the "saturation point," when themes, clarity, and salient ideas begin to ring out.[4] But when analyzing this particular set of data—the interview transcripts and notes and the organizational charts—that point never seemed to occur.

Popular descriptions of Islamist movements would have predicted that I would find evidence of subservience—of clear lines of hierarchy. Sociologists of religion, on the other hand, might have wanted to look to these movements' structural evolutions, positing that as these movements grew, I would find well-defined distinctions between religious and political authority, between crisp internal divisions or "dual structures," perhaps even indicating evidence of so-called internal secularization. Similarly, certain political scientists might hypothesize that as these groups become more active in politics, they would bureaucratize—that a focus on building roads, for example, might dilute the power of religious authorities.[5]

Certain historians of political Islam, on the other hand, might even question the utility of such a research endeavor altogether, viewing the role of religious authority as assumed or fixed. One esteemed professor of Islamic history has written of Islamists' longing for classical Islamic society and for its supposedly "seamless webs of Islamic political and religious institutions," with no apparent differences between "the religious and the political aspects of communal life."[6] Still, some cynics might have suggested that I would find specific intents to mislead the researcher, to engage in so-called double talk, to prevaricate or cover up secretive organizations not often open to public perusal, organizations that purportedly manipulate such secrecy to their advantage.[7]

But none of these insights told the whole story. As I began analyzing what was in front of me, I saw no clear evidence of a singular predicted phenomenon. Instead, I saw signs of ambiguity, multiplicity, and even in-consistency. Some activists (as we will see) sought to go out of their way to illustrate that they were not under the control of any kind of religious au-thority, even conceiving something called "religion" as very much distinct from their work. Others blurred these categories, preferring to place their activism under the domain of some kind of religious authority, both ex-plaining and attempting to show how it is part and parcel of their everyday existence. Some failed to mention religion as important to their work at all. Others spoke solely of it. In sum, very few organizational charts were iden-tical; most articulations of religious authority were wholly unique and distinct.

Reigning scholarly representations of Al Adl, for example, tend to sug-gest a unified and charismatically led, top-down organization, with the sheikh or spiritual guide *directing everything.* Leading scholars of Moroc-can Islam have argued that there has long been a "cult of the guide" in Al Adl; and that young members are "disciples" who lent Yassine an "aura of holiness."[8] To support these claims, some cite the fact that activists used to try to get tickets to Yassine's Sunday morning "conferences" when he spoke to, and met with, members; or because they, like many youth who encounter an old person, kissed Yassine's hand when they saw him.[9]

But the interpretations I encountered of Yassine (in life and in death) and of his successor, Mohammed Abbadi, were as varied as the number of young people articulating them. Many portrayed the movement's spiritual guide as hovering above all. Yet others, through the precision and firmness of lines of their organizational charts, sought to show the limitations of Yassine's influence and that of his successor by placing them in separate boxes, on the side of the main organization, or even absent. Some spoke of their guide as their murshid, others spoke of wanting to find their own guide; others no longer spoke of him at all (this was true even while he was alive). One suggested that he was still looking for new forms of *suhba* or spiritual companionship; he had managed to find this with Yassine but not, he said, with Abbadi.[10]

For the youth of PJD, constructions of religious authority were no less mixed or miscellaneous. Some party members often went out of their way to construct religious authority as something tangible, as something bounded by organizational lines. They equated such authority with the power of their still allied religious preaching movement, the haraka—"of religious da'wa over politics," in the words of one. A leading youth wing leader once reprimanded me when answering one of my questions: "I told you," his voice rose in frustration, "the haraka is not the party and the party is not the haraka." Another activist dismissed the words of the former head of the haraka as "just one cleric's opinion." Still another, named Hakim, portrayed the allied religious movement as the party's "mother" and then told me how he listened to his mother.

I once asked a youth outreach staffer at the PJD party headquarters about an upcoming event, inquiring whether there would be discussions of the Qur'an there. (The July 2013 event was scheduled to elect new members to the party's local youth council in Rabat.) "No." he quickly rebuffed me, "that would be religion (*deen*). This is a party event." "If you want religion," he said, "you must go to the haraka"—or the allied movement.[11] Yet, the chart he drew for me suggested a more layered relationship. It was a classic pie chart with the pie itself labeled "haraka," and the party inhabited just one slice, one constituent part, of the movement as a whole. The so-called religious movement swallowed everything. Still others spoke in even greater detail: suggesting that their work was "inspired" or "influenced" by Islam, but was still somehow "separate" from it. One party leader, Lahcen Daoudi, was more pensive: "How," he once asked rhetorically, "can we separate what is not separable? What is religious and what is not?"[12]

I initially thought that what I was seeing might simply represent evidence of confused or incoherent organizations; that Islamist groups were merely disorganized. There was also the possibility, of course, that my data collection was incomplete. But it turned out that there was some semblance of order amidst the piles of transcripts, and notes, and diverse charts sprawled out on my living room floor. In fact, it was only when I matched the charts with the person who drew them, when I studied the charts in context, that I began to be able to understand their multiple renderings.

I want to suggest that, far from being beside the point, this hodgepodge—this ambiguity, this seeming jumble—represents a new and significant development in understanding Islamist mobilization. *The lack of a pattern was a pattern.* The absence of consistency was itself the constant. These myriad representations reflect a rejection of a one-size-fits-all approach to constructing religious authority, a rejection, furthermore, of Weberian understandings of such authority as an all-encompassing "psychic coercion" or "charismatic authority"; and one that belies the obsolete readings of yesteryear, of an omnipotent leader and his supposedly somnolent, almost unconscious followers.[13] Moreover, for the activists I engaged, religious authority is not organizationally fixed, nor is it simply inhabited (or controlled) by certain individuals. Instead, I want to argue that religious authority here is increasingly constructed according to, and depending upon, personal aims and sensibilities, upon individual circumstance and desires. It is, in a word, *personalized.*

★

Try for a moment to visualize a person holding a doll composed completely of salt. Then visualize that person walking slowly into a sea of saltwater. What happens to the doll, the psychoanalyst Sudhir Kakar once pondered, upon submersion?[14] Does it disappear in the midst of the ocean or does it still maintain its form?

The tale of the "salt doll" is the story of religious authority in contemporary Islamist movements. Such authority clearly has not disappeared, nor is it easily divisible or quantifiable. Rather, it is slowly and indistinctly dissolved into each person's ocean of hopes and wishes and goals, and into a movement's span of mobilizational strategies. Each person sees something different, in his or her own way, through his or her own eyes. Religious authority might be there somewhere; it might even be everywhere or all encompassing. But it could also be imperceptible, made to fade. Its construction, in short, depends on the person doing the constructing.

Such flexibility is not accidental. It is also not simply a response to state action. Instead, it represents a kind of purposeful ambiguity, a focused formlessness. I will show in the coming chapters that constructing authority in such a way makes strategic sense: it is a response to a progressively competitive and diverse religio-political marketplace. In the face of unprecedented competition from multiple groups, such constructions preserve each group's mobilizational flexibility. They represent the possibility of a "goldilocks" authority: not too much or too little for everyone, but just right for each person. If religious authority is consistently constructed as too overpowering or fixed, groups run the risk of leaving some potential young people out in the cold: those, in other words, who are interested in specific kinds of largely political activism (say, new recruits with little history with the groups' religious associations). Conversely, if religious authority is tossed aside completely, if it is constructed as absent or fixed, then the possibility exists of scaring away potential or current recruits interested deeply or even solely in religious learning.

Thus, this ambiguity is not a sign of internal secularization, but of individualization.[15] When trying to convince new people to join their group, one PJD activist named Anas told me, "each member highlights the strongest points depending on the personality of the candidate." "There are some people," he said, "who appreciate being talked to as political human beings and others as religious human beings. Everyone is different." As one

entirely separate. The theorist of religion Talal Asad has called such assessments "vulgar."[21]

While sociologists of religion ask us, for example, to look for references to the supernatural—"god talk"—in order to isolate religious authority, such discourse is widespread throughout the Arab world in different forms and manifestations. Many are familiar with the most ubiqituous phrases (as pronounced in Morocco): "lhamdulillaah" (Praise and thanks to God) or "inshaa' Allaah" (God willing). But to converse in colloquial Arabic (*darija*) in Morocco is to verbalize the name of Allah repeatedly. Talking *is* talking about God.

One could conceivably hear the name Allah casually invoked dozens of times within only a few minutes. After a sneeze: "Rehemek Allah" (May God have mercy on you). Before eating or doing anything of consequence: "Besmellah" (In the name of God). When greeting the sick: "Llah yeshaafeek" (May God heal you). To someone at work: "Llah y'aawen" (May God support you). After a kind act: "Llah yekhelef" (May God compensate you). When thanked: "Baraka Llahu feek" (May God grant you grace). When grateful: "Llah yerham lwalideen" (May God bless your parents). Before or after a cigarette: "Llah yefuu 'leek or" (May God illuminate you). When seeing a child: "Llah yeslah" (May God make your child a good person). On a job well done: "Tebarak Llah 'leek" (May God grant you grace). In response to a beggar: "Llah yejeeb" (May God bring it to you). When someone wishes you good health: "Llah y'teek ssahha" (May God give you health). As a sign of appreciation: "Llah yejaazeek bekheer" (May God grant you goodness). After hearing something horrible: "Llah yester" (May God forbid it).

Thus, it is just as vulgar to claim that religious authority can be distinct from other forms of activism, residing in its own conceptual bubble, as it is to proclaim that absolutely no such distinctions exist at all. Many critics and policy makers have pressed Islamist parties to be more upfront about disassociating themselves from the grasps of their allied religious movements, from the ostensible whims of religious authority. They routinely call upon Islamic movements to "separate" emerging political parties from affiliated religious organizations in order to "free" themselves from the "control of clerics."[22]

But there can never be a zero-sum game, with religious or political authority "winning" in their respective jurisdictions.[23] Rather, the dividing lines between the two are continually being re-drawn and re-negotiated. There are no universal or static roles here. It is futile, the intellectual historian Wilfred McClay has written, "to imagine that the proper boundaries between religion and politics can be fixed once and for all, in all times and cultures, separated by an abstract fiat."[24] What Islamists come to understand as the "religious" and the "political" is constantly in flux; negotiations are, by their very nature, neither absolute nor permanent. And it is this dynamic process that interests me: the ways in which young people push and pull apart domains that are far from fixed.

To better understand how to think about the (non)existence of these dual agency structures, it is worth harking back to earlier debates over how to conceptualize the nature of an organization itself—insights first culled not near the sands of the Sahara, but in a rural community in the American Great Lakes in the middle of the last century. It was from there that the sociologist Alvin Gouldner took direct aim at the reigning functionalist models of his elder colleagues. The debates that transpired would lay the foundations for what is now known simply as organization theory.[25]

Gouldner's contribution was to reject assumptions of organizational clarity—clear lines—where little existed in the day-to-day routine. Instead, he found that modern organizations, of which Islamist movements could later aptly belong, are made up of diverse, heterogeneous subsystems, the independence and interdependence of which are seldom constant. The goals, identities, and strategies that are often ascribed to whole organizations can, more often than not, really only be ascribed to certain strata within them—at times perhaps only to leaders or administrators.[26] To define an organization by its goals alone, therefore, risks elevating organizational beliefs to a misleadingly lofty status: as a "thing in itself." Thus, to speak of an "organization" is merely a reification.[27]

To any economist or even employee, Gouldner's conclusions might today seem obvious, but in the analysis of Islamism, somehow they remain forgotten. Gouldner would likely prod us today to think more carefully about the complex organizations that now represent the contemporary Islamist movement. To assign Qaradawi's views on one particular issue, or that of any single cleric or leader over the whole of the organization and *all* its members, would be at best misleading and at worst deceptive. There is no such thing as singular religious authority, for example, because there is no such thing as a single, immutable "religious" or "political" organization.

Gouldner's work dares us—scholars, policy makers, and interested onlookers alike—to get our hands dirty, to go beyond simply inspecting the chassis or the crude organizations of each Islamist group. One has to examine not just the existence of myriad organizational parts, but also how such parts are conceived throughout the movement—at individual members' *subjective* understandings of intra-organizational power.

★

I asked at the beginning of this chapter whether a single individual could encompass the next Islamist generation's understandings of authority. The answer should be obvious by now. The reasons, as we will see, go beyond newly complicated and layered organizations, beyond recently spawned political wings and multiple shadow organizations, and beyond the existence of diverse avenues to activism. Despite prevailing characterizations of young Islamists as blind followers, of their activism reflecting organizational rigidity, today's activists are, in fact, poised and empowered to personalize religious authority, to interpret and construct authority through their own eyes.

First, Islamist movements no longer share a monopoly on information or can control information flow to recruits and even longtime members. Second, movements find it much more difficult to carve out a single, common, shared experience among members. And with this diversity of experiences comes a diversity of questions. The archetypical young pupil recruited by his teacher or preacher is the exception and no longer the rule. Third, and partly as a result of the previous two, it has become far more difficult for movements to rely on a select few, specifically anointed individuals or teachers as possessors of knowledge. In fact, one result of activism within Islamist groups is a recognition of one's own power and authority, of the ability to question everyone, even one's parents.

Political scientist James Piscatori and anthropologist Dale Eickelman wrote about changes within Islam in general in the late twentieth century, pointing to a fragmentation of authority, a move away from a monopoly of religious authority nestled in the hands of a selected group of religious scholars or ʿulama and toward the masses, toward a glut of individuals, from professors to engineers to military leaders—all seeking to speak in the name of Islam.[28] More broadly, many analysts have reflected on the lack of a central figure in Sunni Islam such as a pope, prompting the publication of books with suggestive titles such as *Who Speaks for Islam? What a Billion Muslims Really Think.*[29]

But for young Islamists, in particular, it is no coincidence that they would grow to question a single, central religious authority: they are trained to interrogate such a monopoly (especially when multiple such movements exist). There has long been a divide, even friction, between Islamists and official religious scholars.[30] Contemporary Islamist movements, after all, are movements that grew not only, in most cases, without official ʿulama as part of them, but with ʿulama in opposition to them. This is especially true of illegal movements such as Al Adl and the Egyptian Muslim Brotherhood.

Islamist leaders rose by wrestling away the authority to interpret religious texts from state institutions and 'ulama; they survive in a competitive milieu by distributing such authority to individual members. For their part, it stood to reason, after seeing that such a thing was possible, that young members would claim authority for themselves.

Despite media portrayals to the contrary, Islamist activists, as discussed in chapter 3, are often highly educated. Young Muslims in general are coming of age during a time when they are witnessing not only the diversification of religious scholars, but also their own ability to question and engage them—and even to assume authority for themselves. Mass education drives instituted in most Arab countries during the second half of the last century brought with them employment challenges to constricting labor forces. But they also brought newfound literacy and, more profoundly, sociological, historical and, indeed, theological knowledge, equipping young people to challenge, question, and interrogate scriptural authority in new and nontraditional ways.

Not only is their upbringing in the movement embedded with additional scriptural teachings; the teachings themselves are conducted by laymen, by nontraditional authorities, by those not trained in major or traditional centers of Islamic learning or Qur'anic schools. When young activists gather weekly or monthly for group meetings to discuss the Qur'an, they are led in textual exegesis by friends, teachers, neighbors—by people like themselves.

Even as adults, members take turns hosting such meetings at their houses. And, in many cases, the owner of the home will be empowered to plan and lead a discussion. Such consistent geographic rotation suggests a certain flexibility: it suggests that learning is not housed in one center, but many. (In the case of Al Adl, it also suggests a necessity to avoid police surveillance.) The significance of this diversification is not only in its quantity, but also in the message that is being sent about authority in the first place. As individuals lay claim to the right to interpret the scripture on their own, they also, in Piscatori's words, "effectively question whether any one individual or group has a monopoly on the sacred—even as they appropriate that right for themselves."[31]

As one young activist in PJD explained to me about her weekly lessons: "We take turns, everybody takes turns leading us." Even in Al Adl, a movement seemingly steeped in the tradition of a central Sufi sheikh figure, authority is delegated. "We read Yassine, and we interpret his work, but we also read the Qur'an and hadith. We also read other authors as well, like Tariq Ramadan or Samuel Huntington." Moreover, recall that usra meetings are often led by young people. One additional outcome of these regular meetings is that women and children are also equipped and emboldened to lead and guide and interpret—even while women and men attend separate meetings.

There is another reason young people question official scholars or even state-appointed imams. Their sermons, I was often told, are "boring." This is largely due to the increasing bureaucratization of religious preaching. On Fridays, imams across the country deliver sermons prepared not by themselves, but by the national ministry.

Listen, for example, to the lyrics of Moroccan rapper Chekh Sar, a PJD supporter who dresses in jeans and hoodies, but refrains from vulgar language. (His oeuvre is sometimes dubbed "halal rap.") In a song called "Wasted Time (Part II)," he speaks of the inability of state-run religious institutions and official scholars to understand the complexity of young people's lives: "the 'ulama that we depend on here / are silent or paid to keep quiet / or they only give us fatwas about sex."[32]

Finally, I wrote earlier about the challenges that the globalization of information poses to Arab states. But it is not only states or 'ulama that face new forms of opposition. If, at the close of the twentieth century, Islamist groups could rely on possessing their membership's attention, they now face myriad competition. Once upon a time, if Islamist leaders or even recruiters gave their members a cassette tape, they could be assured that it would likely be one of the only things that he or she would be listening to. While it is true that there were often numerous cassette tapes floating around, the medium was limited: it was still only other *tapes* they were competing against.

Contrast the experiences of today's activists with those of yesteryear. Take the example of a former Al Adl activist named Aziz who joined the movement in the late eighties. When he first joined Al Adl, he once told me, he did not even know he was joining Al Adl. How could he? Yes, he was bright. The oldest of six children, he was one of the smartest in his class, and seemingly aware of the world around him. But he was only in high school and, as a precondition of his membership, he was told he could not talk to anyone about his membership, not even his parents. "No one could know," his teacher said. "Tell them that you are going to the store or a friend's house." The information relayed to him came in fragments. There was no mention of Al Adl or of the king or of anything about government. At that stage, no one even mentioned the name Abdessalam Yassine.

Even if he had heard the name Abdessalam Yassine, he would have had little means of finding out more about him on his own. There was no Internet and few available outlets existed for his own research. Libraries were either nonexistent or locked up at schools or youth centers, or even if they were open, their limited contents were carefully controlled and sanitized by the state.

In the case of Aziz and young Islamist recruits of yesteryear, the Internet would have given them access to information and the tools to criticize and engage existing authority figures. What university education once did to a few, the Internet with its chat rooms, online courses, and availability of texts, does to the many and even those without any prior formal education. Of course, it also empowers and offers platforms to others—to new and emerging voices (be they religious scholars or pop stars)—often those who would never otherwise be heard from.[33]

But the Internet and satellite television are two-way streets. They help and facilitate new voices to emerge, and offer a dizzying array of new choices and outlets to question and discuss. But they can also sustain and amplify existing voices: offering outlets for supporters to come together to bolster each other's beliefs. Al Adl and Yassine began using blogs and the Internet long before many others in Morocco.

The Internet can even embolden existing authority figures. Take the example of Qaradawi, who has become even more popular due to satellite television and in particular his show on the Al Jazeera network. He has moved from what political scientist Stephen Lacroix calls a "local mufti" to a "global mufti" thanks to the Internet's power to make "one man as influential as a thousand."[34] Many global mullahs existed before the Internet, but what makes someone like Qaradawi so unique is that he rose largely without any institutional backing. The Internet was his institution.

Still, I want to show here that such individual figures are not *everything*—no matter how popular or seemingly powerful they might appear. Each recruiter comes to construct for him- or herself and for his or her potential recruits what "religion" means. Every recruiter becomes a reinterpreter.

In the chapters that remain, I will demonstrate how and why they are reinterpreting religious authority in their own personal ways. Within both movements, such authority is not easily bound to a single leader or organization, but rather is circulated among individual activists in ways they choose and desire. The following two chapters will explore these dynamics and, in the process, illuminate new models of Islamist politics.

Chapter 8

SUITS AND DJELLABAS

Let us imagine that you had spent a great deal of time over the course of your life in homes across Morocco. And then, one day, you suddenly found yourself inside the salon of an Al Adl activist's home. At first glance, you probably would not notice any differences. But there would be (at least) one. In urban and rural settings alike, you would have to look past the mainstays of Moroccan homes: the low wooden coffee tables, the metal-plated tea sets, the bouquets of plastic flowers, the rugs (wool, plastic, reed, or otherwise), and the stiff rectangular cushions. These would still all be there.

Instead, you would have to take note of the pictures on the walls. For most Moroccan families, a photograph of the king is displayed somewhere in the house, but most often in the vaunted position above or beside the television in the salon. Such photos can be purchased anywhere in the country: in multiple colors, shapes, and even poses. (One memorable photo features Hassan II horseback riding with Ronald Reagan, both men in matching starched white dress shirts and khakis.) But to visit a member of Al Adl's house is to be struck either by the absence of the monarch's likeness or even, in that same spot, a picture of someone else entirely: Abdessalam Yassine.

It has long been assumed that photos do not lie: that during his life and even in his death, Yassine plays an overpowering role in members' lives; that he even occupies the same position for movement members that the king does for the vast majority of Morocco's citizens.[1] Making small talk, I once asked an activist if he was from Casablanca. He was a hip-looking guy wearing acid-washed jeans and a t-shirt that read: "4ujeans—for genuine feeling." I phrased my question in casual vernacular, using a common phrase to inquire where one is from—in words that translate literally as "Are you a son of Casablanca" (or Waash nta weld Kasa)? He laughed and responded this way: "No, my brother, I am a son of Yassine!" (Lla, khuya, ana weld Yaasseen!) His friend next to him let out a huge laugh, and immediately grabbed his right hand and embraced it. His was a playful joke, but one with serious and suggestive undertones.

At other times, members have revealed to me, with great pride, the wallpapers on their mobile phones: a smiling picture of Yassine in the background. They had superimposed Yassine and Al Adl over images of the king and Morocco.

An onlooker could easily interpret this iconography to mean that these young people are simply submissive disciples of Yassine's "cult of personality." But my encounters with young members suggest that their constructions of authority are more complex and multilayered. I argue in this chapter that they have personalized religious authority by circulating it away from a single reading of a single figure, even one as supposedly central as their "guide." They have re-appropriated and reconfigured the organization Yassine once established and the scope and the range of the guide's substantive reach. They have even re-appropriated Yassine's memory. From spiritual guide to secular politician to beside the point, the roles assigned to the head of their organization are constructed to fit their own desires.' And, in so doing, they preserve and embrace individual choice, making room for multiple voices within their movement.

★

Al Adl is often characterized as a movement that Yassine, for much of the movement's existence, controlled with a wave of his hand, lecturing, when healthy, to his minions weekly. In this reading, new members are forced to study his work, and are indoctrinated by his words, as part and parcel of their membership. I am certainly not denying or glossing over the unique and ubiquitous role of Yassine in the movement. Young members indeed revere and respect him. Youssef, for one, once paused, almost defensively, when I asked him about Yassine. He declared, in the same way a guilt-ridden adulterous husband might interrupt a conversation to declare his love for his wife, that for the record: "By the way, when I speak of Yassine, I mean Al Adl: you know they are *the same.*"

But I want to suggest here that his supposedly all-encompassing transcendent hold often transitioned to detached leadership of a movement that spawned a sophisticated political organization, officially marked by the creation of a Political Circle in 1998. Even while he was alive (and even more so since his death), institutional oversight and strategy have largely given way to a party-like machine, a cohort of old movement hands and a cadre of influential up and coming young activists.

In their charts, some activists drew and articulated Yassine or his successor, Mohammed Abbadi, as above all. Yet, this was especially true among those who have little interest in politics, who want to be sure to point to the role of the spiritual guide. This was also true for those who have overriding interests in politics, but have reinterpreted Yassine as a political force, as a democratic actor. Still, some went out of their way to separate religious and political circles. This was often the case among those who want to make clear that the spiritual guide, be it Yassine or Abbadi, does not hold sway over their political activism. Still others construct authority in this way because they do not feel the need to spell out religious authority at all. "Where is Yassine or Abbadi?" I would ask. "Inside us," some would answer.

Yet, young members are also eager to show that they are forging their own way, and such sentiment often made its way to the organizational charts they assembled. It became clear early on that Al Adl members were eager to create these charts for two reasons. In stark bureaucratic terms, they could show me the advanced nature and complexity of Al Adl—that they really were more than a mere mirror of a Sufi brotherhood; that they occupied an increasingly sophisticated political and religious organization. But Al Adl members could also clarify for me something else: they could outline the role of Yassine and the murshid/guide position in the movement. Yes, he stands atop the organizational charts, but there are many checks and balances along the way, they would say. He inspires and he teaches, but the movement is composed of far more than just one man. The term "internal democracy," favored by PJD to differentiate their movement from Al Adl, was often used by Al Adl members.

Most writings about Al Adl still rely on its original organizational blueprint, *al-Minhaj*, when discussing the organizational structure of the movement. They look mistakenly to a thirty-year-old book to describe the current state of the movement. They point, for example, to the murshid's role (be it Yassine or his successor) in appointments, which even Yassine no longer wholly possessed. Based on a reading of *Minhaj*, one scholar declared as undeniable fact: "The base of followers has no power and does not participate in the decision-making."[2]

Yet, one young member, Fouad, explained to me that the book is open to interpretation, that it is "not the bible, it is not sacred." And, indeed, it has been extensively reinterpreted, especially beginning in the twenty-first century. A part of the core structure remains as laid out, but it has been built upon and updated.

Its General or Consultative Assembly (Majlis al-Shura) was founded in 1992. But the most dramatic amendment to Yassine's original plan was the aforementioned creation of Al Adl's Political Circle in 1998, which added a new and separate wing to the movement's existing religious circle (originally formed in 1987). In many ways, the very creation of a secondary political circle wears away at the scope of his or any single murshid's authority.

This evolution of Al Adl since its early days is made explicit when viewed in cyber terms. Al Adl now maintains a separate website (http://www.aljamaa.net) from Yassine (http://www.yassine.net) and from his daughter (http://nadiayassine.net). The movement's site (as opposed to Yassine's personal site) has slowly morphed into a party site, regularly featuring postings by young members and political officials reacting to current events and labor disputes. Yassine's site, on the other hand, features sermons and religious material pertaining to Yassine's writings and Qur'anic interpretation. In this sense, young members literally possess and represent the movement—a movement inspired by, but now separate from, Yassine himself. They contribute to forging the movement's agenda—particularly, its political agenda. If one wanted to find sermons or Qur'anic exegesis, one would have to look to Yassine's site—a site that is updated or commented upon with far less frequency than the others, even during his life. To use another example, the Facebook pages that a select few of these young leaders possess tend to link more often to each other than to Yassine or to any clerics.

The movement website is now the website *of* the political circle. And, to be sure, the membership of the whole movement is professionalizing and bureaucratizing—increasingly even offering the kinds of tangible job creation that has helped PJD recruit new members. Activists manufacture conferences to attend, release official-looking press releases, and assign and flaunt new titles to circulate authority, to bolster their own status in the movement and beyond, and to attract new members. A sampling of such titles shared with me include: "national board member of the youth of Al Adl"; "Deputy Secretary and media coordinator of the National Union of Moroccan Students"; "member of the Advisory Board of Al Adl"; "member of the General Secretariat of the Policy Circle"; "member of the National Policy Circle Council"; and "Coordinator of the Moroccan Human Rights Committee of Al Adl."

Thus, the Political Circle is far more instrumental than its religious counterpart, offering more opportunities for self-growth, including new job titles and positions, even website experience. Take the example of Hassan Bennajah, who rose from university student, to university president, to head of UNEM, to head of Al Adl's youth wing. And then in 2012, he was appointed "director general" of the movement's number two official, Arslane. Many activists spoke admiringly of him. Indeed, I was often directed by activists not to "read Yassine," but rather to "talk to Bennajah."

★

While scholars have tended to focus on Yassine's place as a religious leader, parsing his writings and analyzing their diverse ideological content and inspiration, some activists have come to focus more on his outspoken stances on governance and in opposition to the regime. When such individuals refer to him, they do so in decidedly partisan terms, bringing him closer in line with their own hopes, sublimating him into their own fantasies for the movement—a movement that he once singularly founded, but that they now belong to and, in many ways, *guide.*

Even when he was alive, and especially since, many began to move away from constructing their beloved founder as an idealized omnipotent leader with "twinkling eyes" to a pragmatic political one surrounded by new swaths of young activists.[3] This new cadre of youth came to conceive of him as a fallible leader, detached from the political, day-to-day operations of the movement. They praise him increasingly for his political stances, not his religious teachings. Their work, their political goals, their aims of expansion are simply too important to be wholly determined by one man.

Such a transition says less about how Yassine asked to be seen and more about how *they want to see him.*[4] But it also shows how his words no longer represent unquestioned doctrine. Indeed, Yassine once wrote of himself and his position as guide: "A *murshid* [guide] is the cornerstone of the structure, there is no *jama'a* [association] without him; he is the state, man and the [preacher]."[5] One Moroccan political science professor told me that Yassine simply "gave himself too much power." He accomplished this by his own clever machinations: to expand his family's foothold in the movement, he promoted the role of his daughter and his son-in-law. He also seemed to push aside any potentially powerful successors or competitors (Mohamed Bachiri, who died in Casablanca in 1999, is one name that is often mentioned).

Up until his death, the ailing Yassine still maintained what anthropologist Henry Munson called his "grandfatherly" scraggly beard.[6] But Yassine was recognized for most of the 2000s (by supporters and detractors alike) as the most vocal and significant public figure in the country, surpassed only by the king. He came to represent, for many, the sole opposition—the only voice that "had not changed his demands in the face of official pressure."[7] Or as one unaffiliated young person in Casablanca remarked: "Whether you agree or not with his ideas, no-one can deny that Abdessalam Yassine is the only person ever to have said 'no' in Morocco."[8]

Many have come to reimagine Yassine less as a holy spiritual man and more as a courageous anti-tyrannical protester—not that the two have to be mutually exclusive.[9] I often heard a tale about Yassine from his early years as a civil servant with the Moroccan ministry of education. This story was repeated to me by multiple members, and it usually began this way: Yassine's daughter, Nadia, once tried to take a pen from his office desk at the ministry. He told her to put the pen down and explained to her that it did not belong to them. "It is not ours," the father told his daughter. "The pen belongs to the people." He then took money from his own pocket and gave it to her so that she could go out and buy her own pen. In a similar telling, I also often heard how the state offered him a car for business use and that he refused, opting instead to travel with the common man via bus.

It is a tale, no doubt, that extols the virtues of Al Adl's founder—that even when he worked for the state, he was not *owned* by the state. The story, of course, also tries to distinguish Yassine from the king, who is seen by Al Adl members as living lavishly off the money of the people.[10] But such a narrative also makes two larger points: that personal betterment and helping people come necessarily from—and through—opposing the state and its largess, and that Yassine's authority derives not from any kind of special religious standing, but rather from acts of resistance to the state.

One activist was so impressed when he first heard about Yassine's letter to the king that he immediately told his neighbor about him. "As fate would have it," he recalled, "she [his neighbor] was actually a member of Al Adl! She told me all about Abdessalam and about the letter he wrote to the king. Soon after, I actually got a chance to meet with him. And I have been a member ever since!"

The histories of young Al Adl activists are filled with such tales, what psychoanalysts might call personal myths: narratives of their founder, Yassine, playing and replaying their own not so secret fantasies, of standing up to authoritarianism, of sticking it to tyranny.[11] They represent, in short, what they want their movement to be: relayed in chronicles of their first encounters with Al Adl or Yassine, of witnessing unjust repression, or a successful protest march.

Abdou also speaks favorably about Yassine, about his ability to withstand pressure from authorities. "I was so taken by the content of the letter he sent to the king," he said. "Especially because it came at a time when the king was most tyrannical. I think that it is only normal that one should like and admire such a man. When King Hassan died, may he rest in peace, Abdessalam made sure that that new king would receive another letter. There is only one man in Morocco who would do that."

Khalil from Rabat had been exposed to daily prayer by his parents, but it was Al Adl's political project that enamored him. "When I first heard about Abdessalam I was in high school. I heard about how he stood up to the king. What caught my attention the most was his bold attitude towards oppression and tyrannical behavior."

It is important to listen to Khalil and Abdou's specific language. They speak of their founder using his first name, addressing him without formal titles, just as Yassine himself had once addressed King Hassan II. The symbolism is salient: it was as if Yassine was a peer, a political activist just like them.

★

Even in his death, Yassine nonetheless remains the symbol of a movement whose role should not be understated. Yet, he and his writings are increasingly viewed as inspirational rather than directional, constantly being interpreted and reinterpreted by young people who apply them to their own lives and experiences.

Yassine is a "reference," Zahir told me while talking for hours at the café in the Marjane supermarket in the sprawling Casablanca suburb of Ain Sebaa. "It's good to disagree with him." Zahir was visiting family and friends in Morocco after being offered a job with a consulting company in France.

Yassine founded Al Adl, wrote its guiding texts, which young people study and read regularly, and, up until his death, visited and delivered sermons to members. But, simply put, Yassine is not understood in a vacuum. Youth serve as interlocutors for Yassine, placing him in their political context, interpreting his words, taking what is relevant in them to further their political project. As head of the group's Political Circle, Moutawakil, has said, everything should be constantly interpreted. "The fact that we revise our ideas when necessary is something of which we are not ashamed. We do not think we are above criticism or our ideas are sacred. We believe that everything may be subject to revision, improvement or change."[12]

The effect is one where, when young people talk, they invoke Yassine, but in their own terms. Their language is peppered with parentheticals—"bayn qawsayn"—literally meaning "between quotation marks," citing Yassine's words, and then placing his texts in their context. "Ghaadi n'teek mitaal" (let me give you an example), they say, or "wahad lqadeya" (one instance) or "matalan" (for example). Like teachers themselves, they necessarily interpret and translate and explicate their movement's leadership and its goals in ways they see fit.

When I asked activists about the roots of religious authority, they would quote the Qur'an, hadiths, and, of course, Yassine. But they would also speak generally about Islam, in ways that allowed them to use their own lives as testament. It was an issue in which they needed no additional training: they knew themselves. Religious authority understood so generally, decentralized away from the singular guide position, enables each activist to determine what that authority might mean for him or her. If Islam impacts all parts of one's life, then being an authority on *anything* can make one an authority on Islam.

One activist named Amine noted that his organizational chart could not encompass religious authority because, he said, "we are all guided by living piety in all forms." Another, Jalal, said, "We believe that we should *not* keep away from our friends and neighbors even if they disagree with us or do not practice Islam." He then turned to me, looked me in the eyes, and said, "Us speaking with you today *is* Islam. What I am doing now is *as* important as praying or fasting. The narrow understanding of Islam the way the regime and other Islamists tell you is an Islam of rules. That's not our Islam."

In another description, even coming up with good economic policies can be a reflection of these personalized notions of Islam. "For other Islamist movements," Elias said, "Islam means only fasting and praying. How can these things alone elevate you?" He then answered his own question: for a "real Muslim," by which he meant a member of Al Adl, "everything should be under the umbrella of Islam. If you engage in fair free trade practices, then you are being a good Muslim. If you treat your wife well, then you are being a good Muslim."

The flexibility extends to recruitment. Within what they view as the "dire" political context of Morocco—when young people face unemployment, "tyranny," even hunger—some citizens want to hear about how to make their lives better, not necessarily about religious texts. In Bilal's words: "When you talk of Islam only in the language of hadiths and so on, often some people just can't comprehend it."

Bilal even quoted the fourth Caliph, Imam 'Ali ('Ali ibn Abi Talib) as saying: "Poverty leads inevitably to unbelief."[13] He also mustered up another quote to prove that one has to be flexible in Islam—going so far as to write it in Arabic on my notepad so that I would not forget it. "There is a saying that we often repeat," he said. "A hungry person would not hear but a voice that promises him food, and a weak and oppressed person would not hear but a voice that promises him freedom."

On campuses across the country, Al Adl and PJD members campaign for youth support to solve everyday problems: public transportation, health care, even the price of bread. Mimoun, an Al Adl university leader, told me: "Our demands are rational. We try to keep apart our union work as students and our private life with the Jamaʿa (Al Adl). I will later give you this written statement, and you will not feel that it is written by Al Adl." He predicted that I would be surprised that it was their document because it included no mention of Islam. This arrangement not only allows Al Adl to mobilize on campus and beyond (minimizing the wrath of the authorities); it also allows activists to mobilize more broadly, reaching wider audiences than before.

Beyond the university, such constructions bolster their ability to engage strangers. "I might be taking the train from Casablanca to Rabat," Ridouane explained, "and I might catch the attention of a passenger simply because of my long beard. But then, I will talk about whatever he wants to talk about." "If," he said, "the person wants to talk about Yassine, I will; if he wants to talk about tyranny, I will; if he wants to talk about the Qurʾan, no problem. After discussing the state of affairs, this person might ask me for my phone number and my address."

★

During a research trip in the summer of 1987, anthropologist Henry Munson wandered speculatively around "several popular quarters" of the northern coastal city of Tangier—often characterized as a regional stronghold of Islamism—and found that only one of the "dozens" of people with whom he conversed had ever heard of a man named Abdessalam Yassine.[14] Now, if the experimental sojourn were repeated, it would be a surprise if Munson could find many who had *not* heard of Yassine—even though Yassine died in 2012. The number would likely not be as many as would have heard of him during the first decade of the twenty-first century, however.

Of course, a certain amount of decentralization of authority—some circulation—is inevitable in the wake of Yassine's death. The person selected by the movement to replace him is said not to possess his same "aura" (how could he really: he was not responsible for its founding or its seminal texts). In some ways, the movement now possesses two spiritual guides—

one living and one deceased. But Yassine still manages to endure: some have taken to calling him the "renewed Imam" and his work is still widely read and studied and cited.[15] No official counts are available, but Yassine's funeral supposedly attracted tens of thousands. And, anecdotally, participants relayed that traffic between Casablanca and Rabat was disrupted.

A certain amount of recognition—and perhaps authority—erodes with death. At a PJD meeting at the Mehdi Ben Barka center in Rabat, for example, I asked youth there if they knew who Ben Barka was. I thought it was ironic and even humorous that Islamists had taken over a center named after the most famous Leftist in the country's history—a man that the current king's father had allegedly "disappeared" in 1965. But few had heard of him. At different times, I also asked them if they knew who Abderrhame Youssoufi, the country's first Socialist prime minister, was; most did not.

But even in his movement's responses to Yassine's death, an overriding desire for mobilizational flexibility is evident. Following its founder's passing, the movement was at a crossroads. How could it continue without its spiritual guide—without the man who founded the movement in the first place? They had a number of options. They could have chosen (a) a cleric as successor and replacement to Yassine; (b) a lay leader to preserve Yassine's authority, signaling that Yassine was not replaceable; or (c) a caretaker of Yassine's legacy such as his daughter, Nadia, or his son-in-law, Abdallah Chibani. In the end, the movement went with a modified version of option (a): they appointed a cleric, but changed his title from "supreme guide" to "secretary general."

The cleric they chose, Mohammed Abbadi, shares Yassine's greyish beard and traveled often for the movement while Yassine was under house arrest (Abbadi's home in the northern city of Oujda has long been boarded up by authorities). And like Yassine, he has roots in Sufism—in his case, the Darqawiyya brotherhood. But the way the movement selected Abbadi was done in a manner that resembled a political election. The movement first accepted nominations and then held an election, with the winner requiring a two-thirds majority of the General Assembly, or Majlis al-Shura. Members were careful to point out that the council had a 98 percent attendance, of which 26 percent of the attendees were women.[16]

At the news conference to announce Abbadi's appointment, the imagery suggested the challenges at stake. At first glance, the pictures seemed to imply a palpable divide between two camps: it was, as one Moroccan writer described to me, the "djellabas vs. the suits."[17] At first glance, the djellabas appeared to be the clerics; the suits were the professional appointees and managers, the head of the Political Circle and the spokesperson. Arslane, the longtime spokesman and newly appointed deputy secretary general, wore a black suit and a black tie; Moutawakil, the political circle head, wore a dark suit with a grey tie. And Abbadi wore a more formal, traditional white djellaba, similar to the ones the king wears for religious festivals. A large banner with Yassine's picture hung above them. Also wearing a djellaba was Abdelkrim Alami, the head of the Majlis al-Irshad (Guidance Council).

"Look at the faces of the suits," the writer told me, "they are not looking at Abbadi the way they looked at Yassine. They don't respect him. The djellabas are finished." He seemed to have a point: Arslane and Moutawakil could almost be seen rolling their eyes at some of Abbadi's words. I was even told quietly that young members do not heed Abbadi. I was also told that they did not think of Abbadi as a replacement for Yassine; and that they winced at some of Abbadi's seemingly naïve political statements. Some said that they trusted Arslane and Moutawakil more. The suits, for their part, also got promotions: Arslane was named deputy secretary general; Moutawakil was named "president" of the political circle (his title changed from secretary general of the political circle so as not to be confused with Yassine's successor).

But these responses raise a related and no less interesting question: why go through the charade of even appointing Abbadi anyway if no one expected him to be able to fill Yassine's shoes? Of course, an organization focused on a leader must try to replace him, but appointing Abbadi preserves the most options for personalization; it preserves the possibility of offering something for everyone. Appointing a lay leader would have risked alienating those who desired a more religiously oriented organization. Choosing a Yassine family member would have risked disaffecting those who desired more openness. Instead, the movement preserved all available resources, including symbolic ones. Choosing not to appoint a clerical successor to Yassine would have been too great of a risk: it would have risked losing a part of its base, losing the ability to recruit and maintain some segments of youth. For its continued success, it had to keep all constituencies satisfied.

The symbolism of the suits and djellabas had little to do with clothing, but everything to do with diversifying and blending authority, with opening up avenues of activism. It also had little to do with drawing clear divisions of labor: religion could hardly be segmented by attire. Instead, like in the organizational charts drawn by activists, the picture of the stage was telling new stories: there were four individuals, from different backgrounds and professional domains (five counting the poster of Yassine). Even if there had been doubts before, there could be no longer: authority was ambiguous and multiple. It was up for grabs, ready to be made by members.

Chapter 9
STRATEGIZING THE SACRED

Abdelali Hamiddine is a former deputy of the PJD youth wing who has risen within the party to be a member of parliament. He was born in Fez to an established family, one that even had the same surname as the Moroccan dynasty, Alaoui. His father was a former educator at the famed al-Qarawiyyin, one of the oldest centers of learning in the world. When he was younger, his father changed their name to ensure that they would not be treated like royalty (they are not).

During his university years, Hamiddine spent time in jail for a crime he did not commit. One day when he was studying law at the university in Fez, he got caught up in a student protest that turned violent. He was soon implicated in the death of a student who died that day—a death that was more likely the fault of police who went in to stop the riot. He spent two years in jail for the attack, but was ultimately acquitted. He still has a scar on his head from where a stone hit him that day.

Perhaps hardened by this experience, he has a reputation for telling it like he sees it. He does not hesitate to criticize party members and often even the palace. He has said that he disagrees with the management style of the prime minister, Benkirane, and even speaks dismissively of some party members' fears of "disturbing the royal entourage."[1] Largely as a result of this independence, he shares wide popularity among young activists. In 2008, he was elected to the party's general secretariat with the highest score of any candidate.

Hamiddine once asked me to meet him at a mosque in the stylish Agdal neighborhood of Rabat. When I got there, I called him on his mobile phone to ask where he was, and he, in turn, asked me to meet him at a nearby café—one that I was unfamiliar with. It turned out that it was a block away, but on a bad mobile phone connection it was difficult to make out the directions. He lost his patience, and I could hear him repeatedly calling me "crazy" under his breath. When I finally found the café, he was wagging his arms intensely in the air.

In his forties, Hamiddine still shows the vigor and frustrations of his youth. When I saw him in the summer of 2013, he was wearing a baggy black suit, drinking his coffee quickly; his constantly buzzing mobile phone was nearly glued to his ear.

He spoke admiringly about how the founding of his party offers a constructive lesson in the relationship between religion and politics in modern political Islam. He also spoke definitively about how the once allied religious movement, the haraka, is an entirely "separate" entity from the political party, just as they imagined it would be in 1998.

When I asked him if it was also something "separate" for him, in his own life, he nodded his head. "I am a child of the movement," he said, "but I am no longer associated with it." Does he still attend Qur'anic study sessions (jalasaat tarbawiyya)? "I wish I could," he said with a grin, "but I am just too busy."

The organizational charts of many PJD activists often mirrored these sentiments. In those cases, the religious movement and political party were either drawn in entirely different categories or even on separate sheets of paper, sometimes under the headers of religion or politics. Activists also talk of "doing religion" or "doing politics," as if they were distinct things. "We are separate; there is no relationship," the party leader Benkirane once said.[2] Aziz Rabbah often echoed these distinctions. "It is not my job . . . to interpret Islam," he once noted.[3] "I am a politician," he told me with pride.

This separation is suggested on paper, in historical recollection, and even in official discourse. But is the "preaching movement" really "separate" from their lives as party members? Do those in PJD really not "do religion" or "interpret Islam"?

When I asked an eminent scholar of Moroccan Islamism about this relationship in 2013, he maintained that these party members were simply not being truthful. They were, he said, trying to prove to the outside world that they were no longer influenced by religion. But, he said, they don't believe in "the separation of religion and politics."

The scholar's explanation for this seeming contradiction was straightforward. "Lying," he said, "is just part of politics."[4]

I want to suggest a different interpretation. I want to suggest here that the representations of religion in young Islamists' lives are not the product of prevarication, but rather of personalization. Religious authority has become circulated to such an extent that it has come to mean multiple things to multiple members. In the midst of this diversification, party members increasingly appropriate the authority to interpret and represent what "Islam" means or should mean to others. As far as I can tell, none of these myriad representations constitutes "lies." Instead, these words and constructions represent and reflect members' own strategic desires for themselves.

In the pages that follow, we will see how the haraka represents for some a site for religious study, a place of Qur'anic learning unfettered by politics. For others, it is a place to make contacts and to get ahead: an instrumental, not ideological, site. For still others, it serves as a strategic site, a place to try out new ideas, and even as a convenient scapegoat. And, yet, for others, it is completely ignored; it simply has no place in their lives as party members.

For many among them, the meaning of "separating" religion and politics is even more layered. Just because one might be a member of the party and have little to do with the haraka does not mean that she does not "do Islam." Instead, members appropriate Islamic authority on a daily basis and they do so in ways that allow others to do so as well. In order for anyone to find a place for herself or feel comfortable as a member, members often speak of "Islam" as general, fluid values and morals.

Thus, in the end, it is the "Islamic" or "preaching" movement that has become more flexible and more movable than the political party, which itself remains largely a space for self-improvement.

★

Some have argued that as the years have passed and as PJD has become more active in electoral politics, the political party has simply grown more "autonomous" from its allied religious movement, the haraka.[5] But this is not the precise term. It is true that publicly and even formally, PJD has seemingly all but overshadowed the haraka—in tone, organizational composition, leadership, and membership crossover. Yet, PJD is not autonomous in the sense of existing entirely separately and on its own in the context of two distinct, co-equal organizations. Rather, the haraka—and the authority it once possessed—has slowly dissolved into the party and into a sea of members' individual wishes, there to be constructed as each member sees fit, commensurate with his or her experiences, orientations, and desires.

While membership with the haraka was once a precondition or even a given of PJD membership, today it does not seem to be—at least on paper.[6] Officially, the vast majority of PJD members now have no previous, formal affiliation with the party's allied religious organization. And even in the case of those who do (who joined the haraka between 1992 and 1999, before the party even existed), their relationship to the haraka has almost been erased from their public personas. They have sought to gain their public stature from being independently elected to PJD's general secretariat via internal PJD elections.[7] This is even more pronounced for new members: membership with the haraka is no longer necessary for membership in PJD.

As PJD increased its popularity, party members even came to downplay publicly their membership with the religious movement. In 2002, a PJD member of parliament noted that his prior position with the haraka was nothing "special," something that was simply part of his past, such as his work as a labor and educational activist. The MP had been, in his words, "a member of many things."[8] In fact, by 2009, a spokesman of the party was even less oblique: "We left the haraka behind," he said, "We're not here to impose the veil or prohibit alcohol."[9]

These PJD members appear to dismiss the haraka not because it is un-important—or because it had no influence over the party. Rather, they speak in this way and advertise the haraka in this way because they are eager to signal to fellow and potential members that it is not the only path to the party.

For their part, members flout their multiplicity, their ability to come from anywhere, from outside the bounds of the "religious movement." Most charts reflected these multiple paths to the party. One highlighted a flowchart showing three paths to the party: from the youth wing (JJD), from the student wing (OREMA), and, finally, from the haraka. Listen to Karima discuss her own personal path. "Many of us," she said, "used to be-long to the haraka. That is how we came to PJD. We were active in their youth activities." But then, she continued, "the haraka started changing its orientation toward politics and most of the activities we went to were about political issues. The events addressed young people in particular. Soon, the movement became a party and consequently we as members moved directly from the movement to the party." There was no longer a reason, then, to also be a formal member of the haraka.

For Souad, a young medical student with little interest in spending time learning about the Qur'an, the haraka is meaningless in her life and invisi-ble on her chart. "When I was searching for a party to support, I was look-ing at all the parties," she said. "And compared to all of them, PJD is much more serious and transparent. For this reason people trust it—I trust it. The increasing number of PJD supporters has nothing to do with the fact that it is an Islamic party. It is just because PJD has more transparency and cred-ibility; that's all. That is why I am here."

A religiously inspired party possesses specific challenges. How does it handle religious authority when the party grows out of a movement once oriented around religious teaching and dominated by clerics? It risks alien-ating current members if it dismisses such authority too summarily, but it also risks alienating future ones or broader or different ones if it holds on too tightly. The risk, moreover, is as Olivier Roy once claimed of Islamist parties in general—that the "religious sphere" becomes "emptied of its values as a place of transcendence, refuge and protest, since it is now identified with the new power."[10]

PJD tries to tackle this problem by maintaining the *possibility* of the haraka for all individual members. Even if they do not formally join it, members have its activities and services and even rhetoric at their disposal.

★

During one PJD convention, I noticed Badir sitting with his arms resting in his lap. He looked bored. A young man in his early twenties, he wore blue jeans, a white, long-sleeved buttoned down shirt with the sleeves rolled up, and brown leather lace-up shoes. The sea of young people around him were waiting for the next speaker, biding their time by cheering for Palestine and hoisting flags in the air. The greens and reds of the Moroccan flag and the greens, whites, and blacks of the Palestinian flag filled the room like confetti. Young people chanted at the top of their lungs: "ashsh'ab yureed tahreer filistin!" "The youth demand the liberation of Palestine!" (These same chants could be heard in front of the parliament building in Rabat during protests in the summer of 2014, during renewed conflict between Israel and Hamas.)

Badir was still noticeably apathetic, and I could not figure out why. But then a young woman slowly made her way to the front of the auditorium. She came from the right side of the room where the women were seated, and she gently took hold of the microphone on the left side of the room, in front of where the men were seated. A petite fourteen-year-old with a shiny blue and white veil, she began chanting in beautiful tones. Her powerful voice belied her small stature. "God is great," she belted out and then the crowd repeated after her. "God gives us mercy."

Badir leapt from his seat. *This* is what he had come all this way for. The hourly seminars or *warashaat*—on issues from administrative law, human rights, and electoral strategy—that captivated the majority of the young activists, held little interest for him.[11] "I didn't come here for *these* things," he pointed dismissively to the flags on the floor. "I came here for Islam."

But, although Badir was not totally satisfied, he knew he could still find formal Qur'anic training in his weekly sessions with other haraka members. Party conferences like this one were bonus activities. Yet, for the party, this formulation allows them to have their cake and eat it too: they could recruit certain kinds of supporters in party settings and still have the haraka to appeal to others.

Maintaining the haraka as a seemingly distinct entity allows members to prove to new recruits that they are free to join the party sui generis—that they do not need to be a part of the haraka club, and, more profoundly, that they are free to practice politics autonomously. But this organizational flexibility also makes sense from the other side of the coin. Take, as an example, the experience of Aboubakr, a twenty-eight-year-old graduate student in Rabat, originally from the nearby town of Bouznika. In his chart, he showed very clear dividing lines between the movement's religious and political wings. This was not because he was an avowed believer in secularism or because he believed religion should not inform politics. To the contrary, he did not want politics informing his religious practice. He liked it that way, he told me, because he had no interest in the party. He would occasionally go to party events, and would support its agenda—voting for it, marching with it—but he was not an active member. He considered himself, instead, a "son of the haraka," particularly because he enjoyed going to its educational sessions to discuss the Qur'an and listen to short sermons.

The organizational distribution of authority allowed him to experience something he had never experienced before—something many activists termed "freedom." "You cannot control young people," Hamiddine told me. "What they demand is freedom—this is true even for religious youth. If youth have an inclination towards religion, if they want to go to the mosque or a Qur'anic school, let them do it."

"You cannot forbid religious practice," he also said. But just then he let out a huge roar, laughing at his near Freudian slip. The Moroccan Arabic word for "give" and "forbid" are nearly identical—only one letter differentiates them. He almost said: "You cannot give religious practice." But he corrected himself. "Let everybody," he quickly recovered, "live the way they want."

For some, the haraka, and with it Qur'anic study, have come to be understood purely as instrumental, as a tool for advancement. In the case of the burgeoning Islamist party, how could it appear to be open to everyone while at the same time still maintaining some semblance of order? The answer: the haraka. It is increasingly viewed as a training device, a "minor league" for cultivating future leaders, a mechanism for ensuring loyalty that is necessary for advancement in the party, and even as an inculcator of "moral" education and training. In the 2009 local elections, for example, all the heads of the party lists were also reportedly members of the haraka. When asked about this, party members claimed simply that it was a "coincidence."

One frustrated former member named Ashraf said that after attending a number of internal elections for the party, he kept seeing the same people winning: "They were all from the haraka." Either by design or simply as a result of social networks (they knew more people), the message, for him, was palpable: to rise in the party, the haraka still plays an important role. One professor told me of a colleague who was beginning to show interest and enthusiasm in PJD. Will she also, I asked, begin to attend regular Qur'anic study sessions—the jalasaat tarbawiyya? "She will eventually," he said, "if she wants to get ahead." One former member named Ayman was explicit: "If you want to be someone in the party, you have to go the educational sessions."

Others have come to recognize this reality, expressing it in the complementary benefits that each avenue provides: "the party protects you," Ayman reflected, "and the haraka educates you." Which is to say that the party enables professional growth, but the movement allows for personal betterment—and they are interrelated because one needs the education in order to ensure professional growth.

In the elections to choose the leader of the youth wing—the JJD—the head of an association devoted to young people alleged to me that the secretary general of the party was given a list of possible names and that he chose three who could stand for elections—only those active, even informally, in the haraka—especially by attending jalasaat tarbawiyya. Even if this was not the case, the perception is still telling.

One high-ranking activist almost seemed to suggest this when he spoke of the importance of a certain "ethic" in picking party leaders. The effect was transitive. If one needed that ethic to succeed in the party, and the haraka was tasked with ensuring that ethic, then experience with the haraka was essential to success. "The general atmosphere within the party is an educational one. It is an ethical one," he said. "The party is open to everybody, but the party has a climate and that climate usually affects people. The person who displays inappropriate behavior is free to be there, but that person will not get the people's votes." Then he paused: "a person cannot succeed in internal elections if he doesn't fulfill the conditions of these principles and of competency. But when it comes to the future, that is something only God knows."

Because of this unstated role of the haraka, in the spring of 2013, for example, party members in Fez staged what can be thought of as a minor rank-and-file rebellion, when they publicly burned their party membership cards. They were frustrated that they were not rising fast enough in the party. And the reason they gave was because they were not spending enough time with the haraka. They said they were considered "mad dogs" by the party because they did not attend Qur'anic lessons.[12]

The charts also showed other organizational quirks, illustrating additional ways in which party and movement are difficult to disentangle, even on paper. The party newspaper, *Attajdid*, is one example. The paper is said to reside formally under the organizational purview of the haraka, but it has become the de facto publishing agent of the party: its central forum, sounding board, and outlet for policy. Most citizens routinely refer to it as "PJD's newspaper."

Once, when I had to hunt down an old issue of the paper, I called the party headquarters. They then gave me the number of the printing office. When I made it to the street of the printing office, I asked a man for directions and he said, "The PJD paper? Cross the street and take a left."

But when *Attajdid* staff go off the rails and veer into politically imprudent territory (such as when its writers declared infamously that the devastating Asian tsunami was Allah's punishment for bad behavior), party leaders can easily distance themselves from such rhetoric. Like any slick modern party machine, having plausible deniability at your disposal is smart politics.

When *Attajdid* declared public music festivals to be "dens of iniquity," party officials could suddenly appear as the voice of reason. They could distance themselves from the newspaper and instead note, as one party official did, that "one cannot be against festivals, but they should be cleaned if there are drifts."[13]

Under this formulation, haraka figures could sporadically talk of desiring an "Islamic State" even while party leaders would speak only of a political party of "Islamic reference."[14] Maintaining the groups as different "units" allows members to have it both ways—to be open to as many viewpoints as possible. It also offers the party the opportunity to distance itself officially, but to still rally youth who might be interested in hearing the more heated rhetoric. For the same reason, the university wing is technically housed under the haraka, not the party.

Even if leaders publicly denounce such rhetoric, the rank and file has reason to question the denunciations. When PJD wanted to disseminate its new proposals for educational policy, for example, or the results of a PJD-led parliamentary committee, it published them in *Attajdid*.[15] Its longtime editor, Mustapha Khalfi, once disputed the *Attajdid*/PJD connection in a 2007 interview. "I want to clarify one thing. Our editorial policy is not dictated by PJD, and we have no connection with that party." But complicating matters even further is that Khalfi also maintained a leadership role in PJD's policy commissions. And when PJD formed its first government in 2012, it chose none other than Khalfi to be the minister of communications and the chief government spokesman.

The chief religious authority of the entire movement, and the longtime head of the haraka, often made statements contrary to the official party rhetoric. Following PJD's strong showing in the 2002 elections, for example, Raissouni laid out conditions for the party joining a possible government. Among the conditions stipulated were that PJD should not participate in a government that did not promote respect for Islam and the Arabic language, and more specifically the establishment of *zakat* (charity) and Islamic banking principles. Moreover, his 2002 interview in a party publication, *al-ʿAsr*, read like a last will and testament from a man who knew that his authority (and that of his sub-movement) was shifting.[16] While taking pains to stipulate that "he did not speak for the party," he also implored it to refuse to join a government that did not maintain the same commitment to Islam that he had.

Raissouni was eventually forced to resign, not because he challenged the party—that became his strategic role—but because he questioned the religious authority of the state itself. A year later, he went too far. He proposed a theory whereby the king would be stripped of his sole religious authority. The task of issuing fatwas, under this plan, would instead be delegated from a single Commander of the Faithful to a set of "Commanders" of the Faithful. He told a Moroccan newspaper in 2003 that "the current King [Mohammed VI], based on his training, is unable to issue fatwas, which is the principal task of the Commander of the Faithful."[17]

★

Does this strategic organizational arrangement mean that the party simply relegates public talk of religion to those within the haraka? Do party members really, as some claimed, not "do Islam"? Once again, the reality is more layered. Those in PJD speak of Islam in general terms, in purposefully ambiguous and general language, of "values" and "morals." Such talk provides for many possible different individual sensibilities and desires within the umbrella of the party. It also allows for (a) multiple interpretations; (b) the ability to satisfy those who are still looking for religion even in the party; (c) a mechanism to mobilize a variety of youth; and (d) the ability to empower current and future party members as authority figures themselves.

In her study on Qur'anic interpretation, Asma Barlas points out that religious authority in Islam "derives not from closing the canon, or even from 'fixing its contents,' but from certain ways of interpreting them."[18] In this case, because of the way Islam is increasingly constructed by party members—in generalist terms, not as something culled from formal study of hadiths but sustained by moral leadership and activism—anyone, young or old, can lay claim to that authority. Such arrangements are both empowering and diluting: authority is everywhere, but nowhere. Thus, it is by its new nature personalized, left in the hands of each individual activist.

Listen, for example, to a typical recruiting speech delivered by a party elder, Saad Eddine El Othmani, to a large gathering of current and potential PJD rank-and-file members in 2006. The term "elder" here is relative. When Othmani became secretary general of PJD in April 2004, he took over from the ailing eighty-four-year-old Abdelkarim Al Khatib. At the ceremony to pass the reins of the party, Khatib made clear why he was stepping down. It was time, he said, "to make way for the youth."[19] Othmani, though forty-eight at the time, was nonetheless often noted for his "youthful smile." And compared to the heads of every other political party, Othmani was indeed a "youth"—both in relative age and in experience, a leader who came largely from outside the political arena, hailing from a long career in the annals of psychiatry. Othmani's story of professional ascent was well known and celebrated among party faithful: he grew up in an Amazigh family in a transport hub in the south, a town known largely for its multitude of bus and taxi terminals, went on to earn a medical degree in Casablanca, a certificate in Islamic jurisprudence in Rabat, and then, ultimately, the leadership of the party.

When Othmani addressed party audiences, he often made a point of saying: "my fellow *shabaab*," or "my fellow youth." He was just like them, he seemed to be saying, and they, in turn, could be just like him. This intimate yet prepared speech was closed to the press. I was the only non-party member in the room. His speech was not for foreign consumption: this was intended for the audience of a few hundred young people. He spoke in casual language, in the colloquial dialect, as if he were speaking with friends or family.

He recognized that many were still considering movements—not yet members of PJD and there to hear from, and learn about, the party. "I would like to greet our youth in general and those of PJD in particular," he said. He then urged all of them to first take note of the political problems facing the country. "I want you to pay special attention to the current difficult period [in Morocco] and the responsibility we all share." He spoke for fifteen minutes, in very general terms, about corruption, about world events, and, in particular, about "Palestine and its Israeli invaders."

But toward the very end of the speech, he began to speak briefly about Islam. Othmani reminded his guests what at one time would have been obvious: that there was also a religious component to their activism. His wording was deliberate. "PJD," he said, "is also a party that has a religious background like other similar political parties in the Islamic world that work very hard for democracy and political reform according to the main teachings of our religion in our respective countries."

"We," he continued, "are also a party that seeks renewal [*tajdid*], and we view our Islamic background from this perspective. We are not a conservative or a traditional party, but a party that is determined to build the future along modern, scientific and intellectual lines. I want our youth to acquire and develop these principles because the country needs science and knowledge at their best to build the future."

In his address that day, Othmani was careful to talk about religion in general terms. If one came to the speech waiting to hear about Islam, it was there to be heard, and like a coda, shaping everything that came before it. But if one was not interested in that component of the party's activism, it was tucked away at the end, easily ignored by an antsy audience. It was like ambient music played during the closing credits of a film—both by way of order (it came last in his speech) and by way of substance (it seemed to hover ambiguously somewhere merely in the atmosphere of their work). For those still making up their mind, he was sure to point out that his party had a religious background (that fact was irrefutable), but he wanted to remind potential recruits that this background should not be viewed in isolation. Islam had to be thought of in the context of the work they did to "renew" the country—or the faith. The message was purposefully ambiguous, left open to interpretation. For the term "renewal," or "tajdid," itself has deep Islamic undertones and significance, a theme at the heart of Islamic revivalism.[20] Moreover, lest one think that this religious background made the party backwards, it also contributed to the truly important realms of science and knowledge. Once again, if one was so inclined, the term "science" could be understood as Islamic sciences.

PJD activists are often careful to leave open as many interpretations as possible, to leave open the door for myriad understandings. Listen, for example, to an interview with Rabbah in 2008. "We make a point of establishing a strict distinction," he said, "between politics and da'wa, religious preaching." This, at first, sounds straightforward enough, but he then

Rabbah, for one, has settled on a new force for mobilization, what he calls "moral education." And there was a thirst, he recognized, even a market, for this morality.

To grow without any moral backing is difficult, I often heard. "Believe me, politics without a moral base is very difficult," one party leader said. "If you have no moral base—I know from people in other parties—this can be catastrophic. I have contacts, I know people in other parties in Morocco, and they also try to mobilize the youth, but without a moral grounding this is impossible. Without a system of ethics underlying your party, youth will not be active. They will burn away the future. That is why we focus on moral values."

Having an Islamic reference thus becomes a resource to recruit "better" activists. It helps attract more "intelligent" leaders, "clean" people, and "loyal" people. As Salma reiterated: "Though PJD claims not to be an Islamic party, it has an Islamic background. And we feel comfortable with a party that has Islamic principles. Compared to other Moroccan political parties, PJD has the advantage of having very intelligent leaders." Intelligence here could follow from Islam or it could follow from general political knowledge.

These were not simple ideological transformations. There were strategic calculations involved. When Islam is framed so generally, it also becomes easier to expand, to reach across party lines, to reach out to more voters, and to not offend anyone. "That is why we work with other parties," Rabbah said. "We need to try to apply these social and economic values to create a better environment for Moroccans."

Indeed, the biggest problem in Morocco, under this reading, is not the lack of religion or the need to instill Islam. The chief difficulty is a lack of values and "corruption." "We are," Salma said, "looking for uncorrupt, clean people to lead. Citizens know that they can only find this in a modern party."

Such values are so elastic, so general, that they can even be found among Socialists. PJD leader Lahcen Daoudi spoke in 2006 about the similar visions of his party and the main Socialist party—in their "fight against corruption and squandering of public funds" and for "entrenching a culture of transparency."[22] The Islamists and the Socialists, he went on, "have several common values that can be a basis for developing a platform for joint work in advance of the municipal elections." And so it was that PJD's "values" had become so broad that a party leader could declare publicly that the unlikeliest of partners—the main Islamist party and the main Socialist party—had come to share them in common.[23]

Party members uttered similar sentiments in 2012 when, in order to form a governing coalition, they were compelled to join forces with the center-right Istiqlal party and then after that coalition collapsed, with the National Rally for Independents in 2013—a secular-leaning, pro-palace party whose head Benkirane had once labeled "corrupt and incompetent."[24]

Back at that hard-to-find café in Rabat in 2013, following the coup against the Egyptian Muslim Brotherhood, Hamiddine bragged about this flexibility, comparing it favorably with the Egyptian Muslim Brotherhood. "That was their problem," he said. "The reason they failed." "They were too selfish for their own good." Simply put, he said, "they did not have the long experience of learning how to share power that we had—learning how to be flexible." That, he said, was the secret to his own party's success: not lying, but being strategically supple.[25]

Conclusion
THE NEXT ISLAMIST GENERATION

Books about political Islam often tend to end with predictions of its demise. Olivier Roy declared its "failure" in 1994, but newly formed Islamist parties went on to dominate Arab politics. Analysts narrated its decline in the wake of the Muslim Brotherhood's dethroning in Egypt in 2013, but the Islamist project continues.[1]

Like social movement organizations everywhere, Islamist movements adapt in order to survive. When Arab states outlawed them, they went underground. When they were barred from politics, they stepped into the social sphere. When challenged from others or given opportunities to do so, they entered political processes. And, in this newest phase, when they face intensifying competition from fellow Islamists, they move, as I showed in the preceding chapters, to expand their base.

Competition pushes them to pluralize: not only are movements more diverse, but the members within them are as well. As rivalries deepen, as they did in Morocco during the last decade and as they are now most everywhere else, groups begin to do something unexpected: they compete with each other to make room for multiple individual identities and orientations to flourish within their teeming organizations.

In the midst of new battles for limited resources, offering maximum opportunities to young people makes strategic sense. Islamists do not, as so many still assume, simply woo youth with new services or even overwhelm them with doctrine. Instead, groups are keenly attuned to the demands of the market and to the realities of demography. Even before the Arab Spring propelled these concerns to the fore, they recognized that, in the midst of authoritarianism and patriarchy, young people wanted what they did not have: the ability to rise, to ascend, to become someone new. Choosing between and within Islamist groups was often the closest thing to freedom young people experienced. In the absence of democracy, this was their democracy.

The irony, of course, is that those who most successfully offered young people the freedom to choose—Islamists—were the very ones that outsiders long feared would deprive others of that very right. And while many actors and analysts over the last two decades were glossing over such youth, ignoring them altogether or dismissing them as *encadré* or nonsubstantive, these movements recognized their power, seizing upon it, going out of their way to appeal to it.

They were determined. PJD's Action Plan—its strategic mission—for the last *three* election cycles made youth mobilization an "absolute priority." "The average age of PJD activists is below 40," the longtime PJD youth head Aziz Rabbah declared back in 2007, "and we do not hide the fact that we try to recruit the maximum number of young people. We are strongly committed to widening our support among Moroccan youth."

Non-Islamist incumbents and regime loyalists bet against demography. Drunk with power, they too often neglected to invest in the future: they failed to recognize that growing swaths of young people would one day demand rights and responsibilities for themselves. In 2006, I sat in an office within the walls of the royal palace in Rabat, when a top official at the ministry of Islamic affairs put his hand on my shoulder, looked me straight in the eyes, and nearly admitted defeat. "Youth are now the target," he said. "Youth are the future. There are many who want to capture their attention, but the competition is hard." When asked about his chances in 2008, Abbas el Fassi, the former head of one of the country's oldest political parties, the Istiqlal party, also sounded dejected: "It is clear," he said, "that we will not match them [Islamists] in direct recruitment."[2]

Alternatively, when I met an activist from either of Morocco's main Islamist groups, I would often hear versions of the same joke. "What are you studying?" they would ask. I always responded, at first, with my safe, stock answer: "the political mobilization of youth." Then they or someone in the crowd would invariably chime in with a version of the following: "So your work is now complete!" And everyone then laughed uncontrollably because the underlying truth was so obvious it was funny: yes, there were other bit players, but no other groups, and especially none of what they called the "aging" and "elitist" official political parties, came close to mobilizing the nation's youth. Election results, protest turnouts, and opinion polling all confirmed their confidence.

But the most curious aspect of their behavior is not that Islamists leaned toward self-preservation; it's *how* they went about it. Why did they not, as many predicted, work to hold on even tighter to a base they already had? Why not double down on certain elements of their activism, offering specific "products" to certain sets of supporters? Research within the peace movement, the women's movement, and the environmental movement, for example, has all shown that interorganizational competition tends to lead to "specialized tactical repertoires" or, in other words, to organizations working to "appeal to a particular set of potential participants or benefactors."[3] Studies of religious organizations in America have shown similar paths. According to sociologists Rodney Stark and Roger Finke, competition "forces each religious body to appeal successfully to some segment of the religious market," leading to the formation of all sorts of newly specialized organizations, to a cafeteria-type setting.[4]

Why, then, did Islamists pluralize when others have specialized? One reason is that most Islamist groups in the Middle East and North Africa may, surprisingly, be prone to internal pluralism. They already share a Sunni Muslim tradition, hailing from shared historical milieus and from traditions and environments prone to synchronism. Competition is highly "concentrated," therefore, because all potential recruits hail from the same religion. They are bounded to one other by a "common identification": because of how they identify themselves, how they are viewed or perceived by others, and how they are treated by the state, overlap is unavoidable.[5] This is especially the case in the context of the kind of niche competition in which Islamist movements endure—where groups compete against each for a broad set of supporters: youth.

Also, and perhaps most critically, their competition is tightly regulated. Stark and Finke write about specialization in America in the midst of an "open religious economy." But the marketplace in Morocco, as we saw in chapters 5 and 6, is closely monitored and guarded. Recall that any new voice that tries to emerge—be they Shi'i, Christian, or even Muslims who challenged a nationalized Islam—are routinely barred from the public sphere. Under such conditions, pluralism might be less cumbersome than limited specialization.

Last, Islamists may have been greedy, especially because they labored for many decades to thrive. If expansion was possible, they pursued it. The groups I studied might employ different tactics, but both still hope for nothing short of eventual wholesale political change. They aspire to transform how citizens engage with the world around them: from moralizing public life to adding political dimensions to spiritual practice to discrediting entrenched economic forces to judging how pornographic websites are surfed in public. These far-reaching and diverse aims, after all, are what helped them recruit so widely—but they are also often incongruent, with small, narrow offerings.

In the end, there is little question that Islamists have long managed to adapt and endure. But by expanding their ranks in the face of new competition, have they gone one step too far? Have they grown too big *not* to fail?

CONCLUSION

★

Social scientists are not soothsayers. And attempting to foretell the future of political Islam is an especially humbling endeavor. But in these final pages, I do want to carefully reexamine what we have learned about the next generation of Islamist activists and suggest some very real implications of their emergence.

I want to close with this overarching conclusion: power dynamics within Islamist organizations are changing rapidly and dramatically. And these changes are happening, as they always have, not only from external constraints, but from internal pressures (chapter 2). This book offers new evidence not of the demise of Islamist movements, but of their lasting transformation. Young activists are poised to assert more control within their organizations, even initiate internal rebellions of their own, and perhaps also help break apart the very movements they helped grow.

This is the case for four main reasons. First, making room for *many* might also mean laying the foundation for *discord*. By appealing to large groups of young people, the ranks of Islamist movements are now filled with unprecedented range. No single appearance or outlook or living space characterizes the rank and file (chapter 3). While organizational theorists have shown that cultivating group cohesion is critical for survival, we see Islamist individuals increasingly looking out for themselves, embracing the collective only as far as it can improve their own lot in life (chapter 4).[6] Flexible paths to activism or clever reorganizations of allied religious groups could prove to be only temporary solutions (chapters 8 and 9). As one longtime Al Adl activist told me in the summer of 2013, "The new people are not like before."

Second, Islamist successes are increasingly replicable. Youth are not only mobile experimenters, but they are searching for something that could potentially be found elsewhere. New identities are no longer uniquely Islamist identities (chapters 3 and 4). Islamists and non-Islamists alike could learn, for example, to embody the ideals of self-improvement and empowerment. Islamists no longer own these traits, especially in the midst of new protest movements such as *Tamarod* (rebellion) which helped bring down Egyptian president Morsi in 2013. On Moroccan campuses, for example, where Islamist movements have long dominated, other channels for activism, including ethnic and regional movements, are slowly emerging.[7] At universities that I first visited in 2006, *Sahrawi* (Saharan) and Amazigh (Berber) movements are now offering new outlets for personal empowerment.

Third, internal lines of religious authority are growing murky. Young activists were raised to question nationalized or "official" religious authorities (chapter 7) and, as we saw, they are now poised to question their own (chapters 8 and 9). As they continue to personalize Islam—to reinterpret for themselves what their faith means—they come to rely less on those seeking to guide them. Under these circumstances, religious authority is unavoidably fragmented. "I don't need a guide in order to talk to God," an Al Adl member named Samir said matter of factly, "I can talk directly to God myself."

Young Islamists are not caricatures, not following fixed lines or linear paths, not all suddenly more or less "extreme" than those in the generation behind them. Rather, they are independent individuals: the most educated, technologically equipped, and globalized generation in the history of political Islam. Their lives are multilayered; their faith is fluid; their choices are varied (chapters 3 and 4). In the end, such elasticity helps recruitment, but it may hinder movements' abilities to instill discipline, control, and even a single ethos—all of which are imperative for cohesion, especially in the midst of continuing state repression and oversight.

Fourth, and finally, skepticism of omnipotent central authority abounds. For members of the next Islamist generation, the Arab Spring is now part of their histories, just as independence struggles were for their grandparents. Even in countries where leaders were pushed from office, where what political scientists call top-down "authoritarian breakdown" transpired, true regime change is still far off.[8] Those with deep-seated interests—what Abdelilah Benkirane has termed "ghosts"—loom.[9] These governments still look and even act a lot like they used to, but the way young people look at them has changed. Etched in their memories is not that authoritarianism can be overcome quickly, but that it can at least be challenged. Theirs is the post-submission generation.

This skepticism invariably affects the way they look at their own movements, where vestiges of old control also still remain. The final day of the 2012 PJD youth convention was broken up by authorities after activists criticized the relationship between party elites and the monarchy. One delegate named Abdelaziz called the closing "a humiliation," noting that "we must not stand by with our arms folded."[10] Later, after President Morsi fell in Egypt, Omar from PJD told me: "No one should have absolute power, that was Morsi's problem."

A young Al Adl member named Hassan admitted that, in the wake of Yassine's death, he was not satisfied with the group's officially named successor, and that he was still looking for "someone new to learn from." Who might it be? I asked. "I don't know," he said. Could it be anyone, I inquired, even a woman? "Yes," he said. Then I asked what would happen if he or she does not hail from Al Adl? He paused. "I have thought a lot about that," he said.

The early twentieth-century founders of the Muslim Brotherhood used to rail against feeble Arab leaders who "forgot their glory, their history, and their past."[11] They often called for a "restoration," a return to Shari'a, a return to the Caliphate, a return to a way of life that was or might have been. But if their predecessors wanted to build a just, Islamic society from the bottom up, many of today's activists simply want the chance to build *something*—usually by building up themselves or, more to the point, in order to build up themselves. If these opportunities do not present themselves, they will continue to do what they have already begun doing: look to other groups, even perhaps broadening their search in the face of more options. Or they will stay and challenge existing power structures, breaking apart movements in the process. Or they will form their own movements, especially as traditional modes of state control struggle to curtail new forms of expression (chapter 5).

"Until we find something else," Mohammed from Al Adl declared, "Islamism is the best model out there." "It's just like what Churchill said about democracy: it's the worst form except for everything else that's been tried." Yes, his friend nodded, "Things are changing every day."

"Islam is the solution"—the famous Islamist slogan—no longer simply means that Islam encapsulates *the* solution; rather, it has come to mean that there is *a* solution out there. These were the organized opposition groups that this generation inherited. They did not create these movements or develop their infrastructures. They did not write their cardinal texts. When they were growing up, mostly in the 1990s and the 2000s, at high schools and universities, at mosque and on streets, on buses and on trains, these were the movements that were already in place, poised to battle for their support.

They did not build these movements, but they will remake them for themselves—or they will simply move on. Whatever they choose—and the choice is theirs—one outcome is certain: the Islamist project will never be the same again.

ACKNOWLEDGMENTS

How does one thank a population—the countless Moroccans who invited me into their homes, who fed me, who shared the stories of their lives with me, who answered my questions even when they were wary of talking to an outsider? Or those who helped me understand how their faith is practiced in politics when the faith in question is not my own? Or the people of Egypt, Jordan, Palestine, Israel, and the United Arab Emirates, who, along with Moroccans in Spain, England, Italy, France and the Netherlands, offered their assistance and helped me to see their world in all its diversity? Most of them must remain nameless here, but this work would not exist without their help.

This book also would not exist without the scholars who provided indispensable guidance along the way, and whose generosity I hope one day to emulate: Michael Willis, Noah Feldman, Tariq El Allami, and Hassan Rahmouni. Other teachers and colleagues shared vital insights at various points, including Abdullahi An-Na'im, Ali Anouzla, Walter Armbrust, Ahmed Benchemsi, Karim Bejjit, Lisa Bernasek, Julia Cantzler, Daoud Casewit, Harvey Cox, Mohamed Darif, Del Dickson, Asmaa El Allami, Youniss El Cheddadi, Tajeddine El Husseini, Moha Ennaji, John Entelis, Nadia Guessous, Jay Footlik, Myriam Francois-Cerrah, Cecily Heisser, Aboubakr Jamai, George Joffe, Jordan Kaye, Stephen Kosack, Touria Khannous, James Lindsay, Ellen Lust, Ziba Mir-Hosseini, Vidya Nadkarni, Vijaya Nagarajan, Pete Peterson, James Piscatori, Ilhem Rachidi, Eugene Rogan, Fatima Sadiqi, Theresa Sanders, John Joe Schlichtman, Susan Sered, Kathryn Statler, Theodore Way, Catherine Weaver, Carrie Wickham, and Mike Williams.

Special thanks to Marc Lynch and the editors at *Foreign Policy,* who offered helpful feedback and allowed reproduction of several paragraphs from my work in their publication. Erin Grimes provided unfaltering research assistance. The students in my Middle East politics courses consistently challenged me to think about how to present my findings. Norma Tilden taught me to appreciate the beauty of nonfiction. Thanks also to Deans Noelle Norton and Mary Boyd, and all the faculty and staff in the Department of Political Science and International Relations at the University of San Diego. At Princeton University Press, Fred Appel, Juliana Fidler, Sara Lerner, Karen Verde, Chris Ferrante, and the press's anonymous reviewers all provided thoughtful and significant assistance. Heather Schroder offered important early advice.

Multiple institutions and grant-making bodies have funded portions of my research, and I am grateful for their generous support. These include the Smith Richardson Foundation; Robert S. Strauss Center for International Security and Law at the University of Texas at Austin; American Institute for Maghrib Studies; Brookings Institution; Fulbright Scholar Program; Ali Pachachi Scholarship and Peter Fitzpatrick Scholarship at St. Antony's College, Oxford University; Frederick Sheldon Traveling Fellowship at Harvard University; Horowitz Foundation for Social Policy; Sir Richard Stapley Educational Trust; Spalding Trust; and Harvard University Club of the United Kingdom.

Finally, my deepest gratitude goes to my family: my wife, Adina, and our daughter, Lilia; my parents, Steven and Fredelle; my sisters, Mira and Nina; and my in-laws, Solomon and Mickey.

Adina and Lilia brought to this endeavor, as they do to everything, joy, laughter, and splendor. Lilia's sense of curiosity will always be inspiring (she wanted to learn how to read so she could read this book!). Adina contributed so much, far too much to list. As a social scientist and a best friend, her insights were immeasurable, her encouragement, endless. This book is dedicated to them both: to Adina and Lilia, my everythings.

NOTES

A NOTE ON LANGUAGE

1. I focus on two varieties of Arabic here for the purposes of clarity, but the linguistic realities of life in Morocco are actually far more complex. There is a case to be made that at least four varieties of Arabic permeate everyday life, even within a single hour: colloquial Arabic (e.g., among friends, at home); modern standard Arabic (on the news or at school); classical Arabic (at the mosque); and educated colloquial Arabic (among educated citizens or even when discussing certain topics or listening to certain politicians). This does not take into consideration regional colloquial distinctions (of which there are many), nor does it include varieties of Amazigh, Hassaniya Arabic, and/or French and Spanish. For fascinating discussions of the diglossia/triglossia/quadriglossia debate, see three seminal pieces by Moha Ennaji: "Arabic Sociolinguistics and Cultural Diversity in Morocco," in *Perspectives on Arabic Linguistics XIX: Papers from the Nineteenth Annual Symposium on Arabic Linguistics*, Urbana, April 2005, ed. Elabbas Benmamoun (Amsterdam: John Benjamins Publishing, 2007), 267–76; "Aspects of Multilingualism in the Maghreb," *International Journal of the Sociology of Language* 87 (1991): 7–25; and "De la diglossie à la quadriglossie," *Langues and linguistiques* 8 (2001): 49–64.

2. The schwa in Moroccan Arabic is a source of particular academic interest and debate. See, e.g., Abdelaziz Boudlal, "The Special Behavior of Schwa in Moroccan Arabic," *8th Old World Conference in Phonology* (January 2011): 1–6. The use of the "e" to indicate the schwa in transliteration is also debated. Richard Harrell embraces it; Jeffrey Heath eschews it. See Richard S. Harrell and Louis Bunot, *A Short Reference Grammar of Moroccan Arabic* (Washington, DC: Georgetown University Press, 1991); and Jeffrey Heath, *Ablaut and Ambiguity: Phonology of a Moroccan Dialect* (Albany: State University of New York Press, 1987). These two authors also embrace the schwa: Jamila Bargach, *Orphans of Islam: Family, Abandonment, and Secret Adoption in Morocco* (Lanham, MD: Rowman & Littlefield, 2002); and Deborah A. Kapchan, *Traveling Spirit Masters: Moroccan Gnawa Trance and Music in the Global Marketplace* (Middletown, CT: Wesleyan University Press, 2007).

3. For their assistance in thinking through questions of language and transliteration, I am grateful to Youniss El Cheddadi, Moha Ennaji, Stuart Sears, Erik Bakovic, and, in Morocco, Meriam, Mohammed, Mubarak, and Ahmed (first names used for privacy). Their help was profound, but the responsibility for accuracy is mine alone.

A NOTE ON ANONYMITY

1. For more background on these concerns, see "World Report 2013: Morocco/Western Sahara," *Human Rights Watch* (2013). See also, e.g., "Morocco: Activists Jailed for Reporting Torture Must Be Released Immediately," *Amnesty International* (August 14, 2014).

2. In Hosni Mubarak's Egypt, for example, political scientist Carrie Wickham was told she could not even take notes. See Carrie Wickham, *Mobilizing Islam* (New York: Columbia University Press, 2002), 232, n. 34.

3. Often, the targets of prosecution are seemingly random: some activists, for example, post criticism online regularly with little consequence; others are arrested after their first time. But this unpredictability is even more reason to be wary of speaking out: no one can guess who will be punished, and no one seems off limits.

4. This compares to the "Partly Free" designation of Algeria and Tunisia. "Freedom of the Press: 2014 Freedom of the Press Data," *Freedom House* (2014), 1–28.

5. For a further discussion of the Ali Anouzla case, see chapter 5.

6. "Jail Terms for King's Online Critics Upheld on Appeal," *Reporters Without Borders* (March 28, 2012); "Annual Report 2013: Morrocco/Western Sahara," *Amnesty International* (2013); "Morocco: Unjustly Jailed Rapper to Go Free," *Human Rights Watch* (November 11, 2014); "Morocco: Human Rights Gatherings Blocked," *Human Rights Watch* (November 7, 2014).

Introduction ISLAMIST PLURALISM

1. For a snapshot of recent work on Arab youth in general, see, e.g., Mounia Bennani-Chraïbi and Rémy Leveau, *Soumis et rebelles: Les jeunes au Maroc* (Paris: CNRS éditions, 1994); ed. Asef Bayat and Linda Herrera, *Being Young and Muslim: New Cultural Politics in the Global South and North* (New York: Oxford University Press, 2010); Philippe Fargues, *Générations arabes: L'alchimie du nombre* (Paris: Fayard, 2000).

2. See, e.g., Abdessalam Yassine, chapters on *huwiyya iḥsāniyya* ["A Charitable Identity"], and *shuʿab al-īmān* ["Branches of Faith"] in *al-iḥsān*. Pamphlets published by Jamaʿat al-ʿAdl wa-l-Ihsan [The Justice and Spirituality Movement], Casablanca, Morocco; Alexander Bienert, "The Concept of *jihād* in the Writings of Abdessalam Yassine," Unpublished Master's thesis, Worcester College, University of Oxford, 2007, 60, 103; Bruce Maddy-Weitzman, "Islamism, Moroccan-Style: The Ideas of Sheikh Yassine," *Middle East Quarterly* (Winter 2003): 43–51.

3. For a discussion of a "theology of unity," see Roxanne Euben, *Enemy in the Mirror: Islamic Fundamentalism and the Limits of Modern Rationalism. A Work of Comparative Political Theory* (Princeton: Princeton University Press, 1999), 93–122. For a critical discussion of unity, including the work of Jamal al-Din al-Afghani and Mohammad Abduh, see Nikki Keddie, *Sayyid Jamal al-Din "al-Afghani": A Political Biography* (Berkeley: University of California Press, 1972); and Elie Kedourie, *Afghani and ʾAbduh: An Essay On Religious Unbelief and Political Activism In Modern Islam* (London: Frank Cass and Co. Ltd., 1966).

4. A brief note on acronyms and abbreviations. Works on political parties and social movements—and on Islamist movements in particular (because of translation issues)—often include a sea of acronyms. To avoid this, I tried to compose shortened forms that (a) make the text more readable, and (b) stay as close as possible to popular usage. As a result, some abbreviations take liberties with rules of Arabic grammar and transliteration. "Al Adl wal Ihsan" becomes simply "Al Adl" (and not "al-ʿAdl"). The aim is to avoid confusion among English-language readers, for in English-language texts the movement is referred to by a variety of different acronyms—acronyms usually only employed in English—such as JCO, JSO, and even AWI. The Party of Justice and Development is referred to here as PJD (just as it is often called in Morocco). For readability's sake, the definite article "al-" is dropped in all other shortened Arabic forms of groups or books.

5. On cooperation, see Michael J. Willis, "Between *Alternance* and the *Makhzen*: At-Tawhid wa Al-Islah's Entry Into Moroccan Politics," *Journal of North African Studies* 4, no. 3 (1999): 45–80. Note that Mustapha's movement is also referred to in English as the Justice and Spirituality Organization or the Justice and Charity Organization.

6. Even though social scientists have long been grappling with social movement theory, and resource mobilization theory in particular, still "relatively few scholars have attempted to understand the effects of interorganizational competition on social movement organizational processes." Sarah A. Soule and Brayden G King, "Competition and Resource Partitioning in Three Social Movement Industries," *American Journal of Sociology* 113, no. 6 (May 2008): 1570.

7. This is discussed in far greater detail in chapter 1. My research began with an initial trip in the spring of 1997, when I first started formulating preliminary research interests. I then spent two years, 1998–2000, learning about local culture and customs and studying Arabic as a Peace Corps volunteer living and working alongside young people at a local youth center, or *dar shabaab*. (I was not formally conducting research during this period, but my time in the Peace Corps was an extremely useful way of laying the groundwork for later fieldwork and contributed, in the eyes of the people I was working with, to "putting in my time"

20. On the "species" analogy, see Pamela E. Oliver and Daniel J. Myers, "The Coevolution of Social Movements," *Mobilization* 8, no. 1 (2003): 1–25.

21. See, e.g., Quintan Wiktorowicz, *Islamic Activism: A Social Movement Theory Approach* (Bloomington: Indiana University Press, 2004).

22. Yael Navaro-Yashin, *Faces of the State: Secularism and Public Life in Turkey* (Princeton: Princeton University Press, 2002), 16.

23. Saba Mahmood, *Politics of Piety* (Princeton: Princeton University Press, 2005), 189.

24. Ibid. See also Robert W. Hefner, *Civil Islam: Muslims and Democratization in Indonesia* (Princeton: Princeton University Press, 2000).

25. Talal Asad, "The Construction of Religion as an Anthropological Category," in *Genealogies of Religion: Discipline and Reasons of Power in Christianity and Islam* (Baltimore: Johns Hopkins University Press, 1993), 27–54.

26. See, e.g., Henri Lauzière, "Post-Islamism and the Religious Discourse of 'Abd al-Salam Yasin," *International Journal of Middle East Studies* 37, no. 2 (2005): 241–61. For an exception to the rule, see Charles Hirschkind, *The Ethical Soundscape* (New York: Columbia University Press, 2009).

27. Gloria Raheja and Ann Gold, *Listen to the Heron's Words* (Berkeley: University of California Press, 1994), 33.

28. Alberto Melucci, *Challenging Codes: Collective Action in the Information Age* (Cambridge: Cambridge University Press, 1996), 335–37.

29. Antoine Sfeir, *The Columbia World Dictionary of Islamism* (New York: Columbia University Press, 2007), 226.

30. Ahmed Benchemsi, "Feb20's Rise and Fall: A Moroccan Story," *Le blog de Ahmed Benchemsi* (July 17, 2012); see also ed. Lina Khatib and Ellen Lust, *Taking to the Streets: Activism, Arab Uprisings, and Democratization* (Baltimore: Johns Hopkins University Press, 2013).

31. *Al-Massae* (Morocco), November 13–27, 2006.

32. Within the last decade, PJD has itself spawned two offshoots. And Al Adl and PJD themselves sprung, as we will see, from earlier movements, and have origins in yet others. Also, illegal and violent groups exist. These include Salafia Jihadia and assorted Salafi groups throughout the country, especially in the south, such as the Moroccan Islamic Combatant Group (GICM), and Takfir wa-l-Hijra. Yet, while there are other Islamist movements, Al Adl and PJD remain, by far, the largest.

33. On the Brotherhood and on PJD's "family resemblances" to it, see Wickham, *Muslim Brotherhood*, 3.

34. He was referring to the group al-Shabiba al-Islamiyya, which I will discuss in chapter 2. Quoted in David Cook, *Understanding Jihad* (Berkeley: University of California Press, 2005), 259.

35. As is often the case with illegal movements, estimates of Al Adl's size are notoriously unreliable. PJD's secretary general once shrewdly speculated that his rival only had around 5,000 followers; authorities have suggested that it's closer to 50,000. I've heard Al Adl activists invoke the term "million." The actual number of activists probably doesn't exceed 200,000, but again, that is purely an estimate. Avi Spiegel, "The Unknown Moroccan Islamists," *Foreign Policy* (June 13, 2011). Another challenge is the lack of secondary sources. In Arabic and French, see Mohamed Darif, *Al-'Adl wa al-Ihsan*. Other works that reference and concern the movement include: Mohamed Darif, *al-Islamiyyun al-Maghariba: Hisabat al-Siyasa fi al-'Amal al-Islami 1969–1999* [Moroccan Islamists: Political Calculations in Islamist Action] (Casablanca: Al Najah al Jadida, 1999); Okacha Ben Elmostafa, *Les mouvements islamiques au Maroc: Leurs modes d'action et d'organisation* (L'Harmattan, Paris, 2007); Ahmed Chaarani, *La mouvance islamiste au Maroc: Du 11 septembre 2001 aux attentats de Casablanca du 16 Mai 2003* (Paris: Editions Karthala, 2004).

36. For more on definitions, see "Is Islamism a Threat? A Debate," *Middle East Quarterly* 6, no. 4 (December 1999): 29–41.

37. Noah Feldman has called some in this group "Islamic democrats" in *After Jihad* (New York: Farrar, Straus and Giroux, 2003); and *The Fall and Rise of the Islamic State*. William McCants has called them "Islamist parliamentarians" in "Al Qaeda's Challenge: The Jihadists' War with Islamic Democrats," *Foreign Affairs* (September/October 2011): 20–32.

38. Others have noted the term "Islamist" itself, sans modifier, is often used as signifier for radical. See, e.g., Khaled Abu Fadl, *The Great Theft: Wrestling Islam from the Extremists* (New York: Harper Collins, 2005).

39. Their conferences featured panels highlighting and seeking to situate their place in the wider movement, with speakers from places such as Egypt and Sudan.

40. For an extremely helpful typology, one which inspired my own, see Tamara Cofman Wittes, *Freedom's Unsteady March: America's Role in Building Arab Democracy* (Washington, DC: Brookings Institution, 2008).

41. On Jihadi movements, see Angel Rabasa et al., *The Global Jihadist Movement: Part I* (Santa Monica, CA: Rand Corporation, 2006); Marc Lynch, "Islam Divided between Salafi-jihad and the Ikhwan," *Studies in Conflict and Terrorism* 33, no. 6 (2010): 467–87.

42. Examples of inter-Islamist competition are both omnipresent and multiple, across and within all of these streams. In July 2014, for example, ISIS released a video attacking PJD and Al Adl by name and anyone who supported "democratic brothers" and not "the initiatives of real jihadists." The video, and the coverage it received, is an instructive example of how mainstream movements receive

less attention than terrorist ones. When such a video appeared (featuring just three individuals), its release was detailed by major think tanks. Yet, when tens of thousands march in an Al Adl-led demonstration regarding, say, local economic policies, as they do regularly, such protests receive scant attention in policy outlets. On ISIS video, see Vish Sakthivel, "The Islamic State Goes After Morocco's Islamists," *Washington Institute* (July 15, 2014); On specialized coverage of a typical march in Morocco, see Moroccan Organization for Human Rights (OMDH), "Rapport de la commission d'enquête de l'OMDH sur les événements de Sidi Ifni," July 1, 2008.

43. Some even allege that Morocco should not be considered an "Arab" state because people speak French there. Of course, such a criterion would have to eliminate all of North Africa and Lebanon from the region. And, of course, it fails to recognize that French remains a language of the elite in Morocco. And a large percentage of the citizens of North Africa also speak one of many indigenous Berber or Amazigh dialects.

44. Paul Bowles, *Without Stopping* (New York: Ecco Press, 1985), 125.

45. In typical language for a U.S. government official, Madeleine Albright called the North African kingdom a "leader in democratic reform"—boasting that "other countries are moving in the right direction, but Morocco is showing the way." Press Conference with Secretary of State Madeleine K. Albright and Moroccan Prime Minister Youssoufi, September 2, 1999.

46. Ellen Lust, drawing on Larry Diamond's famous paradigm, classifies Morocco, much like the rest of the region, as "hegemonic electoral authoritarian." See Ellen Lust, "Institutions and Governance," in *The Middle East*, ed. Ellen Lust (Washington, DC: CQ Press, 2000), 118. In 2014, Morocco's Freedom House ranking, for example, was "Partly Free"—as it was for the prior decade. Its "aggregate score" was 42 (lower than Tunisia and Lebanon, but one point higher than Libya, six higher than Jordan, and 11 higher than Egypt.) "Freedom in the World 2014: The Democratic Leadership Gap," Freedom House (2014): 1–28; and "Worldwide Governance Indicators: Country Data Report for Morocco, 1996–2012," *World Bank* (2012): 4. In a 2014 study of global anti-Semitism, Morocco ranked in the middle of the region (above Palestine and Iraq but behind Egypt, Saudi Arabia, and Iran). "ADL Global 100: A Survey of Attitudes Toward Jews in Over 100 Countries Around the World," *Anti-Defamation League* (2014): 1–49. On the realities of Morocco's record when it comes to women's rights, see Katja Žvan Elliott, "Morocco and Its Women's Rights Struggle: A Failure to Live Up to Its Progressive Image," *Journal of Middle East Women's Studies* 10, no. 2 (Spring 2014): 1–30.

47. For election results, see "*Election Guide:* Kingdom of Morocco," *United States Agency for International Development* (2014); available at http://www.electionguide.org/countries/id/146/.

48. Confidential documents available at http://www.guardian.co.uk/world /us-embassy-cables-documents/239525.

49. Julie Taylor, "Prophet Sharing: Strategic Interaction Between Muslim Clerics and Middle Eastern Regimes," *Journal of Islamic Law and Culture* 10, no. 1 (2008): 41–62.

50. Even secularism can very much be "a modality of political rule that seeks to transform religious subjectivity and give it a certain modular form." Saba Mahmood, "Secularism, Hermeneutics, and Empire: The Politics of Islamic Reformation," *Public Culture* 18, no. 2 (2006): 323–47, 328; on a "constitutionalization of the shari'a," see Feldman, *The Fall and Rise of the Islamic State*, 12; and Clark Lombardi, "Constitutional Provisions Making Sharia 'A' or 'The' Chief Source of Legislation: Where Did They Come From? What Do They Mean? Do They Matter?" *American University International Law Review* 28, no. 3 (2013): 733–74.

51. Data at "National Profiles: Compare Countries' Religious Freedom," *Association of Religion Data Archives* (2010), available at http://www.thearda.com /internationalData/MultiCompare3.asp?c=73,%20155,%20217,%204,%20225, %20119,%20,#S_1.

52. In the Arab Spring, regime type was only one factor in a leader's vulnerability. See Avi Spiegel, "Predicting the Future of the Middle East—the Easy Way," *Huffington Post*, February 9, 2011. See also Jillian Schwedler, "The End of Monarchical Exceptionalism," *Al Jazeera* (June 22, 2011).

53. Lahcen Achy, "Morocco's Economic Model Succeeds Where Others Fail," *National*, August 3, 2010.

54. These disparities partly explain Morocco's low ranking in the 2014 UN Human Development Index, in which Morocco ranked 129 on the list of 187 countries (with 1 being the highest ranking). Morocco was the second lowest ranked Arab country on the list, higher than Yemen (154), but lower than, for example, Iraq (120), Syria (118), Egypt (110), Algeria (93), and Jordan (77). "Human Development Report 2014," United Nations Development Program (2014): 160–63. Available at http://hdr.undp.org/sites/default/files/hdr14-report-en-1.pdf.

55. "Economic Brief: Poverty and Inequality in Tunisia, Morocco and Mauritania," *African Development Bank* (2011).

56. "Labor Force Participation Rate, Female," *World Bank* data available at http://data.worldbank.org/indicator/SL.TLF.CACT.FE.ZS.

Chapter 1 SHUTTLE ETHNOGRAPHY

1. The rail line between Rabat and Casablanca, or "Casa" as it is known to locals, will likely be supplemented by a new system of extended tramway lines. In 2011, trams began operating within large sections of Rabat.

2. For the most cogent analysis of the urban scope of contemporary Islamism, see Olivier Roy on the "Sociology of Islamism" in *The Failure of Political Islam*, 48–59.

3. Translations are as follows: *al-Waha*—oasis; *al-Manar*—source of light.

4. Many assumptions in English-language publications about Al Adl's political activism trace back to a single piece written in 1986 (by Henry Munson)—which itself relied, in part, on a 1984 doctoral dissertation (by Mohammed Tozy). This was long before the movement even spawned a political wing in 1998. Henry Munson, "The Social Base of Islamic Militancy in Morocco," *Middle East Journal* 40, no. 2 (1986): 269–84; Mohammed Tozy, "Champ et contre-champ politico-religieux au Maroc," doctoral dissertation, Faculté de Droit et de Science politique d'Aix-Marseille (1984).

5. Mark C. Taylor, "The Real Meaning of Deconstruction," *New York Times*, October 15, 2004.

6. Freud is speaking specifically about the preconscious; see Sigmund Freud, "The Origin and Development of Psychoanalyisis," Lecture One, Clark University (September 7, 1909). See also Janet Malcolm, *Psychoanalysis: The Impossible Profession* (New York: Random House, 1977), 30.

7. Walter Hollitscher, *Sigmund Freud, an Introduction: A Presentation of His Theory and a Discussion of the Relationship between Psycho-analysis and Sociology* (New York: Oxford University Press, 1947), 18.

8. The idea of applying this metaphor to the realm of political institutions is not unthinkable, considering that the term "inadmissible to consciousness" is plucked from German courts, rooted in the term *hoffahig*, meaning "admissible to court." José Brunner, *Freud and the Politics of Psychoanalysis* (New Brunswick, NJ: Transaction Press, 2001), 57.

9. James Crawford and Susan Marks, "The Global Democracy Deficit: An Essay in International Law and Its Limits," in *Re-imagining Political Community: Studies in Cosmopolitan Democracy*, ed. Daniele Archiburgi, David Held, and Martin Köhler (Stanford, CA: Stanford University Press, 1998), 80.

10. Confidential Cable, U.S. Department of State, December 18, 2008 (Cable Time 17:26). Available at http://wikileaks.org/cable/2008/12/08RABAT1169.html#.

11. See Janet Malcolm, *The Journalist and the Murderer* (New York: Knopf, 1990).

12. Stephen A. Mitchell, *Relational Concepts in Psychoanalysis: An Integration* (Cambridge, MA: Harvard University Press, 1988), 11.

13. Gerald J. Gargiulo, "When Is the Unconscious, Conscious?" Revised version of speech "When Is the Unconscious, Conscious?" New York Center for Psychoanalytic Training (1988).

14. This is the other side of what Brooke Harrington suggested when she

wrote that "the interest of the researcher can be interpreted as conferring a flattering aura of 'specialness' on the group" in "The Social Psychology of Access in Ethnographic Research," *Journal of Contemporary Ethnography* 32, no. 5 (October 5, 2003): 610.

15. One of the constraints I faced related to gender. To live among young people, to visit them where they lived and worked and hung out, required a certain intimacy that I simply could not have achieved with women in Morocco. That is not to say that I did not interview young female Islamists, but I almost always did so at public events. I do not wish to suggest by the disproportionate number of male voices in my account that women are absent from modern Islamism; they almost surely are not. For important work on the subject, see Ziba Mir-Hosseini, *Islam and Gender: The Religious Debate in Contemporary Iran* (Princeton: Princeton University Press, 1999); Saba Mahmood, *Politics of Piety*; Lara Deeb, *An Enchanted Modern: Gender and Public Piety in Shi'i Lebanon* (Princeton: Princeton University Press, 2006); and Sherine Hafez, *An Islam of Her Own: Reconsidering Religion And Secularism In Women's Islamic Movements* (New York: New York University Press, 2011).

16. See Antonius Robben, who experienced a similar dynamic as he moved between Argentine generals and their victims, as "each party . . . tried to draw me into their camp" in "Ethnographic Seduction, Transference, and Resistance in Dialogues about Terror and Violence in Argentina," *Ethos* 24, no. 1 (March 1996): 85.

17. I engaged in what the anthropologist Walter Armbrust calls a "scaffolding of methods." This also captures what James Clifford notes has long characterized fieldwork as "a mix of institutionalized practices of dwelling and traveling." Studying multiple movements necessarily requires constant movement on the part of a researcher—a combination of "dwelling" and "traveling" in *Routes: Travel and Translation in the Late Twentieth Century* (Cambridge, MA: Harvard University Press, 1997), 67. Anthropologist Julia Paley notes that studies of contemporary political activism are enhanced by ethnographic fieldwork "in that it captures people's lived experience amid conditions of . . . 'dramatic political change.'" This approach, she writes, "reveals the complexity of conditions that might otherwise be assumed to fit predetermined teleologies," in "Toward An Anthropology of Democracy," *Annual Review of Anthropology* 31, no. 1 (2002): 469–96.

18. Of course, there are drawbacks to such research endeavors. The world of qualitative research is often chaotic and disordered, replete with nonrepresentative samples and the repeated use of direct word-of-mouth referrals, or what social scientists call snowballing. You meet one person, who introduces you to another person, who then introduces you to still more people; and as your circle of acquaintances grows, so too does your web of knowledge of the movement. But

is that web by definition limited? I worked hard to avoid this even though some degree of snowballing is often unavoidable when dealing with "hidden populations." While being aware and honest about limitations, I was, in the end, convinced that the data I gathered provides a unique, rarely heard (if not imperfect) view into understanding Islamist change. On snowballing and hidden populations, see Rowland Atkinson and John Flint, "Accessing Hidden and Hard-to-Reach Populations: Snowball Research Strategies," *Social Research Update*, Issue 33 (2001): 1–7. I should add that studies relying on quantitative data in this context are also not without their own distinct set of pitfalls, especially among populations for whom responding truthfully (especially in writing) to surveys or strangers is often viewed with fear and suspicion. See, e.g., Robert Satloff, "Survey Says: Polls and the Muslim World," *New Republic Online*, September 30, 2005.

19. On "lived experience," see Gianpaolo Baiocchi and Brian T. Connor, "The Ethnos in the Polis: Political Ethnography as a Mode of Inquiry," *Sociology Compass* 2, no. 1 (2008): 141; on Tilly and political ethnography, see Charles Tilly, "Afterword: Political Ethnography as Art and Science," in *New Perspectives in Political Ethnography*, ed. Lauren Joseph, Mathew Mahler, and Jaavier Auyero (New York: Springer, 2007), 248. Interestingly, anthropologists of Morocco became famous for foregrounding their own roles in their research in the 1970s and '80s (even while such practices were adopted a half century earlier by Bronisław Malinowski). See, e.g., Paul Rabinow and Robert Neelly Bellah, *Reflections on Fieldwork in Morocco* (Berkeley: University of California Press, 1977). For two classic ethnographies of Morocco, see Kevin Dwyer, *Moroccan Dialogues: Anthropology in Question* (Baltimore: Johns Hopkins University Press, 1982); and Vincent Crapanzano, *Tuhami: Portrait of a Moroccan* (Chicago: University of Chicago Press, 1980).

20. Lisa Wedeen, "Concepts and Commitments in the Study of Democracy," in *Problems and Methods in the Study of Politics*, ed. Ian Shapiro, Rogers M. Smith, and Tarek E. Masoud (New York: Cambridge University Press, 2004), 5.

21. For fascinating insights into this temporal nature of fieldwork, see John L. Jackson. *Thin Description: Ethnography and the African Hebrew Israelites of Jerusalem* (Cambridge, MA: Harvard University Press, 2013).

22. Even as far back as 1958, Norwood Russell Hanson noted that "People, not their eyes, see," in *Patterns of Discovery: An Inquiry into the Conceptual Foundations of Science* (Cambridge: Cambridge University Press, 1958), 6. See, e.g., George Steinmetz, "Toward Socioanalysis: The 'Traumatic Kernel' of Psychoanalysis and Neo-Bourdieusian Theory," in *Bourdieu and Historical Analysis*, ed. Ed Gorski (Durham: Duke University Press, 2013), 124–25.

23. These interpretive biases exist, whether we choose to reflect upon them

or not. Unfortunately, space does not permit the necessary discussion and depth that such subjects warrant. I will thus explore at length issues of reflexivity, identity, and subjectivity, especially related to my American nationality and my Jewish background, in a forthcoming publication. I should also add that the history of Jews in Morocco is complex and multilayered. For fascinating accounts see Emily Gottreich, *The Mellah of Marrakesh: Jewish and Muslim Space in Morocco's Red City* (Bloomington: Indiana University Press, 2006); Michael Laskier, *North African Jewry in the Twentieth Century: The Jews of Morocco, Tunisia, and Algeria* (New York: New York University Press, 1997); Norman Stillman, "The Language and Culture of the Jews of Sefrou: An Ethnolinguistic Study," *Journal of Semitic Studies Monograph*, no. 11 (Manchester: University of Manchester Press, 1988); Aomar Boum, "Saharan Jewry: History, Memory and Imagined Identity," *Journal of North African Studies* 16, no. 3 (2011): 325–41.

Chapter 2 COEVOLUTION

1. Eric Laurent, *Hassan II: La mémoire d'un roi* (Paris: Librairie Plon, 1993).

2. See, e.g., Cathy Sweet, "Democratization Without Democrats," University of California, Los Angeles, Department of Political Science, unpublished dissertation, 1999; Lisa Anderson, "The State in the Middle East and North Africa," *Comparative Politics* 20, no. 1 (October 1987): 395–418; Saloua Zerhouni, "Elite Change and Political Transformation in Morocco," in *Arab Elites: Negotiating the Politics of Change*, ed. Volker Perthes (Boulder, CO: Lynne Rienner, 2004)

3. See also Leila Hallaoui, "Itimad Zahidi, une parlementaire nouvelle génération," *Le Soir* (August 23, 2012).

4. Aboubakr Jamai, "Quand la Boutchichiya fait de la politique," *Le Journal Hebdomadaire*, February 3, 2005.

5. I am indebted here to the work of Pamela Oliver and Daniel Myers for pioneering the theory of "coevolution" in the context of social movements.

6. According to sociologist Sidney Tarrow, "It also results when groups make gains that invite others to seek similar outcomes: when someone else's ox is gored by demands made by insurgent groups; and when the predominance of an organization or institution is threatened and it responds by adopting contentious collective action," in *Power in Movement: Social Movements and Contentious Politics* (Cambridge: Cambridge University Press, 1998), 24.

7. Oliver and Myers, *Co-Evolution of Social Movements*, 2–3.

8. Ibid., 19.

9. See Yassine's conception of such pluralism during the *tanfidh* phase. Alexander Bienert, "The Concept of *jihād* in the Writings of Abdessalam Yassine."

10. Hassan II allowed some members of the Brotherhood to seek refuge in Morocco. Kassem Bahaji, "Moroccan Islamists: Between Integration, Confrontation, and Ordinary Muslims," *MERIA* 15, no. 1 (March 2011): 1–6.

11. Dieter Nohlen, Michael Krennerich, and Bernhard Thibaut, *Elections in Africa: A Data Handbook* (Oxford: Oxford University Press, 1999), 632.

12. Except for this, it read very similar to Tunisia's. See Erwin I. J. Rosenthal, *Islam in the Modern Nation State* (Cambridge: Cambridge University Press, 1965), 331.

13. See, e.g., Henry Munson, *Religion and Power in Morocco* (New Haven: Yale University Press, 1993); Dale F. Eickelman, *Knowledge and Power in Morocco: The Education of a Twentieth-Century Notable* (Princeton: Princeton University Press, 1992); Susan Gilson Miller, *A History of Modern Morocco* (Cambridge: Cambridge University Press, 2013).

14. Quoted in Patricia J. Campbell, "Morocco in Transition: Overcoming the Democratic and Human Rights Legacy of King Hassan II," *African Studies Quarterly*, no. 1 (2004): 38–58.

15. Quoted in Marvine Howe, *Morocco: The Islamist Awakening and Other Challenges* (New York: Oxford University Press, 2005), 127.

16. Abdessamad Dialmy, *L'islamisme marocain: Entre révolution et intégration*, EHESS, Archives de Sciences Sociales des Religions 110 (April–June 2000).

17. Emad Eldin Shahin, *Political Ascent: Contemporary Islamic Movements in North Africa*, 183–84.

18. Susan Gilson Miller, *A History of Modern Morocco*, 189.

19. See, e.g., Amr Hamzawy, "Party for Justice and Development in Morocco: Participation and Its Discontents," *Carnegie Endowment Paper* 93 (July 2008): 7. Al Adl, he writes, "is unique in that it has no organizational or ideological links with older Moroccan or Arab Islamist movements."

20. Mohamed Darif, "Interview with Beat Stauffer," *Qantara Magazine*, Germany, 2007.

21. Shabiba (as well as the Egyptian Muslim Brotherhood) also began as a secretive organization in some ways mirroring the shape of Sufi brotherhoods that Yassine himself once belonged to and would later leave (1965–1972).

22. Mohammed Tozy, *Monarchie et islam politique au Maroc*.

23. Such a background steeped in education was not unique for the Islamist leaders of Yassine's generation. Olivier Roy, "Changing Patterns among Radical Islamic Movements," *Brown Journal of World Affairs* 6, no. 1 (Winter–Spring 1999): 109–20.

24. Abdessalam Yassine, *Al-Islam aw al-Tufan: Risala Maftuha ila Malik Al-Maghrib*, Public Letter, Marrakesh, 1975, 5.

25. The Boutchichiya gather every year for the *Mawlid*, technically meaning "the birth," which celebrates the birth of the reigning Sufi saint, in this case Sheikh Abbas. Celebrations continue to this day.

26. Sheikh Hamza, the man who edged out Yassine for the brotherhood's leadership, traces his spiritual lineage through Sheikh Moulay Abd al-Qadir Al Jilani (1077–1166), back to the Prophet Muhammed's grandson Hassan.

27. See "Biography of Imam Abdessalam Yassine," *The School of Imam: Abdessalam Yassine* (2007), available at http://archive.today/M5lej.

28. Yassine himself wrote of his dissatisfaction with the Boutchichiya in the beginning of his 1974 letter following his departure from the brotherhood.

29. This was relayed to me in conversations with Michael Willis in 2008. Moreover, a senior member of Al Adl recognized how the movement came of age in a competitive environment: it was not as if, he writes, Al Adl "had been alone at the time, with no competitors in the land." Abdelwahid Moutawakil, *Al-Adl wal-Ihsan*, thesis for the Degree of Doctor of Philosophy in Arab and Islamic Studies, University of Exeter (January 2014), 11. He writes also how the movement continues to appreciate these realities: young people, he notes, know that "there are other options, that is, other Islamic groups like Unity and Reform and PJD and others" (273).

30. Mohammed Tozy, *Monarchie et islam politique au Maroc*, 228.

31. Defining "ihsan" in English is challenging, and its meaning was often explained to me in polyvalent terms to suggest not only *ruhaniyyah* (spirituality), but also generosity, virtue, and even excellence. "Ihsan" is also sometimes translated in the group's name as "charity," adding to the confusion.

32. Mohamed Darif, *Al-Islam al-Siyasi fi al-Maghrib*, 351.

33. This was relayed to me in her office in Rabat in 2006; she died in 2012.

34. Malika Zeghal, "On the Politics of Sainthood: Resistance and Mimicry in Postcolonial Morocco," *Critical Inquiry* (Spring 2009): 587–610.

35. These institutional antecedents can be seen in clear focus in the original letter Yassine wrote to the king in 1974. See Henry Munson, *Religion and Power in Morocco*, 168. See also pages 5–7, and 19 of Yassine's letter, *Al-Islam aw al-Tufan*, for further discussion of these themes.

36. Ellen Lust-Okar, *Structuring Conflict in the Arab World*, 167.

37. Malika Zeghal, *Les islamistes marocains*, 12–13.

38. Abdessalam Yassine, *Al-Islam aw al-Tufan*, 5.

39. See also Nadia Yassine, "Modernity, Muslim Women, and Politics in the Mediterranean," *Princeton Readings in Islamist Thought: Texts and Contexts from Al-Banna to Bin Laden*, ed. Roxanne Leslie Euben and Muhammad Qasim Zaman (Princeton: Princeton University Press, 2009).

40. Malika Zeghal, *Les islamistes marocains*, 143.

41. Relayed to me by Ahmed Benchemsi, 2013.

42. For background on the case, see "Letter to Moroccan Minister of Interior Regarding Abdelkrim Mouti," *Human Rights Watch* (August 22, 2011).

43. Anneli Botha, "Terrorism in Morocco," in *Terrorism in the Maghreb: The Transnationalisation of Domestic Terrorism Monograph*, no. 144 (June 2008): 85–110.

44. Abdessalam Yassine, *Winning the Modern World for Islam*, Martin Jenni, trans. (Iowa City: Justice and Spirituality Publishing, 2000), 149. On Yassine's complicated and often contradictory notions of violence, and on the distinctions in his writings between uprising (*qawma*) and revolution, see Jaafar Aksikas, *Arab Modernities: Islamism, Nationalism, and Liberalism in the Post-colonial Arab World* (New York: Peter Lang, 2009), 107.

45. Four of these are considered the most important by activists. These are often referred to as the "mother books" or the *ummahāt al-kutub*.

46. Abdessalam Yassine, *al-Minhaj al-Nabawi*, Casablanca, 1981. (The new organization itself was only made public in 1987, six years after the book's publication.)

47. Mohammed Tozy, *Monarchie et islam politique au Maroc*, 199.

48. For more background on women in the movement, see Nadia Yassine, "Modernity, Muslim Women, and Politics in the Mediterranean," in *Princeton Readings in Islamist Thought: Texts and Contexts from Al-Banna to Bin Laden*, ed. Roxanne Leslie Euben and Muhammad Qasim Zaman (Princeton: Princeton University Press, 2009), 302–17.

49. Benkirane's eventual status in his movements is certainly different from that of Yassine, Sheikh Hamza, or even the Moroccan king. (After all, of the four, Benkirane is the only one not able to trace his ancestry back to the Prophet.) Still, his narrative is an important lens for examining the complex development of the modern PJD.

50. For vivid details, the Moroccan magazine *TelQuel* published excerpts of official documents from Benkirane's formative years; see Redouane Erramdani, "Enquête: L'histoire secrète du PJD," *TelQuel* (December 21, 2007).

51. The former head of Shabiba's military wing, who was aligned with Mouti (Abdelaziz Noumani), also went on to form his own offshoot movement, Harakat al-Mujahidin al-Maghariba (Moroccan Mujahedeen Movement). Yet, it was later stamped out by authorities after being implicated in an overthrow attempt of the Moroccan regime (October 1985). Emad Eldin Shahin, *Political Ascent*, 184–88.

52. Ibid., 189. For more background on these multiples groups, see also Mohamed Darif, *Al-Islam al-Siyasi fi Al Maghrib*, 257–76; Mohammed Tozy, *Monarchie et islam politique au Maroc*, 234–36.

53. "Morocco Muslim Party Aims High," *Al Jazeera* (September 07, 2007).

54. Ellen Lust-Okar, *Structuring Conflict in the Arab World*, 173.

55. On Algeria, see Michael J. Willis, *The Islamist Challenge in Algeria a Political History* (New York: New York University Press, 2007); George Joffé, "The Role of Violence within the Algerian Economy," *Journal of North African Studies* 7, no. 1 (2002): 29–52; Luis Martínez, *The Algerian Civil War, 1990–1998* (New York: Columbia University Press in Association with the Centre D'études et de Recherches Internationales, 2000); Hugh Roberts, *North African Islamism in the Blinding Light of 9–11* (London: Crisis States Programme, 2003).

56. Michael J. Willis, "Between *Alternance* and the *Makhzen*," 45–80.

57. John Entelis, *Islam, Democracy and the State in North Africa*, 53.

58. The extent of many of these transgressions has come to light during hearings for Morocco's first ever truth commission. See Susan Slyomovics, *The Performance of Human Rights in Morocco* (Philadelphia: University of Pennsylvania Press, 2005).

59. Michael Willis, among others, notes that certain Islamists had begun to petition for electoral participation beginning in the mid-'80s; see "Between *Alternance* and the *Makhzen*."

60. Quoted in *Libération* (Paris), June 5, 1996.

61. The PJD's Abdelkarim Al Khatib had long sought to court a relationship with the palace; by focusing on Benkirane here, I by no means intend to gloss over Khatib's specific role. Stephen O. Hughes, *Morocco Under King Hassan* (Reading, UK: Ithaca Press, 2001), 304.

62. Ibid.

63. Quoted in Emad Eldin Shahin, *Political Ascent*, 190–91.

64. Malika Zeghal, *Islamism in Morocco*, 167.

65. I refer to it by the shorthand "haraka" in this book over the more common "MUR" because I found this to be the term used by activists themselves. The shorthand has the added benefits of delineating between movement and party, and not overwhelming the reader with acronyms (e.g., MUR vs. PJD). See, e.g., Abdelilah Benkirane, *Al-Harakat al-Islamiyya wa-Ishkaliyyat al-Minhaj* [Islamist Movements and the Modalities of Method] (Casablanca: Matba'at al-Najah al-Jadida, 1999);

66. Abdelkarim Al Khatib was MPDC's founder and went on to become PJD's first secretary general.

67. Quoted in *Liberation* (Paris), June 5, 1996.

68. Emphasis added. Michael Willis suggests the haraka maintained its independence as a safety measure. If the authorities changed their mind and Islamist electoral activity was later frowned upon and MPDC banned, the haraka would still be protected. In "Between *Alternance* and the *Makhzen*," 48.

69. Ibid., 64.

70. Saad Eddine El Othmani expressed similar sentiments in 1986: "The political arena is the most dangerous area for Islam, where, by dealing with politics, it could corrupt itself, thereby undermining the Islamic ummah's values," in "Fi al-siyasa al-shar'iyya" ["On Islamic Governance"], *Al-Fourqaan* (1986), 2. Quoted in Matt Buehler, "The Threat to 'Un-Moderate': Moroccan Islamists and the Arab Spring," *Middle East Law and Governance* 5 (2013): 1–27.

71. For a picture of a campaign poster of women vying for PJD's seats in the 2011 elections, see http://twitpic.com/7go6jl. Like most official political parties at the time, in 2007 PJD agreed to a mandate to "encourage political participation among women and children." PJD now reserves at least 15% of party posts and local sections for women. See Laurel Rapp, "The Challenges and Opportunities Moroccan Islamist Movements Pose to Women's Political Participation," Center for the Study of Islam and Democracy (May 14, 2008), 21. In 2004, the party also paved the way for the direct election of its secretary general, granting the National Council the ability to preselect acceptable candidates before the congress delegates. Eva Wegner, *Islamist Opposition in Authoritarian Regimes* (Syracuse, NY: Syracuse University Press, 2011), 41–42.

72. Quoted in Nadia Lamlili, "Université: Guerre Froide Sur Le Campus," *Tel Quel*, no. 251 (December 2006). Indeed, when PJD took the helm of government in 2012, crackdowns against Al Adl-led UNEM intensified and links between PJD and OREMA flourished, including senior party officials speaking at OREMA conferences. One news outlet referred to this intensification as a "battle." See "Organisation du renouveau estudiantin vs l'UNEM: Suite à des 'instructions d'en haut,' la bataille devient inégale," *Aufait Maroc* (March 26, 2013).

73. The circle is known as the *Da'ira Siyasiyya*. The session was held in July 1998; the official announcement was made in July 2000. Al Adl documents available at http://Yassine.net/en/Default.aspx?article=political_circle_EN&m=1&sm=17.

74. Ibid.

75. Abdessalam Yassine, *al-Minhaj al-Nabawi*.

76. Jaafar Aksikas, *Arab Modernities*, 61.

77. Of course, I am not suggesting that Zahidi would have signed up for political activism within Al Adl, but rather that this formal option did not exist for anyone, let alone Zahidi.

78. See, e.g., Remy Leveau, "A Democratic Transition in Morocco?" *Le Monde Diplomatique* (December 1998), 5. Francesco Cavatorta, "Neither participation nor revolution: the strategy of the Moroccan *Jamiat al-Adl wal-Ihsan*," *Mediterranean Politics* 12, no. 3 (2007): 381–97; Jon B. Alterman, *Arab Reform and Foreign Aid: Lessons from Morocco* (Washington, DC: CSIS, Center for Strategic and International Studies, 2006), 52.

79. Michael Willis, "Between *Alternance* and the *Makhzen*," 71.

80. Ibid., 61; Michael Willis, "Morocco's Islamists and the Legislative Elections of 2002," 72.

81. For a flavor of this attention, see Avi Spiegel, "The Pollbearer: A Letter from Rabat," *American Interest* (May/June 2007): 128–32.

82. Hannah Allam, "Moroccan Woman Favors Cultural Revolution." *McClatchy DC* (September 9, 2007).

83. In elections in 2012 for the political circle's guiding council, twelve men and three women were chosen to serve. The council includes the movement's most well-known members—Hassan Bennajah, Omar Iharchane, and Omar Amkassou—not to mention Moutawakil himself. In a rare practice, the movement even released the first ever photo of the political circle's guiding council (Moutawakil is pictured in the middle with a black suit and no tie). It can be viewed at http://tinyurl.com/myu554n.

Chapter 3 RANK AND FILE

1. On the concept of an "extended youth," see Federico M. Rossi, "Youth Political Participation: Is This the End of Generational Cleavage?" *International Sociology* 24, no. 4 (July 2009): 467–97. For more on Arab youth, see ed. Navtej Dhillon and Tarik Youssef, *Generation in Waiting: The Unfulfilled Promise of Young People in the Middle East* (Washington, DC: Brookings Institution Press, 2009); Ted Swedenburg, "Imagined Youth," Middle East Report (2007); and Linda Herrera, "Youth and Generational Renewal in the Middle East," *International Journal of Middle East Studies* 41 (2009): 368–72.

2. Dale Eickelman, "Mass Higher Education and the Religious Imagination in Contemporary Arab Societies," in *The Book in the Islamic World*, ed. George N. Atiyeh (New York: State University of New York Press, 1995); Brahim Boudarbat and Aziz Ajbilou, "Youth Exclusion in Morocco: Context, Consequences, and Policies," Middle East Youth Initiative Working Paper. Wolfensohn and Center for Development Dubai School of Government, September 5, 2007.

3. For an analysis on the failures of the Arab educational system itself, particularly in Egypt, see Ahmed Galal, "The Paradox of Education and Unemployment in Egypt," Egyptian Center for Economic Studies (March 2002); Gregory Starrett, *Putting Islam to Work* (Berkeley: University of California Press, 1998).

4. African Development Bank, "Poverty and Inequality in Tunisia, Morocco and Mauritania," 5.

5. Emad Eldin Shahin, *Political Ascent*, 195; Henry Munson, *Religion and Power in Morocco*, 173.

6. Voting data clearly show that college-educated voters are more likely to either vote for PJD or to spoil ballots or even to abstain from voting altogether—the latter two, I should point out, directly heed Al Adl's call. See Miquel Pellicer and Eva Wegner, "Socio-economic Voter Profile and Motives for Islamist Support in Morocco," *Party Politics* (March 2012): 1–31.

7. Alan Richards and John Waterbury, *A Political Economy of the Middle East*, 3rd ed. (Boulder, CO: Westview Press, 2008), 368. See also Nader Habibi, "The Economic Agendas and Expected Economic Policies of Islamists in Egypt and Tunisia," *Middle East Brief*, Crown Center for Middle East Studies, Brandeis University, no. 67, October 2012.

8. International Labor Organization, "Global Employment Trends 2012," available at www.ilo.org.

9. Soraya Salti, "Extended Interview," *PBS Frontline World*, 2009. Temporary or 'urfi marriages, common in Egypt in particular, are perhaps the most salient example of a sexual, rather than political, response to this liminality.

10. Brahim Boudarbat and Aziz Ajbilou, "Youth Exclusion in Morocco: Context, Consequences, and Policies."

11. "Youth at the United Nations" available at http://social.un.org/index/Youth/YouthintheUN.aspx.

12. On the social scientific study of youth, see Mary Bucholtz, "Youth and Cultural Practice," *Annual Review of Anthropology* 31 (2002): 525–52. For more on defining youth in the Moroccan context, see Hassan Rachik and Rahma Bourqia, *La sociologie au Maroc, Sociologies, Théories et recherches*, October 11, 2011.

13. For more on women and social movements in the Arab world, see Valentine M. Moghadam, *Modernizing Women: Gender and Social Change in the Middle East* (Boulder, CO: Lynn Rienner, 2003). On the political economy of gender, see Ragui Assaad and Fatma El-Hamidi, "Women in the Egyptian Labor Market: An Analysis of Developments, 1988–2006," in *The Egyptian Labor Market Revisited*, ed. Ragui Assaad (Cairo, Egypt: American University of Cairo Press, 2009); Lisa Blaydes and Drew Linzer, "The Political Economy of Women's Support for Fundamentalist Islam," *World Politics* 60, no. 4 (July 2008): 576–609.

14. For a fascinating discussion, see Jean Comaroff and John Comaroff, "Reflections on Youth: From the Past to the Postcolony," in *Frontiers of Capital: Ethnographic Reflections on the New Economy*, ed. Melissa Suzanne Fisher and Greg Downey (Durham: Duke University Press, 2006).

15. Hassan Rachik "Jeunesse et changement social," in *50 ans de Développement humain et perspectives 2025* (May 7, 2008). See also Rahma Bourqia, *Les jeunes et les valeurs religieuses* (Casablanca: Eddif, 2000).

16. Although as far back as 1930, the Shebab Watani were also an active political youth group.

17. I am referring here to *Jeunesse istiqlalienne* and *Parti Démocratique et de l'Indépendance*, "PDI," respectively.

18. For definitive work on student movements in the region, see Ahmed Abdallah, *The Student Movement and National Politics in Egypt, 1923–1973* (London: Al Saqi, 1985).

19. For discussion, see John Voll in preface to Richard Mitchell, *Society of Muslim Brothers* (London: Oxford University Press, 1993), xxi.

20. For more on this hadith, see *Adab al-Mufrad*, 21: 388.

21. See, e.g., William E. Shepard, "Sayyid Qutb's Doctrine of Jāhiliyya," *International Journal of Middle East Studies* 35, no. 4 (November 2003): 521–45.

22. For more on this hadith, see *Sahih Muslim*, "Kitab Al-Iman," 1: 270.

23. Homa Hoodfar, *Between Marriage and the Market: Intimate Politics and Survival in Cairo* (Berkeley: University of California Press, 1997), 15.

24. This generational divide is high in Morocco (a difference of 18%) but the difference exists everywhere: 8% in Egypt and 23% in Palestine. Pew Forum on Religion and Public Life, "Full Report: The World's Muslims: Unity and Diversity," *Pew Research Centers Religion & Public Life Project*, August 9, 2012. A January 2013 published poll by Pew in Egypt found those under 30 were the least likely of any age group to believe that "laws should strictly follow the Qur'an." Numbers were 68% of those 50+, 60% of those 30–49, and 54% of those below the age of 30. Richard Wike, "The Tahrir Square Legacy: Egyptians Want Democracy, a Better Economy, and a Major Role for Islam," *Pew Research Centers Global Attitudes Project* (January 24, 2013).

25. These findings were supported by a nationally representative sample of 1,156 Moroccans, conducted in 2007 by leading Moroccan sociologists. The survey found that 87% of Moroccans possess a Qur'an at home; almost 60% do not believe that someone should be considered a Muslim if he/she does not fast on Ramadan; and 84% approved of the hijab. Almost two-thirds (65.7%) pray regularly. Mohammed El Ayadi, Hassan Rachik, and Mohammed Tozy, "L'islam au quotidien—Enquête sur les pratiques religieuses au Maroc," ed. *Religion et société* (Casablanca, 2007).

26. These beliefs are not outside the regional mainstream. In a 2012 Pew survey of Arab Muslims, more than two-thirds of respondents believed that religion should primarily be a "private matter"—up almost fifteen percentage points since the prior decade. Pew, "The World's Muslims."

27. See François Burgat, *Modernizing Islam: Religion in the Public Sphere in the Middle East and Europe* (New Brunswick, NJ: Rutgers University Press, 2003), for example, on the dangers of over-ideologizing Islamist movements. See also Stathis N. Kalyvas, "Commitment Problems in Emerging Democracies: The Case of Religious Parties," *Comparative Politics* 32, no. 4 (July 2000): 379–99.

28. This is true even though Al Adl's boycott of elections is not founded on a Salafi-like tantamount rejection of politics; in fact, as we will see, Al Adl is intimately involved in politics at the national and student levels without formally participating in national elections.

29. Daniel Lav, "The Next Proving Ground for Political Islam," 1–3.

30. On how Al Adl "became reminiscent of a Sufi order," see Ellen Lust-Okar, *Structuring Conflict in the Arab World*, 161.

31. Richard P. Mitchell, *The Society of the Muslim Brothers*, 165.

32. Malika Zeghal notes that Sufi and Salafi narratives together represent "salient elements" in Moroccan political life in *Les islamistes marocains*, 17–21. The extent of these Moroccan intra-Islamic collisions was captured in the anthropological studies of the late sixties and mid-seventies by Geertz, Eickelman, and Gellner. Clifford Geertz, *Islam Observed: Religious Development in Morocco and Indonesia* (New Haven; London: Yale University Press, 1968); Dale Eickelman, *Moroccan Islam: Tradition and Society in a Pilgrimage Center* (Austin: University of Texas Press, 1976); Ernest Gellner, *Muslim Society* (Cambridge: Cambridge University Press, 1981). On patterns of Moroccan culture, see John P. Entelis, *Culture and Counterculture in Moroccan Politics* (Boulder, CO: Westview, 1989).

33. Even Hassan al-Banna used to discuss Sufism in his early, weekly educational sessions on which both Al Adl's usra and PJD's jalsa tarbawiyya are modeled. Richard P. Mitchell, *The Society of the Muslim Brothers*, 196, 214–17.

34. Polling data also show the extent to which certain rituals not normally ascribed to the mainstream masses are actually far-reaching, even nationalized— not relegated to certain groups or even rural residents. In one survey, 66% claimed to believe in *jinn* and 59% in *sehuur* (sorcery). Mustapha Akhmisse, *Rites et secrets des marabouts à Casablanca* (Paris: SEDIM, 1984).

35. Profiles from www.facebook.com, viewed September 2014. Specific links withheld out of privacy concerns.

36. See, e.g., *The Minerva Initiative: Fostering a Community of Strategic Scholarship*, Forces Transformation and Resources Seminar, Fort Lesley J. McNair, Washington, DC, September 16, 2010.

37. Mohamed El Ayadi, Hassan Rachik, and Mohammed Tozy, "L'Islam au quotidien: enquete sur les valeurs et les pratiques religieuses." Khalid Bekkaoui, Ricardo René Larémont, and Sadik Rddad, "Survey on Moroccan Youth: Perception and Participation in Sufi Orders/Evaluation and Interpretation," *Journal of the Middle East and Africa* 2, no. 1 (May 27, 2011): 47–63.

38. For a thorough and thoughtful discussion of the veil, see Leila Ahmed, *A Quiet Revolution: The Veil's Resurgence from the Middle East to America* (New Haven: Yale University Press, 2012).

39. David D. Kirkpatrick or @ddknyt, "In Cairo, a lot of protestors today do not look like Islamists," August 30, 2013, 1:47 p.m. Twitter.

40. For more on the 2008 conference, see Omar Dahbi, "Islamisme: Abouzaid accuse l'Etat de perfidie," *Aujourd'hui le Maroc* (August, 25, 2008). For a description of PJD's 2014 gathering, see its website: http://www.pjd.ma/regions/page-17435. In another example, PJD's affiliated newspaper, between the summer of 2006 and the summer of 2007, called on its readers to boycott American products. The appeal, which superimposed photos of suffering Palestinians onto the logos of famous American brands (such as Pizza Hut, Marlboro, and McDonald's), featured a caption that read: "If you can't support the mujahideen, don't pay for the criminal Zionists' bullets." For his part, Yassine's writings are also laced with diatribes against, for example, the Moroccan king's "Zionist Jewish friends" or "Judaeocracy." See Daniel Lav, "The Next Proving Ground for Political Islam: The September 7, 2007 Parliamentary Elections in Morocco," MEMRI 3846 (September 6, 2007), 1–3; and Abdessalam Yassine, "Memorandum to Whom is Concerned: The King of the Poor" (2000), available at http://www.Yassine.net/en/document/4873.shtml.

41. Egypt is third. "Annual Remittances Data: Inflows," *World Bank* (April 2014).

42. "Power to Some Other People," *Economist*, March 17, 2012.

43. The Middle East and North Africa have urbanization rates higher than the world average; its rates are only slightly below Europe and Central Asia, and more than twenty percentage points higher than sub-Saharan Africa. Only in Egypt and Yemen do more people still live in rural areas. Data available at http://data.worldbank.org/indicator/SP.URB.TOTL.IN.ZS.

44. The term for the ubiquitous sitting cushions, "ponge," derives from the French word for "sponge": "éponge."

45. On Asef Bayat and the "quiet encroachment of the ordinary," see "From 'Dangerous Classes' to 'Quiet Rebels': Politics of the Urban Subaltern in the Global South," *International Sociology* 15 (September 2000): 533–57. see also Diane Singerman, *Avenues of Participation: Family, Politics, and Networks in Urban Quarters of Cairo* (Princeton: Princeton University Press, 1996).

46. See, e.g., Miquel Pellicer and Eva Wegner, "Socio-economic Voter Profile and Motives for Islamist Support in Morocco," *Party Politics* 20, no. 1 (March 15, 2012): 116–33.

47. Quintan Wiktorowicz, *Islamic Activism: A Social Movement Theory Approach*, 7.

48. Incoming high school teachers are able to select ten districts or "delegations" (out of 82 in the country); and data from 2014 show that many receive one

of these first ten. Married female teachers get first priority (ostensibly because the ministry does not want them to live alone or away from their husbands). A new high school teacher can "switch" job locations with another teacher after serving in the job for at least four years. The ministry even has a website in place to make it easier for teachers to find someone to "switch" with. According to ministry officials, priority is given to married female teachers to join their husbands. But there are, indeed, some cases of male teachers who are accepted to join their wives. This information is culled from two documents I obtained from the ministry of education: "Natijat Taʿyinat Khariji al-Marakiz al-Jihawiya li-Mihan al-Tarbiyya wa-l-Takwin li-Sanat 2014 (al-Taʿlim al-Thanawi al-Taʾhili)" [Outcomes of Graduates of Regional Centers for Careers in Education and Training for 2014 (Vocational Secondary School Education)]; and "Natijat al-Haraka al-Wataniyya al-Intiqaliyya al-Taʿlimiyya li-Sanat 2014" [Outcomes of the National Transitional Educational Movement for 2014].

49. On anomie, see Émile Durkheim, *The Division of Labor in Society* (New York: Free Press of Glencoe, 1964).

50. William Axinn, Amie Emens, and Colter Mitchell, "Ideational Influences on Family Change in the United States," in *International Family Change: Ideational Perspectives*, ed. Rukmalie Jayakody, Arland Thornton, and William G. Axinn (New York: L. Erlbaum Associates, 2008).

51. A compromise option, cheaper than home Internet but more expensive than the Cyber, would be a pay-as-you-go "wifikey" inserted to the USB port on a laptop. For raw numbers, "Internet Users by Country (2014)," Internet Live Stats, The Official World Wide Web Anniversary Site (2014), available at http://www.internetlivestats.com/internet-users-by-country/.

52. Only on April 2, 2014 did the youth wing of Al Adl post a "get to know us" letter announcing its Facebook and twitter pages. Facebook here: www.facebook.com/chabibaj; Twitter here: https://twitter.com/chabibajs; see announcement of their launch here: http://www.aljamaa.net/ar/document/79090.shtml. Al Adl launched its website (www.aljamaa.net) in 2000, initially, to disseminate Yassine's writing. See chapter 5 for further discussion of this. PJD launched its website (www.pjd.ma) in 2002; and its affiliated religious organization (www.alislah.ma), launched its in 2003.

53. Khalid Bekkaoui, Ricardo René Larémont, and Sadik Rddad, "Survey on Moroccan Youth: Perception and Participation in Sufi Orders/Evaluation and Interpretation." In a larger survey of 3,500 Arab youth aged 18–24 across 16 countries, 75% report that they get their news from "television" (up from 62% in 2012 and 72% in 2013). This is higher than from all other sources (including "social media" at only 29%). "A White Paper on the Findings of the ASDA'A Burson-Marsteller Arab Youth Survey 2014," ASDA'A Burson-Marsteller (2014): 1–29.

54. Research on young Arabs often tends to focus on their relationship to terrorism or how they become "radicalized. " See, e.g., Jessica Stern, *Terror in the Name of God: Why Religious Militants Kill* (New York: Ecco, 2003); Mia Bloom, *Dying to Kill: The Allure of Suicide Terrorism* (New York: Columbia University Press, 2005); Robert Anthony Pape, *Dying to Win: The Strategic Logic of Suicide Terrorism* (New York: Random House Trade Paperbacks, 2005); Marc Sageman, *Understanding Terror Networks* (Philadelphia: University of Pennsylvania Press, 2004); Mohammed M. Hafez, *Why Muslims Rebel: Repression and Resistance in the Islamic World* (New York: Lynne Rienner, 2003).

55. *The Economist*, for example, in language used regularly in the Western and Arab press, refers to Al Adl as the "more radical Islamist party." "Power to Some Other People," *Economist*, March 17, 2012.

56. The emphasis by commentators on the "hittistes" in Algeria is another salient example. See, e.g., Gilles Kepel, *Chronique d'une guerre d'Orient* (Paris: Gallimard, 2002).

57. The Arab Human Development Report has long described the bleak situation facing youth throughout the Arab world, with rampant unemployment and more than half of older youths wishing to emigrate. The International Labor Organization has consistently shown how unemployment in the region sits at the bottom of global rankings, with higher figures than even sub-Saharan Africa (data available at http://www.ilo.org/global/statistics-and-databases/lang—en /index.htm).

58. David R. Francis, "The Mideast 'Bomb' No One Talks About," *Christian Science Monitor* (November 4, 2004): 16.

59. Isobel Coleman, "The Arab World Is Experiencing the First Tremors of a Youthquake," *Council on Foreign Relations* (February 5, 2006).

60. For more on the flawed nexus between poverty and radicalization, see Alan Krueger and Jitka Maleckova, "Does Poverty Cause Terrorism? The Economics and the Education of Suicide Bombers," *New Republic* (June 24, 2002): 53.

61. James Traub, "Keep Calm and Carry On," *Foreign Policy*, September 21, 2012.

62. See, e.g., Charles Kurtzman, *The Missing Martyrs* (New York: Oxford University Press, 2011). If one were to count the young people who went to wage jihad in Iraq, and later Syria, the numbers of course would be slightly higher. See Rogelio Alonso and Marcos García Rey, "The Evolution of Jihadist Terrorism in Morocco," *Terrorism and Political Violence* 19, no. 4 (2007): 571–92.

63. My findings are supported by two national surveys conducted in Morocco: one for the newspaper *L'Économiste* and a second for the ministry of the interior. The survey in *L'Économiste* was the first nationally representative poll ever completed in Morocco on political and religious views of young people.

"Youth" (split evenly by gender) was defined as ages 16–29 for purposes of the survey (N=776). The results of a 2007 poll administered by the ministry of the interior were stunning for a government-issued survey—produced by a ministry that has historically been tasked with quelling any signs of opposition. In a representative sample of 1,204 Moroccans in rural and urban areas, only 24% of those surveyed trusted political parties; politicians had the confidence of 17%; and the government itself enjoyed the support of just 55%. "Grande enquête L'Economiste-Sunergia 57% des jeunes sont pour le hijab," *L'Économiste*, no. 2199 (January 24, 2006). Also, *Le Journal* in 1998 showed that only 3.1% of Moroccans trusted politicians and 3.9%, the police. Nine out of 10 people surveyed in the runup to the 2002 elections were unable to identify by name or ideological orientation any political party. John Entelis, "Le Maroc: Un courant populaire mis à l'écart," *Le Monde Diplomatique* (September 2002), 22–23.

64. Hassan II, *The Challenge: The Memoirs of King Hassan II of Morocco* (London: Macmillan, 1978), 169.

65. Laila Lallami's fictionalized account of a boat journey to Spain explores the personal side of this phenomenon in *Hope and Other Pursuits* (Chapel Hill, NC: Algonquin of Chapel Hill, 2005).

66. For historical context, see Janet Abu-Lughod, *Rabat: Urban Apartheid in Morocco* (Princeton: Princeton University Press, 1980).

67. A person seeking to migrate illegally is often termed a *harraga* from the root "burn," as in "burn" one's well-being trying to cross a border clandestinely.

68. Rising numbers of sub-Saharan migrants are also attempting this, including around 3,000 migrants between January and September of 2013 (1,400 more than during the same period the year before). "Morocco repels 1,000 Migrants Trying to Reach Spain," *Morocco World News* (November 20, 2013).

69. The promise of the Arab Spring has done little to abate this trend, in Morocco and elsewhere. Associated Press, "Arab Spring Increases Migration to EU," June 1, 2012. Boualem Sansal writes of a saying popular among Algerian youth: "Mourir ailleurs plutôt que vivre ici" (Die elsewhere rather than live here) in *Le village de l'Allemand ou le journal des frères Schiller* (Paris: Éditions Gallimard, 2008).

70. Quoted in Hassan Hamdani and Hicham Oulmouddane, "Décryptage: Génération perdue," *TelQuel*, June 13, 2013.

Chapter 4 WHAT YOUTH WANT

1. E. Burke Rochford, *Hare Krishna in America* (New Brunswick, NJ: Rutgers University Press, 1985), 54–55.

2. See, e.g., *Guide to Islamist Movements, Volume 1*, ed. Barry M. Rubin (New York: M.E. Sharpe, 2010), 439.

3. Emile A. Nakhleh, *A Necessary Engagement: Reinventing America's Relations with the Muslim World* (Princeton: Princeton University Press, 2009), 14.

4. Dieter Fuchs and Dieter Rucht, "Support for New Social Movements in Five Western European Countries," in *Social Change and Political Transformation: A New Europe?* ed. Chris Rootes and Howard Davis (London: UCL Press, 1994). Doug McAdam, "Social Movements and Culture," in *Ideology and Identity in Contemporary Social Movements*, ed. Joseph R. Gusfield, Hank Johnston, and Enrique Laraña (Philadelphia: Temple University Press, 1994), 36–57.

5. Carrie Wickham, *Mobilizing Islam*, 120. My research project itself is indebted to Wickham's book, which, in many ways, inspired my own fieldwork.

6. Mancur Olson, *The Logic of Collective Action: Public Goods and the Theory of Groups*, Rev. ed. (Cambridge, MA: Harvard University Press, 1965).

7. See, e.g., Quintan Wiktorowicz, *Islamic Activism: A Social Movement Theory Approach.*

8. See, e.g., James Jasper's *Art of a Moral Protest* for a discussion of how certain explanatory models (like resource mobilization theory) that deconstruct mobilization down to cost-benefit analyses do not adequately contend with the fact that emotional and cultural contexts determine what represent costs and benefits in the first place, in *The Art of Moral Protest: Culture, Biography, and Creativity in Social Movements* (Chicago: University of Chicago Press, 1997).

9. See, e.g., Matthew Levitt, *Hamas, Politics, Charity, and Terrorism in the Service of Jihad* (New Haven: Yale University Press, 2007).

10. See Lisa Wedeen, "Beyond the Crusades: Why Samuel Huntington (and Bin Ladin) Are Wrong," *Contemporary Conflict* (March 26, 2004): 54–61.

11. Donatella Della Porta and Mario Diani, *Social Movements* (Oxford: Blackwell, 1999), 102.

12. Quoted in Stephanie Willman Bordat, Susan Schaefer Davis, and Saida Kouzzi, "Women as Agents of Grassroots Change: Illustrating Micro-Empowerment in Morocco," *Journal of Middle East Women's Studies* 7, no. 1 (Winter 2011): 90–119, 98.

13. For a discussion of the variety of solidary, emotional, and material incentives, see, e.g., Lynn G. Bennie, *Understanding Political Participation: Green Party Membership in Scotland* (Aldershot, Hants, UK: Ashgate, 2004).

14. Donatella Della Porta, and Mario Diani, *Social Movements*, 149–50.

15. Hanspeter Kriesi, Willem E. Saris, and Anchrit Wille, "Mobilization Potential for Environmental Protest," *European Sociological Review* 9, no. 2 (September 1993): 155–72.

16. Nathan Teske's work in United States on the "identity construction model" was pathbreaking, finding that through activism, individuals are "able to be and become someone that they would not otherwise be able to be and become," in "Beyond Altruism: Identity-Construction as Moral Motive in Political Explanation," *Political Psychology* 18, no. 1 (1997): 71–91, and *Political Activists in America: The Identity Construction Model of Political Participation* (Cambridge: Cambridge University Press, 1997).

17. Jacquelien van Stekelenburg and Bert Klandermans, "The Social Psychology of Protest," *Sociopedia.isa* (2010), 3.

18. Ibid.

19. This is consistent with collective identity construction literature; see Jackie Smith, Charles Chatfield, and Ron Pagnucco, *Transnational Social Movements and Global Politics: Solidarity beyond the State* (Syracuse, NY: Syracuse University Press, 1997).

20. Significantly, each movement appeals to all of these ideal typical identities, but in different ways, thus demonstrating the tactical aspect of movement recruitment. One might assume that if the movements were looking for members with different values, each would look to a particular type of recruitment. Yet, each movement is engaging in strategic framing to recruit as many adherents as possible by creatively aligning themselves with what the movements perceive to be relevant to the youth.

21. On "moral obligation," see Carrie Wickham, *Mobilizing Islam*, 232.

22. See Alberto Melucci, "Domanda di qualità, azione sociale e cultura: verso una sociologia riflessiva," in *Verso Una Sociologia Riflessiva: Ricerca Qualitativa E Cultura*, ed. Alberto Melucci (Bologna: Il Mulino, 1998), 15–31, 8; on a "pleasure in agency," Elizabeth Jean Wood, *Insurgent Collective Action and Civil War in El Salvador* (Cambridge: Cambridge University Press, 2003), 231.

23. I am grateful to the funding agency for first bringing this to my attention, although, as a result, this example was narrated secondhand and thus the specific details cannot be independently confirmed. I have withheld the organization's name for confidentiality purposes.

24. Avi Spiegel, "The Future of Arab Democracy?" *Huffington Post* (June 23, 2011).

25. On "encounters with unjust authority," see Hank Johnston, *States and Social Movements* (Cambridge: Polity, 2011), 112.

26. Video available at https://www.youtube.com/watch?v=zvV8zJK7IlU.

27. See, e.g., Driss Bennani, "Rencontres: Ces jeunes du PJD," *TelQuel*, November 2005.

28. In most accounts of what is called "high-risk activism," harassment and repression tend to have the precise opposite effect: to dissuade new members and

cripple mobilization. See Doug McAdam and Mario Diani, *Social Movements and Networks: Relational Approaches to Collective Action* (Oxford: Oxford University Press, 2003). In Quintan Wiktorowicz's account of Salafi mobilization in Jordan, for example, he notes that: "It [police harassment] also has a residual effect—the organization is unable to encourage new members because of fear. People are suspicious when the *mukhabarat* interfere and would rather not place themselves in a position where they could become targets. The result is that individuals who *might have joined stay away because of repression*. For a fledgling organization such as the Qur'an and Sunna Society, this is *devastating for organizational survival*" (emphasis added) in *The Management of Islamic Activism: Salafis, the Muslim Brotherhood, and State Power in Jordan* (Albany: State University of New York Press, 2001), 131.

29. For one example, see http://www.aljamaa.net/fr/document/79.shtml.

Chapter 5 UNHEARD VOICES OF DISSENT

1. Susan Slyomovics, *The Performance of Human Rights in Morocco*.

2. Coralie Gardandeau, "Les cachots secrets d'Hassan II," *Libération* (June 9, 2005).

3. On transnational crime, see the work of Louise Shelley, e.g., *Human Trafficking: A Global Perspective* (Cambridge: Cambridge University Press, 2010).

4. Banishing or even eliminating top movement leaders also had little effect. For one example of the Syrian Muslim Brotherhood in Turkey, see Piotr Zalewski, "Islamic Evolution: How Turkey Taught the Syrian Muslim Brotherhood to Reconcile Faith and Democracy," *Foreign Policy* (August 11, 2011). Relatedly, Qatar expelled Egyptian Muslim Brotherhood leaders in September 2014; they will likely resettle in Turkey. See David D. Kirkpatrick, "Muslim Brotherhood Says Qatar Ousted Its Members," *New York Times* (September 13, 2014).

5. First book published in 2000 was Abdessalam Yassine, *Winning the Modern World for Islam.*

6. Edward P. Lipton, *Religious Freedom in the Near East, Northern Africa and the Former Soviet States* (New York: Nova Science, 2002), 76.

7. Ibid.

8. There is a reason, perhaps, why one of Mohammed VI's first acts in 2000 was ending Yassine's eleven-year house arrest. Most assumed it was a conciliatory gesture; but it was also one born out of practicality.

9. Blocking Internet access altogether would have profound economic costs, and filters can be overcome. Blocking access would invite international scrutiny and crack the veneer of freedom and amiableness and invincibility. See Clay Shirky, "The Political Power of Social Media," *Foreign Affairs* (January/February

2011). For more on the Anouzla affair, see Avi Spiegel, "Fear and Loathing in Morocco," *Huffington Post*, September 27, 2013.

10. I am thinking, for example, of Ali Amar's banned underground biography of Mohammed VI. Ali Amar, *Mohammed VI: Le grand malentendu. Dix ans de règne dans l'ombre de Hassan II* (Paris: Calmann-Lévy, 2009).

11. Lena Bopp, "An End to Visas: Tunisia's Book Market after Ben Ali," *Qantara.de* (2011).

12. Marc Lynch, *The Voices of the New Arab Public: Iraq, al-Jazeera, and Middle East Politics Today* (New York: Columbia University Press, 2006).

13. Dov S. Zakheim, "Morocco Deserves Better," *National Interest* (November 13, 2013).

14. Abdellah Hammoudi finds within Morocco, and specifically Sufism, systems of "absolute authority and absolute submission," in *Master and Discipline: The Cultural Foundations of Moroccan Authoritarianism* (Chicago: University of Chicago Press, 1997), 5.

15. Constitution of Morocco 2011, Article 46. According to Ahmed Benchemsi, there is another twist: "In Arabic, it reads: 'The King's person is inviolable, and *ihtiram* [respect] and *tawqeer* are owed to him.' *Ihtiram wa tawqeer* is an ancient expression used to signify the privileged status of those who claim descent from [the Prophet] Muhammad himself—a group that includes the members of Morocco's 350-year-old Alaouite dynasty," in "Morocco: Outfoxing the Opposition," in *Democratization and Authoritarianism in the Arab World*, ed. Larry Diamond and Marc F. Plattner (Baltimore: Johns Hopkins University Press, 2014), 338–50.

16. Fred Halliday, *The Middle East in International Relations: Power, Politics and Ideology* (Cambridge: Cambridge University Press, 2005), 39.

17. Patricia J. Campbell, "Morocco in Transition," 40.

18. Mohammad al-Tagi, "Despite His 'Absence,' Moroccan King Maintains Total Authority." *Al-Monitor* (August 25, 2013).

19. Stephen O. Hughes, *Morocco Under King Hassan*, 292.

20. Susan Gilson Miller, *A History of Modern Morocco*, 214.

21. Susan Waltz, *Human Rights and Reform Changing the Face of North African Politics* (Berkeley: University of California Press, 1995), 104.

22. Abdellah Hammoudi, *Master and Discipline*.

23. In the 1980s, Hassan II looked to Saudi Arabia and Salafi movements there for help in clamping down on domestic Islamic-oriented opposition though admittedly this was not the first occasion. The Sultanate moved toward Wahabism at the close of the eighteenth century—this time not against Islamist oppositions but against "the popular Islam of the Sufi zawiyas." The modern Sultanate itself constructed the monarchy as a religious institution able to transcend,

and stand above, the ethnic (Arab/Berber) and tribal divisions of society. Fascinating insights in Nazih Ayubi, *Political Islam: Religion and Politics in the Arab World* (London: Routledge, 1991), 185; Muhammad Darif, *Mu'assasat al-Sultan al-Sharif bi-l-Maghrib* [The 'Sharifian' Sultanate in Morocco] (Casablanca: Ifriqiya al-Sharq, 1988).

24. For a discussion of these streams, see Clifford Geertz, *Islam Observed*; Dale Eickelman, *Moroccan Islam*; Ernest Gellner, *Muslim Society*; and Malika Zeghal, *Islamism in Morocco*.

25. Patricia J. Campbell, "Morocco in Transition," 39.

26. See, e.g., M. E. Combs-Schilling, *Sacred Performances: Islam, Sexuality, and Sacrifice* (New York: Columbia University Press, 1989).

27. Muhammad Yusuf Faruqi, "*Bay'ah* as a Politico-Legal Principle: Practices of the Prophet and the Rightly Guided Caliphs and Views of the Early Fuquha," *Insights* (Autumn 2009): 33–56.

Chapter 6 REGULATING ISLAM

1. On the NDP under Mubarak, see Jason Brownlee, "The Decline of Pluralism in Mubarak's Egypt," *Journal of Democracy* 13, no. 9 (October 2002): 6–14.

2. Theodore Friend, "The Arab Uprisings 2011: Ibn Khaldûn Encounters Civil Society," *Foreign Policy Research Institute* (July 2011). Available at http://www.fpri .org/articles/2011/07/arab-uprisings-2011-ibn-khaldun-encounters-civil-society.

3. For the definitive study on oppositions in the Arab world, see Ellen Lust-Okar, *Structuring Conflict in the Arab World*. On Hassan and balancing, see John Waterbury, *The Politics of the Seraglio* (Hanover, NH: American University Field Staff, 1972); Francesco Cavatorta, "More than Repression: The Significance of *Divide et Impera* in the Middle East and North Africa—The Case of Morocco," *Journal of Contemporary African Studies* 25, no. 2 (May 2007): 187–203.

4. Examples are numerous. See, e.g., Craig Whitlock, "Feud with King Tests Freedoms in Morocco," *Washington Post Foreign Service* (February 12, 2006); Scheherazade Faramarzi, "Trial of King's Critics Suggests Morocco's New Openness Has Limits," Associated Press (July 4, 2005).

5. Perhaps the oddest accounts of Mohammed VI's "softness" trace this quality back to his father's own harsh treatment of him as a child. See Dan Ephron, "The Survivor," *Daily Beast* (August 29, 2011).

6. Abdelilah Bouasria, "The Second Coming of Morocco's 'Commander of the Faithful': Mohammed VI and Morocco's Religious Policy," in *Contemporary Morocco: State, Politics and Society Under Mohammmed VI*, ed. Bruce Maddy-Weitzman and Daniel Zisenwine (London: Routledge, 2012), 48–49.

7. According to Al Adl activists, the crackdown against it is widespread. For

example, they estimated to me that almost 2000 followers were arrested or prosecuted by authorities between 2004 and 2008; and that 725 members faced charges in 159 cases in courts across the country. The fines leveled totaled over 5 million dirhams. These numbers cannot be confirmed because it is impossible to identify which cases involve members of Al Adl.

8. See, e.g., Mohamed Daadaoui, *Moroccan Monarchy and the Islamist Challenge: Maintaining Makhzen Power* (New York: Palgrave Macmillan, 2011).

9. Quoted in Malika Zeghal, *Islamism in Morocco*, 167. Zeghal references Benkirane as the "Palace Islamist," 175. Yassine called Benkirane a "puppet of the King." Quoted in Henry J. Munson, "International Election Monitoring: A Critique Based on One Monitor's Experience in Morocco," 618.

10. Avi Spiegel, "The Unknown Moroccan Islamists."

11. On Ramid as "younger" and "more radical" because he criticized party leaders, see James N. Sater, *Morocco: Challenges to Tradition and Modernity* (London: Routledge, 2010), 73.

12. Sigmund Freud, Sándor Ferenczi, and Ernst Falzeder, *The Correspondence of Sigmund Freud and Sándor Ferenczi* (Cambridge, MA Belknap Press of Harvard University Press, 1996), 48.

13. This is also not to suggest that this was the first time the government had cracked down on its Islamic opposition. Two examples were during the Iranian revolution and the first Gulf War. Susan Waltz, *Human Rights and Reform Changing the Face of North African Politics* (Berkeley: University of California Press, 1995).

14. On analyzing jokes in authoritarian contexts, see Lisa Wedeen, *Ambiguities of Domination: Politics, Rhetoric, and Symbols in Contemporary Syria* (Chicago: University of Chicago Press, 1999).

15. On the crackdown following the Casablanca attacks of 2003, see Craig S. Smith, "Morocco Has Arrested 56 So Far in Terror Sweep," *International Herald Tribune* (August 1, 2006).

16. The king's remarks in this section come from his official address: King Mohammed VI of Morocco, "Speech to 'Higher Council' the 'Provincial Councils of Scholars,' Royal Palace, Casablanca (April 30, 2004).

17. See also Hassan Rahmouni, "Deploying Legal Instruments to Counter the Terror Threat in Morocco," Presentation at the Near East South Asia Center for Strategic Studies in Washington, DC: July 22–23, 2008, 26–28.

18. Mohamed Darif, "Interview with Beat Stauffer," *Qantara Magazine*, Germany, 2007.

19. Abbadi left the ministry in 2005 to become the head of the Muhammadan League of Religious Scholars.

20. "Morocco: 330 Arrested In Crackdown on Islamists," World Briefing, *New York Times*, May 27, 2006.

21. For an interesting description, see Marvine Howe, *Morocco: The Islamist Awakening and Other Challenges*, 75–77.

22. Stephen O. Hughes, *Morocco Under King Hassan*, 304.

23. Hassan Benmehdi, "Morocco Counters Jihadism with Religion," *AllAfrica* (July 8, 2014).

24. Quoted in "Morocco Hooks Up Mosques to TV to Fight Extremism," *Worldwide Religious News* (June 21, 2006).

25. Hassan Benmehdi, "Morocco Counters Jihadism with Religion."

26. Ahmed Toufiq, minister of Islamic affairs, quoted in "Tous les imams vont être remis à niveau," *Jeune Afrique* (June 25, 2009).

27. Ibid.

28. Quoted in Tom Pfeiffer, "Rabat Bets on Better Imams to Counter Extremist Islam," *Faith World*, July 5, 2009.

29. "Tous les imams vont être remis à niveau," *Jeune Afrique* (June 25, 2009).

30. "Morocco Pledges to Support for Mali," *Daily Trust* (September 24, 2013).

31. Quoted in Ellen Lust-Okar, *Structuring Conflict in the Arab World*, 162.

32. From remarks by Ahmed Toufiq at the Sidi Mohamed Al Hadi Benaissa mausoleum in Meknes, Morocco 2004.

33. "Morocco Women Preachers Appointed," BBC News, May 4, 2006,

34. Richard Hamilton, "Islam's Pioneering Women Preachers," BBC News, February 25, 2007.

35. Hassan Benmehdi, "Morocco Protects Mosques from Religious Extremism," *Magharebia* (June 17, 2014).

36. Saad Eddine Lamzouwaq, "Closing of Marrakesh's Qur'anic Schools: A Miscalculated Decision," Morocco World News, July 5, 2013.

37. Ibid.

38. "Shia Muslim Citizens in Morocco Being Persecuted," *Islamic Educational Center of Orange County, California, USA* (May 25, 2009).

39. Ali Jawad, "The Myth of Sectarianism in the 'New Middle East,'" *Global Research* (April 27, 2009).

40. Ibid.

41. "Stop Preaching or Get Out," *Economist* (July 29, 2010).

42. Eva Wegner and Miquel Pellicer, "Islamist Moderation Without Democratization: The Coming Age of the Moroccan Party of Justice and Development," *Democratization* 16, no. 1 (February 1, 2009): 173.

43. Ibid.

44. Wendy Kristianasen, "Can Morocco's Islamists Check al-Qaida?"

45. Fatama Ashour, "No Mosque Electioneering: Morocco PJD," IslamOnline. net (September 2, 2007).

46. The king issued a decree of July 1, 2014 that even went a step further: it "barred religious leaders, imams and preachers from participating in any form of political or union activities." A member of an anti-Islamist political party praised the move, saying it would prevent mosques from becoming sites of "political one-upmanship." Hassan Benmehdi, "Morocco Counters Jihadism with Religion," Al-lAfrica (July 8, 2014).

47. Jaafar Aksikas, *Arab Modernities: Islamism, Nationalism, and Liberalism in the Post-Colonial Arab World* (New York: Peter Lang Publishing, 2009), 61.

48. "Elections, INDH, islamisme, terrorisme . . . Les dossiers chauds de Benmoussa," *L'Économiste* (December 11, 2006); Anneli Botha, "ISS Today: The Prosecution of Al-Adl Wal Ishane in Morocco," *Institute for Security Studies* (July 20, 2006).

49. Quoted in "Morocco Cracks Down on Opposition," *Al Jazeera* (June 14, 2006).

50. I am indebted here to the work of Human Rights Watch. See "Freedom to Create Associations: A Declarative Regime in Name Only," *Human Rights Watch* (2009).

51. Indeed, the name of organization itself has roots in the Qur'an.

52. HRW, 2009.

53. Diary available in French at http://www.aljamaa.net/fr/document/545 .shtml.

54. Nick Pelham, "Islamists Take to the Beaches," *BBC News* (August 7, 2000).

55. Ibid.

56. Ibid. See also James N. Sater, *Civil Society and Political Change in Morocco* (London: Routledge, 2007).

57. "Court Jails Moroccan Singer for Adultery," *Daily Star* (April 2, 2007).

Chapter 7 EVERY RECRUITER IS A REINTERPRETER

1. Samuel Helfont, "Islam and Islamism Today: The Case of Yusuf al-Qaradawi," *Foreign Policy Research Institute* (January 2010). For more on Qaradawi, see Marc Lynch, "Veiled Truths: The Rise of Political Islam in the West," *Foreign Affairs* (July/August 2010): 138–47. On Morocco, see, e.g., Bruce Maddy-Weitzman, "Islamism, Moroccan-Style: The Ideas of Sheikh Yassine," and Olivier Guitta, "The Moroccan Justice and Development Party, 'Moderate,' Think Again," *Counterterrorism Blog* (October 1, 2007).

2. The attempt to boil down complex ideologies into sound bites of certain

leaders is, almost necessarily, riled with methodological and philosophical problems. See, e.g., Pamela Oliver and Hank Johnston, "What a Good Idea! Frames and Ideologies in Social Movement Research," *Mobilization* 5, no. 1 (2000): 37–54. To use an example from the policy domain: A former colleague of mine at the Brookings Institution, later a high-ranking U.S. government official, once responded to my discussion of Morocco's PJD by saying: "But I overheard some of them speaking favorably about Qaradawi."

3. Elisabeth Wood, *Insurgent Collective Action and Civil War in El Salvador*.

4. See, e.g., Glenn A. Bowen, "Naturalistic Inquiry and the Saturation Concept: A Research Note," *Qualitative Research* 8, no. 1 (February 2008): 137–52.

5. Robert Michels, *Political Parties: A Sociological Study of the Oligarchical Tendencies of Modern Democracy* (New York: Crowell-Collier Publishing, 1962).

6. Ira M. Lapidus, "The Separation of State and Religion, in the Development of Early Islamic Society," *International Journal of Middle East Studies* 3 (1975): 363–85.

7. On "double talk," see Jillian Schwedler, *Faith in Moderation*, 47.

8. See, e.g., Tariq Ramadan, "Shaykh Abdessalam Yassine: Entendre sa voix," *Tariq Ramadan* (February 24, 2013). On Al Adl as "cult," see Fouad Laroui, "Democracy and Islam in the Maghreb and Implications for Europe," in *The Other Muslims: Moderate and Secular*, ed. Zeyno Baran (New York: Palgrave Macmillan, 2010), 75.

9. See, e.g., Malika Zeghal, *Islamism in Morocco*, 129. Yassine himself even wrote of his role as *mab'ūth* or a messenger of God. Abdessalam Yassine, *Al-ʿAdl: Al-Islamiyyun wa-l-Hukm* [Justice: Islamists and Governance] (Casablanca, 2000), 432. Quoted in Malika Zeghal, "On the Politics of Sainthood," *Critical Inquiry* 35 (Spring 2009): 599.

10. Traditionally in a large organization like Al Adl (or Boutchichiya or even Salafi groups), only those in a position of power or close to the *murshid* would have opportunities of real *suhba* with him. Traditionally speaking, the role of the spiritual master was not to provide *suhba* but rather *hidaya* (guidance) and direction (*irshad*). Instead, *suhba* was usually sought with fellow members based on shared interests and personal affinities. But in this case, this activist felt a certain camaraderie with Yassine, and such sentiments were not unheard of. Thus, as we may be seeing in the contemporary Al Adl, these lines are increasingly no longer linear, and the source of companionship is not assumed. On the concept of *suhba* and Al Adl, see Abdessalam Yassine, *al-Minhaj*, 123–24; and http://Yassine.net/en/document/5236.shtml. On *suhba* in general, see Jamil M. Abun-Nasr, *Muslim Communities of Grace: The Sufi Brotherhoods in Islamic Religious Life* (New York: Columbia University Press, 2007), 60.

11. The question of subject matter is certainly not straightforward. On a typical day in September 2014, for example, the haraka's website included articles about the holy pilgrimage to Mecca, but also about: Morocco's prime minister (Benkirane); the status of the Arab Spring; Hamas; "Definitions of Politics"; and the progress of the "democratic transition" in Tunisia. http://www.alislah.ma/ (accessed September 15, 2014).

12. Karim Boukhari, Fahd Iraqi, and Redouane Ramdani, "Islamistes: La démonstration de force," *TelQuel* (November 4, 2008).

13. Mark Chaves, "Intraorganizational Power and Internal Secularization in Protestant Denominations," *American Journal of Sociology* 99, no. 1 (July 1993): 10. Max Weber, Hans Heinrich Gerth, and C. Wright Mills, *From Max Weber: Essays in Sociology* (New York: Oxford University Press, 1946).

14. Sudhir Kakar, *The Analyst and the Mystic: Psychoanalytic Reflections on Religion and Mysticism* (Chicago: University of Chicago Press, 1991).

15. Others have written of a democratization of Islam (which according to Olivier Roy is a non-institutional Islam) or a wholesale relegation of Islam to the private sphere (Jocelyn Cesari points to this in Europe). For a thorough discussion, see Frank Peter, "Individualization and Religious Authority in Western European Islam," *Islam and Christian-Muslim Relations* 17, no. 1 (January 2006): 105–18.

16. Mark Chaves, "Secularization as Declining Religious Authority," *Social Forces* 72, no. 3 (March 1994): 754; and "Intraorganizational Power and Internal Secularization in Protestant Denominations," 3–7.

17. Mark Chaves, "Secularization as Declining Religious Authority," 755–56.

18. Mark Chaves, "Intraorganizational Power and Internal Secularization in Protestant Denominations," 8–10.

19. The exception is *Ennahda* in Tunisia.

20. Mark Chaves, "Intraorganizational Power and Internal Secularization in Protestant Denominations," 10.

21. Talal Asad, "Islam, Secularism and the Modern State," *Asia Society* (2003).

22. See, e.g., Raphaël Lefèvre, "A Falling-Out Among Brothers?" *Sada* (July 30, 2013): "A clearer separation between the Brotherhood's socio-religious wing and its political wing could resolve the dilemma it has been facing regarding who should be the ultimate source of authority on politics."

23. On "jurisdictional battles," see Don Grant, "Neosecularization and Craft Versus Professional Religious Authority in a Nonreligious Organization," *Journal for the Scientific Study of Religion* 42, no. 3 (2003): 483. For a different view on secularization and Islamism, see Asef Bayat, "The Coming of a Post-Islamist Society," *Critique* (Fall 1996): 43–52; Asef Bayat, "Democracy and the Muslim World: the "Post-Islamists" Turn," *Open Democracy* (March 6, 2009): 5.

24. Wilfred McClay, "The Soul of a Nation," *Public Interest* (Spring 2004): 4–19.

25. Gouldner's theories were drawn from fieldwork with the General Gypsum Company in a rural community in the Great Lakes region between 1948 and 1951. See "Reciprocity and Autonomy in Functional Theory," in *Symposium on Sociological Theory,* ed. Llewellyn Gross (Evanston, IL: Row, Peterson and Co., 1959); John Hassard and Denis Pym, *The Theory and Philosophy of Organizations: Critical Issues and New Perspectives* (London: Routledge, 1990); John Hassard, *Sociology and Organization Theory: Positivism, Paradigms, and Postmodernity* (Cambridge: Cambridge University Press, 1995), 53–54.

26. See also Arthur Stitchcombe's work on organizational sociology: "units of analysis should be subparts of organizations that deal with distinctive sorts of uncertainties," in *Information and Organizations* (Berkeley: University of California Press, 1990), 358.

27. Stewart Clegg and David Dunkerly, *Organization, Class and Control* (New York: Routledge, 2013), 209. On goal orientation, see Talcott Parsons, "An Approach to Psychological Theory in Terms of the Theory of Action," in *Psychology: A Study of Science Vol. 3: Formulations of the Person and the Social Context,* ed. Sigmund Koch (New York: McGraw-Hill, 1959).

28. Dale Eickelman and James P. Piscatori, *Muslim Politics* (Princeton: Princeton University Press, 2004). See also Robert W. Hefner, *Remaking Muslim Politics: Pluralism, Contestation, Democratization* (Princeton: Princeton University Press, 2005).

29. John L. Esposito and Dalia Mogahed, *Who Speaks for Islam? What A Billion Muslims Really Think* (New York: Gallup, 2007).

30. See, e.g., Olivier Roy, *Globalized Islam: The Search for a New Ummah*; Malika Zeghal, *Islamism in Morocco*, xxvi.

31. James P. Piscatori, *Islam, Islamists, and the Electoral Principle* (Leiden, International Institute for the Study of Islam in the Modern World, 2000), 4. Dale Eickelman and James P. Piscatori, *Muslim Politics,* 71, 131.

32. Matt Schumann, "The Beats of Morocco's Young Islamists," *Armchair Arabist* (May 2012).

33. Heidi A. Cambell and Paul Emerson Teusner, "Religious Authority in the Age of the Internet," *Center for Christian Ethics at Baylor University* (2011), 59–68.

34. Stéphane LaCroix, "Islamism and the Question of Religious Authority," *DIIS: Religion and Violence* (June 2012).

Chapter 8 SUITS AND DJELLABAS

1. See Abdellah Hammoudi, *Master and Disciple*, 8; Malika Zeghal, *Islamism in Morocco*, 143.

2. Kassem Bahaji, "Moroccan Islamists," 5.

3. On "twinkling eyes," see Henry Munson, *Islam and Revolution in the Middle East* (New Haven: Yale University Press, 1988), 33.

4. This anecdote was relayed to me by Michael Willis in 2005: once at a meeting in Yassine's home, Yassine was so engaged in a discussion with Willis about the problems facing Morocco that Yassine continued talking even in the midst of the call to prayer. Only at the nudging of his daughter Nadia (seated beside him) did he proceed to pray silently. Willis recalled the "conflicted look on his face as he wrestled with whether to continue to talk or pray."

5. Abdessalam Yassine, *al-Minhaj*, 42.

6. Henry Munson Jr., *Religion and Power in Morocco*, 162.

7. See Ellen Lust-Okar, *Structuring Conflict in the Arab World*, 162.

8. Quoted in Michael J. Willis, "Justice and Development or Justice and Spirituality?: The Challenge of Morocco's Non-Violent Islamist Movement."

9. See Henry Munson, *Religion and Power in Morocco*, who places Yassine within a long historical trajectory of "pious" men standing up to "unpious" political leaders.

10. On King's wealth (supposedly five times that of Queen of England), see Dan Ephron, "The Survivor," *Newsweek* (August 29, 2011).

11. On personal myths, see Ernst Kris, "The Personal Myth: A Problem in Psychoanalytic Technique," in *The Selected Papers of Ernst Kris* (New Haven: Yale University Press, 1956).

12. Philippa Newman, "Filling the Void: An Investigation into Abdessalam Yassine's Relationship with Democracy" (Unpublished MA thesis, Durham University, 2005). Nadia Yassine noted at a movement meeting once that their goal was to "desanctify Muslim history, reinterpret it." Quoted in Wendy Kristianasen, "Hard-Won Change in Iran and Morocco: Islam's Women Fight for Their Rights," *Le Monde Diplomatique* (April 2004),

13. On Imam Ali, see M. Ali Lakhani, Reza Shah-Kazemi, and Leonard Lewisohn, *The Sacred Foundations of Justice in Islam: The Teachings of ʿAlī Ibn Abī Ṭālib* (Bloomington, IN: World Wisdom, 2006).

14. Henry Munson, *Religion and Power in Morocco*, 162.

15. Cédric Baylocq and Azziz Hlaoua, "Du religieux au politique? Symbolique des funérailles et chantier de la succession dans le mouvement al ʿAdl wa-l ihsan, au lendemain de la mort du cheikh Abdessalam Yassine," in Centre Jacques Berque, *L'Année marocaine*, no. 8, Rabat, Morocco, March 2013.

16. Press release and photo available on Al Adl's website at http://www
.aljamaa.net/fr/document/4938.shtml.

17. This was relayed to me by Ahmed Benchemsi, 2013.

Chapter 9 STRATEGIZING THE SACRED

1. For more on Hamiddine, see Ali Hassan Eddehbi, "Portrait: L'enfant terri-
ble du PJD," *TelQuel* (May 24, 2013).

2. Interview with Benkirane in Mohammed Radwan, "Moroccan MP: We Are
Not Affiliated with the Muslim Brotherhood," *Al-Monitor* (February 29, 2013).

3. Quoted in Carrie Wickham, *Muslim Brotherhood*, 237.

4. These quotes come from an interview with a public figure in Morocco, but
I am withholding his name in this instance because the quote in question could
conceivably be construed as an "attack" against government officials and thus
would be a punishable offense in Morocco.

5. On "distinct lines," see Hussam Tamam, "Separating Islam from Political
Islam: The Case of Morocco," *World Security Institute* (May 2007). For more discussions of relationship, see Eva Wegner, *Islamist Opposition in Authoritarian Regimes: The Party of Justice and Development in Morocco* (Syracuse, NY: Syracuse
University Press, 2011).

6. The leadership of the party and movements are increasingly overlapping.
At the haraka's annual congress in Fez in August 2014, for example, two of the
main candidates to assume its helm were none other than Saad Eddine El Othmani (the former secretary general of PJD) and Abderrahim Chikhi, an official
advisor to the sitting prime minister, Benkirane. According to *Attajdid*, on August
10, 2014, Chikhi was elected soon after Othmani withdrew. Chikhi promised to
resign his official government position.

7. Malika Zeghal, *Islamism in Morocco*, 178.

8. Quoted in Eva Wegner, *Islamist Opposition in Authoritarian Regimes*, 163.

9. "Les 'Jeunes Turcs' du PJD," *Jeune Afrique* (May 26, 2009).

10. Olivier Roy, *Failure of Political Islam*, 199.

11. Party leader Mustapha Ramid, for one, delivered a remarkably dense two-
hour address on international human rights laws and their application. It was
more of an academic lecture than party propaganda.

12. "Fès: Des militants du PJD brûlent leurs cartes d'adhérent," *Lakome* (May
27, 2013).

13. Anouar Boukhars, *Politics in Morocco: Executive Monarchy and Enlight-
ened Authoritarianism* (London: Routledge, 2011).

14. For more on "Islamic State" rhetoric, see Khadija Moshen-Finan and Ma-

lika Zeghal, "Opposition islamiste et pouvoir monarchique au Maroc," *French Journal of Political Science* 56 (2006): 79–119.

15. When party members wanted to draw my attention to their proposals to reform education, they pointed me in the direction of *Attajdid*, in particular the November 10–12, 2006 issue.

16. Ahmed Raissouni, "Harakat al-Tawhid wal-Islah," *al-ʿAsr* (October 7, 2002).

17. Raissouni's comments were also particularly ill timed, appearing four days before the Casablanca bombings of May 2003. Anouar Boukhars, *Politics in Morocco*, 119–20.

18. Asma Barlas, *Believing Women in Islam: Unreading Patriarchal Interpretations of the Qurʾān* (Austin: University of Texas Press, 2002), 77; Brannon M. Wheeler, *Applying the Canon in Islam: The Authorization and Maintenance of Interpretive Reasoning in Ḥanafī Scholarship* (Albany: State University of New York Press, 1996).

19. A version of this quote was often repeated to me in the course of my fieldwork. It is also noted in this interview: "Congress of Moroccan Islamists," *Sada* (April 22, 2004).

20. For more on Tajdid, see Emrah Çelik, *Renewal (Tajdid) in Islamic Thought: with Special Reference to al-Ghazali and Abduh* (Saarbrücken, Germany: LAP Lambert Academic Publishing, 2012).

21. "Abdelaziz Rabbah: 'La laïcité? Ça se discute!'" Interview by Hamid Barrada Kenitra, *Jeune Afrique* (November 2009).

22. "Habib El Malki: Une alliance avec le PJD est une décision qui revient au congrès national," *Aujourd'hui le Maroc*, July 25, 2008.

23. Benkirane argued that one of the main reasons for PJD's early struggles was its failure to work with other parties. Michael Willis, "Morocco's Islamists and the Legislative Elections of 2002: The Strange Case of the Party That Did Not Want to Win," *Mediterranean Politics* 9, no. 1 (2004): 53–81.

24. Speech available in Arabic at https://www.youtube.com/watch?v=OVKe208m6eQ.

25. Avi M. Spiegel, "The Fate of Morocco's Islamists," *Foreign Policy* (July 9, 2013).

Conclusion THE NEXT ISLAMIST GENERATION

1. See, e.g., Olivier Roy, *The Failure of Political Islam*; Mümtazer Türköne, "Islamism is Dead!" *Today's Zaman* (January 4, 2014); Khaled Abou El Fadl, "Egypt: Is Political Islam Dead?" *Al Jazeera* (July 8, 2013); Jacob Resneck and Jabeen

Bhatti, "Does Morsi Ouster Signal End of 'Political Islam'?" *USA Today* (July 7, 2013).

2. Quoted in *Aujourd'hui le Maroc*, June 20, 2008.

3. Sarah A. Soule and Brayden G King, "Competition and Resource Partitioning in Three Social Movement Industries," 1569.

4. Roger Finke and Rodney Stark, "Religious Economics and Sacred Canopies," *American Sociological Review* 53 (1988): 47.

5. On "common identification," see Pamela E. Oliver and Daniel J. Myers, "The Coevolution of Social Movements," 2.

6. See, e.g., Albert Carron, "Cohesion: Conceptual and Measurement Issues," *Small Group Research* 31, no. 1 (2000): 89–106; Michael Hogg, "Group Cohesiveness: A Critical Review and Some New Directions," *European Review of Social Psychology* 4, no. 1 (1993): 85–111.

7. One Moroccan study from 2003 found that nearly 89% of students believed that Islamists were the most active groups on campuses; Aziz Chahir, "Procès de l'université marocaine," *La Gazette Du Maroc* (February 3, 2003).

8. Eva Bellin, "Reconsidering the Robustness of Authoritarianism in the Middle East," *Comparative Politics* 44 (January 2012): 127–49.

9. Avi M. Spiegel, "The Fate of Morocco's Islamists."

10. "Morocco Bans Ruling Party Youth Ceremony," *Agence France Presse* (September 1, 2012).

11. John Voll in Richard Mitchell, *The Society of the Muslim Brothers*, xv.

INDEX

INDEX

Sahrawi (Saharan), movement, 196
Sa'di Dynasty, 126
Salafis/Salafism, 6, 9, 70–72, 206n32, 207n41,
    222n32, 229n28, 230n23, 235n10
Sar, Chekh, 162
Saudi Arabia, 43, 117, 120, 126, 230n23
secular/secularization, 3,4, 11, 16, 28, 51, 92,
    130, 137, 152, 155, 166, 182, 191, 209n50
select incentives, 90, 91, 130, 131
selective suppression, 129–33
Shabiba, 37–39, 41–44, 46–48, 70, 138, 214n21
Shahin, Emad, 63
Shari'a, 47, 74, 198
Shi'as/Shi'ism, 4, 31, 126, 139, 195
socialism/Socialists, 33, 38, 43, 91, 126, 174, 190
social networks, 61, 69, 92, 183
social services, 4, 88, 91
Spain, 76, 82, 84, 117, 138; illegal immigrants
    to, 85
Stark, Rodney, 195
State Department (U.S.), 16, 139
Sufism, 3, 14, 36, 39–42, 44, 70–72, 94, 126, 135,
    161, 167, 174, 215nn 21 and 24, 222n33,
    230n14, 230n23. *See also* Boutchichiya
    Sufi Tariqa; Darqawiyya brotherhood;
    Royal Islam
Sunnis, 3, 4, 122, 160, 195
Suri, Abu Musa al-, 14

Tangier, 63, 84, 173
television, 1, 2, 82, 85, 96, 120, 137, 141, 147, 163,
    165, 224n53; Al Jazeera, 82, 163; and Qa-
    radawi, 141, 163
Temara, 21, 34, 54, 58, 77, 115, 189
terrorism, 4, 18, 85, 107, 119
Tilly, Charles, 31
Toufiq, Ahmed, 135, 149
Transparency International, 16
Tunisia, 5, 16–18, 81

'ulama, 136, 160–162; Councils, 138

umma, 121, 122
UNEM (Union Nationale des Étudiant(e)s du
    Maroc), 66, 73, 168, 218n72
unemployment, 16, 38, 40, 65, 64, 83, 111, 143,
    172, 225n57
Union of Democratic Youth, 66
urban/urbanization, 21, 76–79, 138, 165,
    223n43
USFP (Union Socialiste des Forces Populaire),
    33, 34
Utvik, Bjørn Olav, 6

veiling, 72–73

Waha, al-, 22
Wahabis/Wahabism, 126, 230n23
Weber/Weberian, 12, 154, 157
Wedeen, Lisa, 31
Wickham, Carrie: on religious obligation, 90
WikiLeaks, 16, 23
Wood, Elisabeth, 151
World Bank, 16, 140

Yassine, Abdessalam, 3, 13, 14, 22, 25, 36, 39–
    48, 54–56, 58, 70, 102, 106, 112, 118, 132, 135,
    138, 145, 151, 153, 161–63, 165–76, 197,
    214n21; "Islam or the Flood," 92; *Al-
    Minhaj al-Nabawi,* 44, 167
Yassine, Nadia, 56, 168, 170, 174, 238n4
Yatim, Mohammed, 49–50
Yemen, 14, 16, 31, 223n40; *Islah,* 14
Youssoufi, Abderrahmane, 33, 34, 179
youth, 7–9, 32, 35, 57, 62, 63, 71, 83, 85, 87–112,
    116, 118, 119, 131, 133, 134, 140, 141–43, 153,
    156, 168, 169, 171, 173–75, 181, 182, 184–88,
    190, 193–97

Zahidi, Itimad, 33–35, 55
Zeghal, Malika, 42
Zohal, Mohammed, 71
Zouanat, Zakia, 42

PRINCETON STUDIES IN MUSLIM POLITICS

Diane Singerman, *Avenues of Participation: Family, Politics, and Networks in Urban Quarters of Cairo*

Tone Bringa, *Being Muslim the Bosnian Way: Identity and Community in a Central Bosnian Village*

Dale F. Eickelman and James Piscatori, *Muslim Politics*

Bruce B. Lawrence, *Shattering the Myth: Islam beyond Violence*

Ziba Mir-Hosseini, *Islam and Gender: The Religious Debate in Contemporary Iran*

Robert W. Hefner, *Civil Islam: Muslims and Democratization in Indonesia*

Muhammad Qasim Zaman, *The 'Ulama in Contemporary Islam: Custodians of Change*

Michael G. Peletz, *Islamic Modern: Religious Courts and Cultural Politics in Malaysia*

Oskar Verkaaik, *Migrants and Militants: Fun and Urban Violence in Pakistan*

Laetitia Bucaille, *Growing Up Palestinian: Israeli Occupation and the Intifada Generation*

Robert W. Hefner, ed., *Remaking Muslim Politics: Pluralism, Contestation, Democratization*

Lara Deeb, *An Enchanted Modern: Gender and Public Piety in Shi'i Lebanon*

Roxanne L. Euben, *Journeys to the Other Shore: Muslim and Western Travelers in Search of Knowledge*

Robert W. Hefner and Muhammad Qasim Zaman, eds., *Schooling Islam: The Culture and Politics of Modern Muslim Education*

Loren D. Lybarger, *Identity and Religion in Palestine: The Struggle between Islamism and Secularism in the Occupied Territories*

Augustus Norton, *Hezbollah: A Short History*

Bruce K. Rutherford, *Egypt after Mubarak: Liberalism, Islam, and Democracy in the Arab World*

Emile Nakhleh, *A Necessary Engagement: Reinventing America's Relations with the Muslim World*

Roxanne L. Euben and Muhammad Qasim Zaman, eds., *Princeton Readings in Islamist Thought: Texts and Contexts from al-Banna to Bin Laden*

Irfan Ahmad, *Islamism and Democracy in India: The Transformation of Jamaat-e-Islami*

Kristen Ghodsee, *Muslim Lives in Eastern Europe: Gender, Ethnicity, and the Transformation of Islam in Postsocialist Bulgaria*

John R. Bowen, *Can Islam Be French? Pluralism and Pragmatism in a Secularist State*

Thomas Barfield, *Afghanistan: A Cultural and Political History*

Sara Roy, *Hamas and Civil Society in Gaza: Engaging the Islamist Social Sector*

Michael Laffan, *The Makings of Indonesian Islam: Orientalism and the Narration of a Sufi Past*

Jonathan Laurence, *The Emancipation of Europe's Muslims: The State's Role in Minority Integration*

Jenny White, *Muslim Nationalism and the New Turks*

Lara Deeb and Mona Harb, *Leisurely Islam: Negotiating Geography and Morality in Shi'ite South Beirut*

Ësra Özyürek, *Being German, Becoming Muslim: Race, Religion, and Conversion in the New Europe*

Ellen McLarney, *Soft Force: Women in Egypt's Islamic Awakening*

Avi Max Spiegel, *Young Islam: The New Politics of Religion in Morocco and the Arab World*